# Wild in ARIZONA
### ~ EXPANDED 2nd EDITION ~

## Photographing Arizona's Wildflowers
### A Guide to When, Where, & How

ANALEMMA PRESS

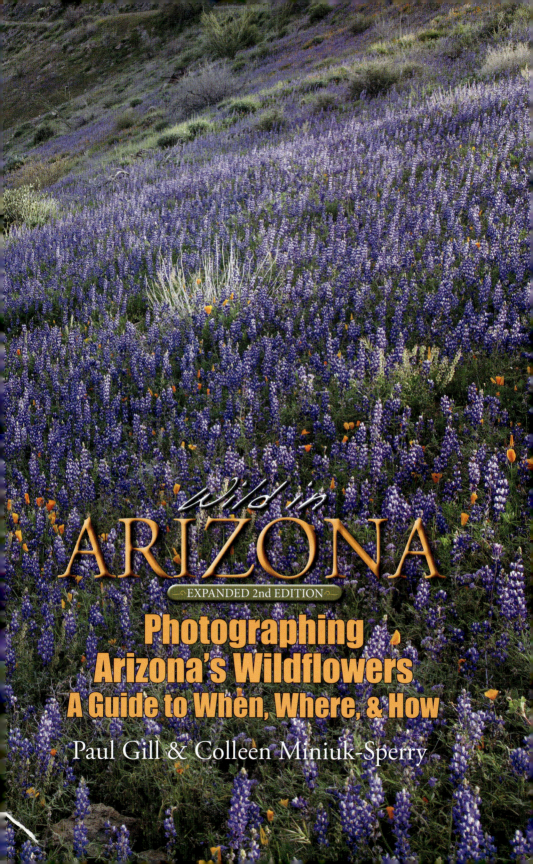

*To my parents, Bob and Jacque; my brother, Rob; the Sperry family; and my husband, Craig, who never think my wild and crazy ideas are all that wild and crazy. Also, to Regina and Sterling Skouson and my friends from the Chandler-Gilbert Community College photography class for changing my life.*
*~ Colleen Miniuk-Sperry*

*To my parents, Roy and Ruth, for encouraging me to follow a life in the arts and to the photographers of Arizona Highways Magazine, especially Peter Ensenberger, Jeff Kida, David Muench, and Jack Dykinga, for their inspiration and mentoring. Also, thanks to Christine for her support.*
*~ Paul Gill*

# Wild in Arizona: Photographing Arizona's Wildflowers A Guide to When, Where, & How (Second Edition)

Copyright © 2015 Analemma Press, L. L. C., Chandler, Arizona
Printed in the United States of America.

All rights reserved. No part of this publication may be reproduced in any form or by any means, electronic, mechanical, photocopying, recording or otherwise, without the prior written permission of the publisher.

**Text:** Colleen Miniuk-Sperry
**Photography:** Paul Gill and Colleen Miniuk-Sperry (credit listed for each photograph)
**Editor:** Erik Berg
**Layout and design:** Gill Photo Graphic

**ISBN:** 978-0-9833804-3-6
**Library of Congress Control Number:** 2014959346

**Disclaimer:** Enjoying the outdoors is not without risk. Because no guidebook can adequately disclose all potential hazards or risks involved, all participants must assume responsibility for their own safety and actions while visiting the locations and participating in the activities suggested in this book. The authors and publisher disclaim any liability for injury, suffering, or other damage caused by traveling to and from a location, visiting a recommended area, or performing any other activity described in this book.

The authors and publisher have conscientiously tried to ensure this guidebook contains the most accurate and up-to-date information at publication time. However, since names, roads, places, conditions, etc. may change over time, please spend time prior to your outing adequately researching and preparing for your trip.

Also, many of the designations used by manufacturers and sellers to distinguish their products are claimed as trademarks. Where those designations appear in this book, and the authors were aware of a trademark claim, the designations have been printed with initial capital letters or in all capitals.

COVER PHOTO: First light on carpets of owl clover in the Eagletail Mountains Wilderness. Originally photographed with a wood Wista 4x5 field camera, 90mm, Kodak VS 100 film, f/32 @ 1 sec., two-stop graduated neutral density filter. Because each film exposure costs about $5.00, I used "twin-checking," where I captured two different images at the same exposure, developing one as shot and pulling (underexposing) the other to capture the sky. Six years later, using High Dynamic Range (HDR) processing, I merged the two images to actually represent the scene as I saw it that morning. Paul Gill

TITLE PAGE PHOTO: Backlit Mexican gold poppy. Canon 5D, 100mm macro, ISO 125, f/3.5 @ 1/320 sec. Colleen Miniuk-Sperry

OVERLEAF PHOTO: Last light across a carpet of Coulter's lupine on the hillsides near Silver King Mine Road. Canon 5DMII, 16-35mm at 35mm, ISO 100, f/22 @ 1/8 sec., two-stop graduated neutral density filter. Paul Gill

# Table of Contents

Locations Listing .................................. 6
Featured Flowers Listing ..................... 8
Photography Tips Listing ................... 9
"Making the Photo" Stories Listing........9
Acknowledgements ............................10

Introduction ...................................... 12
How to Use This Book .......................13
Arizona's Wildflower Seasons ............ 14
Predicting Wildflowers .......................18
Photography Basics ...........................20
Preparing for Your Photo Shoot ........ 26
Caution! ............................................ 27

*Pollen-covered stamen of a strawberry hedgehog cactus bloom. Canon 5DMII, MP-E 65mm 1-5x, ISO 400, f/9 @ 1/800 sec. Paul Gill*

Northern Arizona Locations ............. 28
Western Arizona Locations ............... 66
Central Arizona Locations ................ 98
Eastern Arizona Locations ...............140
Southern Arizona Locations ............184

Additional Resources ...................... 229
Bloom Calendar .............................. 230
Book Sponsors and Contributors ....234
Index ............................................... 242
About the Authors ......................... 248

*Elegant Apache-plume grows in the Sunset Crater National Monument. Canon 5DMII, 100mm macro, ISO 100, f/4.5 @ 1/100 sec. Colleen Miniuk-Sperry*

# Locations Listing

## Northern Arizona — Page 28

1. North Rim: Grand Canyon National Park...30
2. South Rim: Grand Canyon National Park..36
3. Hart Prairie.....38
4. Arizona Snowbowl.....40
5. The Arboretum at Flagstaff.....42
6. Robinson Crater.....46
7. Sunset Crater National Monument.....48
8. West Fork of Oak Creek.....50
9. Schnebly Hill Road.....54
10. Red Canyon.....56
11. Upper and Lower Lake Mary.....58
12. Mormon Lake.....60
13. Ashurst Lake.....64

## Western Arizona — Page 66

14. Oatman.....68
15. Tres Alamos Wilderness.....70
16. Buckskin Mountain State Park.....72
17. Gibraltar Mountain Wilderness.....74
18. Eagletail Mountains Wilderness.....76
19. Saddle Mountain.....78
20. Lake Pleasant Regional Park.....82
21. White Tank Mountain Regional Park.....88
22. Kofa National Wildlife Refuge.....90
23. Cabeza Prieta National Wildlife Refuge...94

## Central Arizona — Page 98

24. Go John Trail.....100
25. Bartlett Lake.....102
26. Lost Dog Wash Trail.....108
27. Desert Botanical Garden.....110
28. South Mountain Park.....114
29. Pass Mountain Trail.....116
30. San Tan Mountain Regional Park.....118
31. Lost Dutchman State Park.....120
32. Silly Mountain.....124
33. Peralta Road.....126
34. Hewitt Canyon.....128
35. Boyce Thompson Arboretum.....132
36. Silver King Mine Road.....134

## Eastern Arizona — Page 140

37. General Crook Trail.....142
38. Fool Hollow Lake Recreation Area.....144
39. Scott Reservoir Area.....146
40. Thompson Trail.....148
41. Hannagan Meadow.....152
42. Forest Service Road 419.....158
43. Black Mesa.....162
44. Cline Cabin Road.....166
45. The Rolls.....168
46. Apache Trail.....170
47. Workman Creek.....176
48. Peridot Mesa.....180

## Southern Arizona — Page 184

49. Treasure Park.....186
50. Pinal Pioneer Parkway.....188
51. Picacho Peak State Park.....192
52. Ironwood Forest National Monument...194
53. Catalina State Park.....198
54. Tohono Chul Park.....200
55. Tucson Botanical Gardens.....204
56. Mount Lemmon.....206
57. Saguaro National Park - West.....210
58. Arizona-Sonora Desert Museum.....214
59. Organ Pipe Cactus National Monument..220
60. Dragoon Mountains.....224

# Wild in Arizona: Wildflower Locations

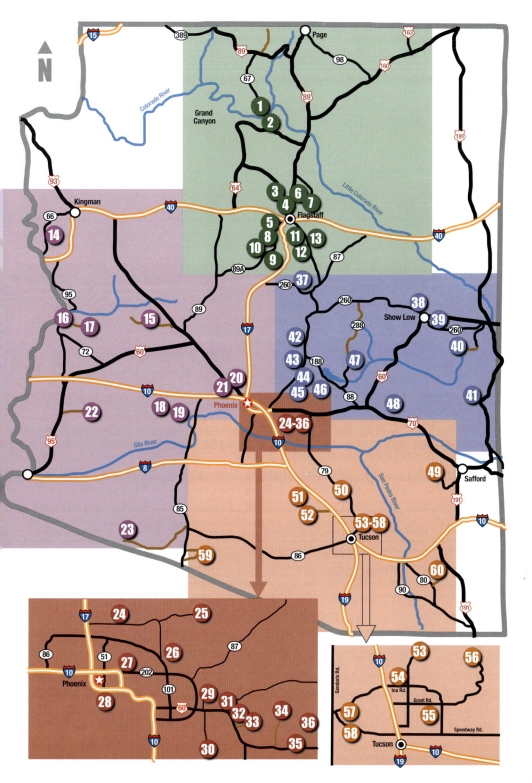

# Featured Flowers

*Sego lilies and owl clover bloom in bunches along Forest Service Road 419 near the Barnhardt Trail. Canon 5DMII, 100mm macro, ISO 200, f/5 @ 1/320 sec. Paul Gill*

## WHITE
Albino Mexican Gold Poppy..103
Cream Cups...........................57
Desert-Chicory................. 181
Desert Primrose................. 95
Flat-Top Buckwheat........... 163
Joshua Tree......................... 71
Lemon Beebalm..................209
Organ Pipe Cactus.............221
Sacred Datura...................... 41
Saguaro Cactus................... 211
Sego Lily............................. 159
Torch Cactus..................... 113
White Tackstem..................117
Yerba Mansa...................... 201

## YELLOW
Annual Goldeneye.............. 147
Brittlebush.........................125
Butter and Eggs................... 59
Calliopsis...........................145
Chocolate Flower................215
Common Sunflower............. 47
Creosote Bush.................... 109
Desert Marigold................... 83
Engelmann's Prickly Pear Cactus. 171
Fiddleneck......................... 79
Littleleaf Paloverde.............. 89
Parry's Century Plant.........143
Tall Goldenrod.................... 31
Western Sneezeweed...........155
Yellow Columbine...............179
Yellow Cups.........................69

## PINK
Apache-Plume...................... 49
Beavertail Cactus................. 73
Boyce Thompson Hedgehog Cactus.133
Desert Ironwood.................195
New Mexican Checkermallow... 149
Pincushion Cactus............... 127
Strawberry Hedgehog Cactus.115
Water Knotweed...................65

## PURPLE
Broad-Leaved Gilia............. 169
Chia................................ 101
Colorado Four O'Clock........55
Coulter's Lupine................. 135
Dakota Verbena.................. 187
Owl Clover.......................... 77
Purple Nightshade.............. 167
Rocky Mountain Columbine..43
Rocky Mountain Iris............61
Scorpionweed....................... 75
Wild Bergamot..................... 51

## ORANGE
Desert Globemallow............ 119
Mexican Gold Poppy.......... 121
Buckhorn Cholla............... 189
California Poppy................. 193
Blanketflower.....................205
Arizona Caltrop..................225

## RED
Arizona Gilia....................... 39
Chuparosa........................... 91
Indian Paintbrush................37
Ocotillo............................. 199

## BLUE
Blue Dicks........................129

# Photography Tips

1. Landscape Photography Basics.................34
2. Macro Photography Basics......................44
3. The Rule of Thirds................................52
4. Where's the Light?................................80
5. Make Friends with the Wind..................84
6. How Low Can You Go?..........................92
7. Reflect the Light..................................104
8. Create an Instant Cloudy Day...............122
9. Focus With Precision...........................130
10. Bring Your Own Background................136
11. The Dutch Tilt.....................................150
12. Polarizer Magic...................................156
13. When Natural Light Isn't Enough..........182
14. Get Perfect Exposures With Grad NDs..190
15. Rain, Rain, Don't Go Away!..................196
16. Extend Your Opportunities...................216
17. Breaking the Rules..............................226

*Wild geranium. Canon 5DMII, 100mm macro, ISO 400, f/5.6 @ 1/200 sec. Colleen Miniuk-Sperry*

# "Making the Photo" Stories

1. Using All 1,000 Words............................62
2. A Bug's View.........................................86
3. Preconception and Discovery..................96
4. Working the Scene................................106
5. Tilting for the Near-Far Technique.........138
6. Telling a Story......................................160
7. What Else is It?....................................164
8. Working Freehand.................................174
9. Visualizing the Possibilities...................202
10. Focus Stacking to the Rescue...............218

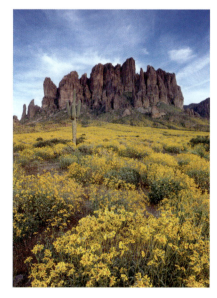

*Yellow brittlebush carpets the landscape below the Superstition Mountains. Canon 5D, 24-105mm @ 24mm, ISO 100, f/22 @ 1/25 sec. Paul Gill*

# Acknowledgements

A project of this magnitude cannot be accomplished alone. We are forever indebted to those who contributed to the creation of this book:

We would first like to thank the members of our "Virtual Focus Group," including Erik Berg, Kelly Pape, Denise Schultz, Bev Secord, Kerry Smith, Holly Smith, and Floris van Breugel who provided outstanding constructive feedback early in this project.

Special thanks to our amazing editor, Erik Berg, whose keen eye and unbelievable wealth of knowledge about Arizona have significantly improved this book.

Thanks also to Colleen's husband, Craig, and mother, Jacqueline, for being ruthless, but honest, editors as well as serving as assistants on many of our trips. We are grateful to our friend Lori A. Johnson for providing an extremely detailed review and excellent feedback during the editing process. And thank you to Colleen's father, Bob, for helping to secure partnerships with our sponsors and for his invaluable sales and marketing expertise.

We also greatly appreciate the financial support and the opportunity to partner with the wonderful sponsors of this book: Arizona Highways Photography Workshops, Boyce Thompson Arboretum, Clik Elite, Hoodman Corporation, Manfrotto, Singh-Ray, Tempe Camera, Tohono Chul Park, and Wimberley. We are equally thankful to those who generously supported our Indiegogo fundraising campaign.

We cannot give enough thanks to Bernadette Heath and Jim Steinberg as well as our fellow Outdoor Writers Association of America members (specifically John Beath, Chris Batin, Michael Furtman, Kevin Rhoades, and Pat Wray) for sharing their priceless expertise and providing guidance throughout the book writing and publishing process.

And finally, we'd like to extend a heartfelt thank you to one another. After meeting at a fateful Arizona Highways Photography Workshop in September 2003 and mutually encouraging each other's photography careers since then, we are truly honored to share in the joy of creating this book together.

~Paul & Colleen

RIGHT: *Claret cup hedgehog cactus bloom. Canon 5DMII, 100mm macro, ISO 100, f/22 @ 1/4 sec., diffuser, and reflector. Paul Gill*

> *"Earth laughs in flowers."*
> ~ Ralph Waldo Emerson

# Introduction

Overhead, the ripping staccato sound of thunder pierces nature's silence. Angry clouds unleash impulsive and torrential downpours, soaking parched forests, thirsty meadows, and desperate deserts. Winter rains ricochet off evergreen needles, tumble through blades of grass, and seep through dry crevasses in baked mud. The passing outburst quenches the land and then restores the stillness in its wake.

A few weeks later, a delicate celebration ensues from Mother Nature's fury. Tiny seedlings sprout from the nourished ground, unfurling slowly, timidly, as the smiling sun graciously radiates its warmth on waking buds. Triumphant blossoms of all shapes and sizes stretch widely to greet the cerulean sky, transforming dull hills into mosaics of color and life. Fields of flowers dance and sway in the gentle spring breeze, drunk with delight. A little giggle pierces nature's silence.

The contagious chuckle starts softly in the southwestern sands and then echoes through nearby desert canyons. Joyous cheers catch on in the lush aspen and conifer-lined meadows. Month by month, the chorus of glee crescendos.

Famed writer Ralph Waldo Emerson once suggested, "Earth laughs in flowers." Come spring and summer, the sweet sounds of happiness also come from photographers, nature lovers, and "petal peekers" giddy over the sight of such an ephemeral event in such an unlikely place.

Those who see this spectacle never forget it and often yearn to visit the wondrous and jubilant blooms year after year. After all, the show is never the same.

When will the poppies bloom at Picacho Peak? Where can I find the best lupine in Arizona? How do I capture an award-winning photo of a saguaro cactus bloom when I visit Saguaro National Park?

After spending a collective 45 years exploring and photographing every corner of Arizona, we are thrilled to share with you—in this expanded second edition—the treasure-trove of information we have collected about when, where, and how to photograph the more impressive wildflower, cactus, tree, and shrub blooms across the Grand Canyon State.

So pack this guidebook, grab your camera, and laugh with the earth as you enjoy and photograph Arizona's unforgettable wildflowers!

*Goodding's verbena blooms near Red Canyon. Canon 5DMII, 16-35mm at 16mm, ISO 640, f/22 @ 1/50 sec. Colleen Miniuk-Sperry*

# How to Use This Book

Though Arizona enjoys a prolonged blooming season, the wildflowers may only show their colors for two or three weeks. When these fleeting blooms occur, we want to get you to the right place at the right time with the right camera equipment. With this guide, you'll become the "poppy-razzi!"

For each location listed in this book, you will find information to help plan your outing, specifically:

*Prairie sunflowers cover Bonito Park. Wista 4x5, 120mm, Fuji Velvia 100, f/32 @ 1 sec., two-stop graduated neutral density filter. Paul Gill*

- **Bloom Time:** The month(s) listed suggest the time of year most likely to produce the best blooms for that spot. From year to year, peak times can vary two to four weeks. Review the "Predicting Wildflowers" section on page 18 to help determine the bloom time.
- **Ideal Time of Day:** Based on the geographic features, the sun's direction, and the usual location of the wildflowers, we have recommended optimal times to visit. That does not mean there are not great photographic opportunities during the other times we omitted! You can make great images anywhere, in any light, and at any time if you work hard enough. Should you find yourself in an area during what seems to be the wrong time of day, challenge yourself to do the best you can with your situation.
- **Vehicle:** If we would drive to the location in a Mercedes-Benz sedan, we rated the drive as "Any," meaning almost all vehicle types are capable of making the journey. If the route is bumpy, rocky, or sandy, we've suggested a two-wheel drive high-clearance (2WD HC) vehicle. If the road is notably steep, narrow, or more dangerous when wet, we recommended a sturdy four-wheel drive high-clearance (4WD HC) vehicle. Because road conditions change frequently, contact the managing agency or local sources to determine the current status before your trip.
- **Hike:** If a location is "road kill" (meaning you can park the car, hop out, and start shooting immediately with little or no effort), we've deemed it "easy." If getting to the flowers requires a long, arduous hike over steep terrain or bushwhacking off-trail, we rated it "strenuous." Everything in between is labeled "moderate." Please consider your own physical capabilities and limitations before hiking.

A summary of these characteristics for all the locations is available in the "Bloom Calendar" starting on page 230.

In each location's description, we suggest must-see trails and places offering the most reliable wildflowers. The 17 instructional photography tips throughout the book suggest additional ideas for capturing eye-catching wildflower pictures in any location. The new "Making the Photo" stories offer a behind-the-scenes glimpse at how we approached 10 different scenarios. We encourage you to explore the areas through your own eyes, though, using this book as a starting point to capturing your own vision.

Though it is not practical to list every flower ever spotted in a place, we list the wildflowers you will most likely encounter as well as a "Featured Flower" to help identify those blooms. For a list of more comprehensive field identification guides, turn to the "Additional Resources" section on page 229.

> *"Our job is to record, each in his own way, this world of light and shadow and time that will never come again exactly as it is today."*
> – Edward Abbey

# Arizona's Wildflower Seasons

**W**hen, where, and why will the flowers bloom this year? That's the million dollar question—one that keeps photographers, nature lovers, and color-chasers guessing each year!

The amount of precipitation received from November to March, the timing of that rain during those months, the temperature, and the location's elevation play into when, where, and why the flowers bloom from year to year. Though wildflowers bloom almost year-round in Arizona, the prevalent season for wildflowers, cacti, trees, and shrubs in the Grand Canyon State generally begins in late February and runs through the end of September. During this time, the state sees four distinct blooming seasons that can overlap.

The **annuals** season kicks off the year-long flowering event in February as the sandy, low-lying deserts in southwestern Arizona start to see dune primrose and desert sand verbena. Classic annuals like the showy Mexican gold poppy, photogenic owl clover, and delicate Coulter's lupine follow in March and April.

These desert annuals—meaning they complete their lifecycle in a single year—need triggering rains from November to January and then steady sprinkles in February and March to germinate. Areas that receive an even amount

*Mexican gold poppy (annual flower) and brittlebush (perennial shrub) grow simultaneously in the Superstition Mountains. Wista 4x5, 120mm, Fuji Velvia 100, f/32 @ 1 sec. Paul Gill*

*Wildflowers from left to right:*
Lupine, Poppy, Wild Onion, Blue Dick, Paintbrush, Fleabane, Chia, Sand Verbena, Desert Marigold, Desert Cosmos

of moisture in January, February, and early March tend to see more prolific flowers even if the total rainfall quantity is below average during this time. Peak blooms traditionally occur in late March or early April in the southern deserts, but the exact timing depends on rain, temperature, and the location's elevation. May normally signifies the end of desert annuals but the beginning of the higher and cooler mountain annuals season, as temperatures warm up in the higher elevations.

Come June, biennial plants like skyrocket and Arizona gilia make a showing in the high country as well. These flowers establish themselves in the first year of life but stay dormant and do not flower until ideal blooming conditions exist during its second year of life before dying.

Sometimes consistent winter and spring rains turn the desert into lush green fields of desert grasses that choke out wildflowers. Extreme downpours can wash delicate flower sprouts out of the ground. An unusual freeze in January or February can stop the necessary wildflower growth dead in its tracks, resulting in few flowers in March and April. Similarly, an overly wet spring that comes too late in March will not arrive in time to produce an endless sea of annual blooms.

*Claret cup cactus. Canon 5DMII, TS-E 24mm, ISO 100, f/11 @ 1/8 sec. Paul Gill*

The perennials season begins in late March as shrubs like desert globemallow spring up alongside perennial flowers like Parry's penstemon. Brittlebush blooms next through early May. Then in June, wild rose starts the perennial show in the higher elevations.

Unlike annuals, **perennials**—meaning the plant lives longer than two years—are not as dependent on a steady rainfall from November to March. Thus, a late rainy season can still produce a good crop of perennial blooms even if the annual season is not spectacular.

Being perennials themselves, the **cacti**

*Arizona caltrop in the Dragoon Mountains. Wista 4x5, Schneider 120mm, Fuji Velvia 100, f/32 @ 1 sec., two-stop graduated neutral density filter. Paul Gill*

*(Continued)*

# Arizona's Wildflower Seasons

TOP: *Mexican gold poppies cover the desert near Four Peaks in March 2009 following plentiful rains in October 2008.*

ABOVE: *The same area in March 2010, where wildflowers were choked out by desert grasses due to heavy late rains. Both by Paul Gill*

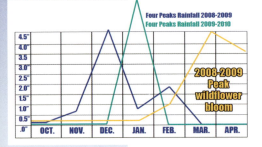

**and trees** begin their season concurrently with the perennial wildflowers. The pincushion cactus blooms in the low desert areas in March, followed by the strawberry hedgehog cactus in April, the stately saguaro cactus in May, and ending with the barrel cactus in August. It is possible to follow the prickly pear cactus bloom from March in the southern half of the state to July in northern Arizona's high deserts. Most cacti and trees produce blooms every year regardless of rainfall.

Towards the end of June, a shift in the wind moves moisture across the dry state and ushers in a wetter **monsoon** season which lasts through September. Triggering the final bloom frequent, but brief, monsoon thunderstorms give annuals and perennials in Arizona's higher elevations the nourishment they need to sprout. Above-average and consistent summer rains can also spark a rare late-summer bloom event in the low deserts as seen in the Dragoon Mountains (see page 224).

Even when all the necessary ingredients come together in the seemingly perfect recipe for a banner bloom, different years seem to produce different flowers. For example, the west central deserts of Arizona received at least a half-inch (1.3 cm) of rain during November and December 2004, then a significant soaking of almost two to three inches (5.1 to 7.6 cm) of precipitation a month during January and February. This moisture, combined with a slow and mild temperature rise from January to March, caused those desert areas around the Eagletail and Saddle mountains to see an incredible owl clover bloom—one that only happens once or twice a decade—in March 2005.

As this great show of color occurred, the Mexican gold poppy bloom was poor in these same spots during the same time frame. However, less than 100 miles (161 km) to the south, the poppies bloomed prolifically in Organ Pipe Cactus National Monument. Later in August, the monsoon bloom in the high country was one of Arizona's finest, producing a broad mix of abundant wildflowers.

Though Mother Nature is the only one who knows what will happen with future blooming seasons, you can keep a pulse on the weather throughout the year for the various elevations using the resources listed in the "Predicting

*March 5: the same day, one year apart in Organ Pipe Cactus National Monument. A steady rainfall from October to March produces colorful wildflowers, but an abundant, late rain produces few blooms (see graph below). Note how the chain fruit cholla droops in a dry year. Both by Paul Gill*

Wildflowers" section starting on page 18. To get an idea of when each place featured in this book typically blooms, consult the individual location description or the summary in the Bloom Calendar on pages 230-233.

### Disturbance Wildflowers

The term "disturbance wildflowers" refers to flowers that move into an area after a large-impact natural or man-made event causes a significant clearing of the pre-existing forest or desert surface. Wildfires and road construction projects are two predominant causes of disturbance wildflowers in Arizona.

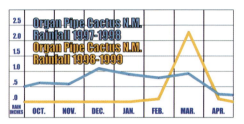

*Slow, steady rain from October 1997 to March 1998 produced carpets of flowers. Late, heavy rains in 1999 led to a poor bloom year in the same area.*

In June 2002, the Rodeo–Chediski Fire charred just shy of 500,000 acres (202, 343 hectares) across the Apache-Sitgreaves and Tonto National Forest lands. In May 2011, the Wallow Fire raced through the White Mountains. Then starting in May 2014, the Slide Fire altered the pristine forest landscapes of Oak Creek Canyon near Sedona. Though these areas may look bleak, with little life seemingly remaining, delicate disturbance wildflowers like fireweed and lupine will thrive here for many years as the process of regeneration unfolds. Locations like the West Fork of Oak Creek (see page 50), Thompson Trail (see page 148), and Workman Creek (see page 176) offer a chance to see a recovering forest in different lifecycle stages.

In addition to wildfires, large road construction projects may result in significant soil disturbance. To restore the area to a more natural state, the Arizona Department of Transportation often uses a technique called "hydroseeding." Hydroseeding is the process of spraying a seed mix —which includes both annual and perennial species of wildflower grasses, shrubs, and trees native to the construction zone—onto the disturbed soil once the project concludes. Not only does this allow for immediate and long term stabilization of the area, but it also makes the area a prime location for wildflower viewing in the years following the hydroseeding.

*"Opportunity dances with those already on the dance floor."*
~ H. Jackson Brown, Jr.

# Predicting Wildflowers

Predicting wildflowers is a lot like forecasting the weather: there are a number of variables involved, none of which occur reliably from year to year. Due to the variations in weather, in one year, the blooms may start in late February; in other years, those same flowers don't start blooming until mid-March.

Since the peak bloom timing for a given area can shift up to four weeks from year to year, it is best to do some research before heading out in the field. A number of resources exist to help develop a best guess as to when and where the wildflowers will bloom in Arizona.

Start by checking the National Oceanic and Atmospheric Administration's (NOAA) Climate Prediction website to review the El Niño or La Niña forecast at **www.pmel.noaa.gov/tao/elnino/forecasts.html**. La Niña indicates drier than normal conditions while El Niño brings an increase in precipitation across the state.

Then, as spring begins to approach, look at the Farmer's Almanac forecast at **www.farmersalmanac.com/long-range-weather-forecast/southwest-us**, which can yield surprisingly accurate long-range predictions based on solar science, climatology, and meteorology. For another opinion of the long term and short term forecasted rainfall, browse NOAA's Climate

**Arizona's Annual Rainfall**
- 35"+
- 25"-35"
- 20"-25"
- 15"-20"
- 10"-15"
- 5"-10"
- 0"-5"

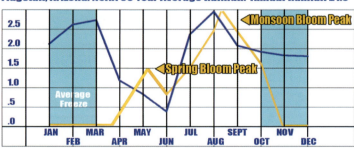

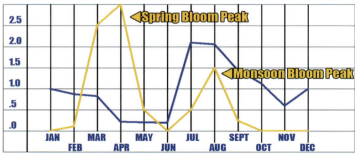

Prediction Center webpage at **www.cpc.ncep.noaa.gov**.

Also, hundreds of rain collectors track rainfall across the state and post their findings on **rainlog.org**. On this site, you can see the total amount of precipitation for a given area on a single day, over a date range, or during a specific month. To pinpoint the historical averages for precipitation and temperature for a specific location within Arizona, visit: **www.wrcc.dri.edu/summary/climsmaz.html**.

Wildflower enthusiast, George Delange, tracks the rainfall and temperatures to provide a yearly wildflower forecast at **www.delange.org/ArizWFlowers/Wf.htm**.

To keep an eye on what's currently blooming, visit the Wild in Arizona blog at **www.wildinarizona.com/wordpress**. Additional websites that post actual wildflower sightings include:
- DesertUSA Wildflower Report: **www.desertusa.com/wildflo/wildupdates.html**
- Arizona State Parks: **www.pr.state.az.us/rangercam/index.html**
- Desert Botanical Garden's Wildflower Infosite:
  **www.dbg.org/gardening-horticulture/wildflower-infosite**

Before your outing, also consult the Weather Channel for the weather forecast at **www.weather.com**. Their Weather in Motion map shows current conditions as well as the predicted forecast for the next six hours for your selected area.

Keeping copious notes about the temperature, rainfall, and peak bloom timing from year to year can pay off in predicting the bloom timing for an area. The graphs below show the average peak bloom times during normal rainfall years.

By putting the various pieces together from these different resources, you can get an idea of whether Arizona will see a phenomenal, decent, or not-so-good wildflower season. However, if you find yourself in Arizona during a sub-optimal bloom year, do not be discouraged. Go shoot anyway! We captured many of the images shown throughout this book in pristine conditions but also made the best of what Mother Nature presented during poor years.

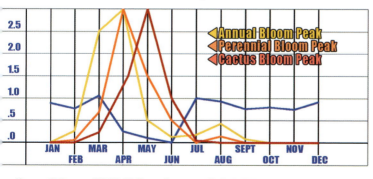

## Average Rainfall

*Rainfall amounts vary from year to year. This variable, along with the temperature and elevation determine if and when a peak bloom will occur. These charts show the average rainfall and the resulting peak bloom. Source: National Oceanic and Atmospheric Administration (NOAA) & the Weather Channel.*

*"You don't take a photograph, you make it."*
*- Ansel Adams*

# Photography Basics

When we suggest camera equipment and possible approaches throughout this book, we refer to a number of different photography terms and camera settings. This section offers insight into those expressions and offers points to consider as you set up your camera for the perfect wildflower shot.

### RAW or JPEG?

You can create a successful photograph in either format! A raw file (also referred to as RAW file) is a large file that captures the entire range of data in an uncompressed format, providing the most options and flexibility in post-processing. The photographer must convert the RAW photograph into a usable, modifiable format before a computer can read it. Since post-processing does not impact the data, this lossless format allows the photographer some leeway in capturing exposure, color balance, and composition when creating the photograph. However, producing the best photograph possible in the field will help increase the efficiency and the effectiveness of your post-processing activities.

A JPEG (which stands for "Joint Photographic Experts Group") is a smaller file that contains a compressed subset of the RAW data that is instantly readable by almost all computers. This format type does not require conversion before post-processing, but requires keeping adjustments to a minimum. Considered a lossy format, each time a photographer modifies and saves a JPEG photograph, the file progressively loses data and image quality degrades. This means there is slightly more pressure on the photographer to capture the image perfect out of the camera.

If you are undecided as to which format to use, shoot in both RAW and JPEG. While it takes up more space on your memory card, you can capture the best of both worlds while deciding which format to pursue.

### Exposure

The word "photography" comes from the Greek words meaning "to paint with light." True to the name, photographers need to record an adequate amount of light to capture a photograph. The term "exposure" refers to the total amount of light collected by your camera when you create a picture.

*Rocky Mountain bee plant. Canon 5DMII, ISO 1250, 24-105mm at 90mm, f/22 @ 1/50 sec. Colleen Miniuk-Sperry*

*Brittlebush blooms on Black Mesa. Canon 5DMII, 16-35mm at 20mm, ISO 100, f/11 @ 1/60 sec., three-stop graduated neutral density filter. Paul Gill*

There are three settings that control exposure: ISO/film speed, shutter speed, and aperture. Measured in "stops" of light, modifications to these exposure settings affect how much light the camera records. When you increase exposure by one stop of light through any of the exposure settings, the camera will record double the amount of light. Consequently, when you decrease the exposure by one stop of light, the camera will only record half the light.

The statement, "open up" means you should add stops of light through one or a combination of these exposure settings. Conversely, "stop down" simply means you should reduce the light the camera records.

Different cameras manage these settings differently. Point-and-shoot and phone cameras automatically adjust these settings without the photographer getting involved. However, some of the fancier compact cameras allow for manual adjustments as well, much like their digital Single-lens Reflex (SLR) cousins which permit photographers to modify the three exposure settings through various camera modes such as program (P), aperture priority (Av), shutter speed priority (S or Tv, which stands for "time value"), and Manual (M). Since camera models vary, please consult your instruction manual to determine your camera's capabilities.

## ISO/Film Speed

The International Standards Organization (ISO) has a widely-used numerical scale for measuring the light sensitivity, or speed, of camera film known as the ISO speed (often called 'ISO' for short). Most modern digital cameras allow you to specify an ISO speed and thus configure the digital sensor to perform similar to film of the same speed. Common ISO speed settings (from slowest to fastest) include ISO 100, ISO 200, ISO 400, ISO 800, and ISO 1600.

Changing the ISO setting affects how long it takes the camera to record an image. Lower numbers indicate the sensor is less sensitive to light and records an image more slowly. On the other hand, higher numbers suggest the sensor will record an image faster because the sensor is more sensitive to light.

To help freeze the motion of a moving wildflower, select a faster ISO speed such as ISO 400 or higher. When photographing static subjects like landscape scenes or when you wish to a

(Continued)

# Photography Basics

*Lone Coulter's lupine surrounded by Mexican gold poppies along the Apache Trail. Canon 5D, 100mm macro, ISO 200, f/5 @ 1/320 sec.
Colleen Miniuk-Sperry*

moving bloom, use a lower ISO speed such as ISO 50 or 100. Use as low of a film speed as you possibly can to achieve your desired image so as to keep unnecessary noise or grain out of your photograph.

ISO/film speed can be summarized as follows:

| 50 | 100 | 200 | 400 | 800 | 1600 | 3200 | 6400 |
|---|---|---|---|---|---|---|---|
| Low | ← | | Sensor's sensitivity to light | | | → | High |
| Slow | ← | | Speed in recording image | | | → | Fast |
| Longer | ← | | Exposure times | | | → | Shorter |
| Lower | ← | | Noticeable grain/noise | | | → | Higher |
| Greater | ← | | Ability to enlarge without noise | | | → | Lesser |

**Shutter Speed and Depicting Motion**

The shutter speed setting determines the amount of time the shutter stays opens during the exposure. Measured in seconds, a fast shutter speed lets in a small amount of light and helps to freeze any action you see in your scene. However, a slow shutter speed allows the camera to record more light and helps to blur motion.

Many cameras permit shutter speeds as fast as 1/8000th of a second and as slow as 30 seconds. Some cameras also have a Bulb mode, which allows the shutter to remain open as long as the shutter is depressed, usually through a locking cable release (historically called the "bulb"). This mode enables photographers to capture images with shutter speeds longer than 30 seconds, so long as the cable release shutter is depressed.

Here are some examples of various shutter speeds and how they affect the way motion is depicted in an image (note that the numbers without the tick mark are fractions of a second and those with the tick mark are in seconds):

| 1000 | 500 | 250 | 125 | 60 | 30 | 15 | 8 | 4 | 2 | 1' | 2' | 4' | 8' | 16' |

| Fast  | ← | Speed                        | → | Slow  |
| Short | ← | Amount of time shutter is open | → | Long  |
| Frozen| ← | Type of motion recorded      | → | Blur  |

## Aperture and Depth of Field

Aperture refers to the circular hole in the front of the camera lens, called the diaphragm, which controls the amount of light allowed to pass on to the digital sensor during an exposure. Even though they refer to slightly different things, photographers use the terms "aperture" and "f-stop" interchangeably.

A small aperture such as f/16 or f/22 will let in a small amount of light during the exposure. However, a wide aperture such as f/4 or f/5.6 allows the camera's sensor to collect a lot more light.

*Richardson's geranium near Mount Lemmon. Canon 5DMII, 100mm macro, ISO 400, f/3.2 @ 1/200 sec. Colleen Miniuk-Sperry*

The aperture setting is one way to control depth of field, which defines the extent to which objects at different distances from the camera will remain in sharp focus. The smaller the aperture number (e.g. f/4), the smaller the depth of field will appear. Only objects near the focal point will stay in focus while objects that are closer or further away will be increasingly out of focus. The bigger the aperture number (e.g. f/16), the deeper the depth of field will seem, meaning objects will stay in focus across a wider range of distances.

In addition to the aperture settings, the focal length of a lens and the camera-to-subject distance also affects depth of field. For a given aperture, the longer the focal length of the lens, the shorter the depth of field will seem. Conversely, the shorter the focal length of the lens, the larger the depth of field will be.

Regardless of the focal length of your lens, if the distance between your camera and subject is small, the resulting depth of field will be smaller. Alternatively, if the space between your camera and subject is large, the depth of field will be larger.

To capture extensive depth of field in your image, focus at the hyperfocal distance (the distance that produces the maximum depth of field for a given aperture, lens, and subject-distance). The hyperfocal distance is the point where everything from half the hyperfocal distance to infinity is acceptably sharp. Because the set hyperfocal distance varies based on the aperture, focal length of the lens, and camera-to-subject distance, it is possible that you might need to focus behind or in front of your subject to get the depth of field you desire. Internet resources such as the Depth of Field Master website (**dofmaster.com**) can help identify this distance for your equipment and composition.

To summarize aperture settings and their impact on an image:

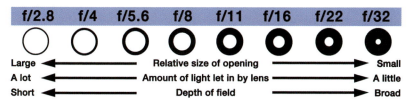

*(Continued)*

# Photography Basics

## Putting Exposure Together

The ISO/film speed, shutter speed, and aperture work together to regulate the amount of light the sensor collects. Specifically, there is an inverse relationship between aperture and shutter speed. As the aperture gets smaller, the shutter speed generally needs to be open longer to record an adequate amount of light. As the aperture gets larger, the shutter speed does not need as much time.

Multiple combinations of aperture and shutter speeds exist to record the same amount of light. While this gives photographers a multitude of options to choose from, how do you know which setting to choose?

Start by adjusting your ISO speed to a single setting such as ISO 200 to keep things simple. Then ask yourself whether you want to depict motion or record a specific depth of field.

If you wish to capture a frozen or blurred wildflower and you care little about depth of field, set your shutter speed first. On the other hand, if you wish to show either a short or broad depth of field in your scene and are not as concerned with motion, change your aperture first. When both motion and depth of field are of equal importance, modify both shutter speed and aperture.

Sometimes conditions aren't conducive to getting the exact settings you want. If you desire faster shutter speeds or smaller apertures (less light), choose a faster ISO speed.

Conversely, if you wish for slower shutter speeds or wider apertures (more light), choose a slower ISO speed.

## The Histogram

Viewed on your camera's screen, a histogram is a graphical chart of how much light your camera captured during the exposure. This instant feedback helps photographers understand whether the camera recorded the appropriate amount of light and how to adjust the exposure if you don't like what you see.

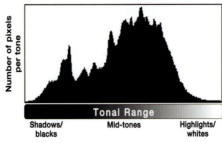

The left side of this graph represents the shadows captured in the image, while the right side shows the highlights. The middle displays the mid-tones.

Generally, a correctly exposed photo will show a balanced distribution of tones towards the center if you are shooting in JPEG format (see "RAW or JPEG?" section) or slightly to the right of the histogram without blowing out the highlights to maximize the amount of data your sensor records in RAW format.

The Exposure Value (EV) compensation function can help either add light or subtract light to an image after evaluating the resulting histogram. If you see a spike on the left-most side of the graph, the image may have areas that are underexposed. To record sufficient detail in those dark spots, add light to the exposure in one of three ways:

1. In Av or Tv modes, increase light through EV compensation ("+").
2. In Manual mode, open up the aperture but keep shutter speed the same. Or slow your shutter speed and keep the aperture the same.
3. Use a faster ISO speed, keeping aperture and shutter speed the same.

However, if you see a spike off the right side of the histogram, the camera has recorded too much light in certain areas. If your camera has the "Highlight Alert" function available and enabled, the overexposed spots will appear as blinking black and white areas when you review the photograph on your LCD screen, which indicates the camera has not recorded data in those places. Post-processing software cannot currently recover or recreate this lost information. In this situation, you will want to subtract light in one of three ways:

*Sego lilies and strawberry hedgehog cactus along Forest Service Road 419. Canon 5DMII, TS-E 24mm, ISO 100, f/22 @ 1/30 sec., diffuser, reflector. Paul Gill*

1. In Av or Tv modes, decrease light through EV compensation ("-").
2. In Manual, stop down the aperture but keep shutter speed the same. Or increase your shutter speed and keep the aperture the same.
3. Use a slower ISO speed, keeping aperture and shutter speed the same.

## White Balance

White balance describes how the camera sees color and makes internal adjustments to render color neutrally in the photograph.

Auto White Balance (AWB) enables your camera to interpret the light and make modifications to deliver what it thinks is the proper color in your photograph. Common preset settings such as Sunny, Overcast/Cloudy, Shade, Tungsten, and Fluorescent offer more control over how your camera sees the light's color. Simply set the white balance to match the conditions you see outside. However, if you would like additional warmth in your photograph, consider changing the white balance to Overcast/Cloudy or Shade when it is sunny, as this tricks the camera into adding an orange tint to your photograph to balance the blues, similar to the effects of a warming filter.

*"You only get one sunrise and one sunset a day, and you only get so many days on the planet. A good photographer does the math and doesn't waste either."*
~ Galen Rowell

# Preparing for Your Photo Shoot

While each location description in this guide suggests appropriate gear to pack for your photographic outing, consult the general gear checklist below for a list of equipment you should consider bringing with you when you set out to photograph Arizona wildflowers.

As they say, "less is more." Give some thought as to the type of photography you are likely to do on your trip and pack only the equipment you need to accomplish those goals.

### General Gear Checklist

- ☐ Camera
- ☐ Tripod (we prefer Manfrotto)
- ☐ Cable release
- ☐ Variety of lenses – from wide angle (less than 28mm) to telephoto (more than 100mm) and macro/micro lenses
- ☐ Extension tubes, close-up diopters, and/or bellows
- ☐ Focusing rail
- ☐ Polarizer
- ☐ Graduated neutral density filters
- ☐ Reflector
- ☐ Diffuser
- ☐ Off-camera flash
- ☐ Lens cloth
- ☐ Boards or shirts in natural colors for artificial background
- ☐ Hoodman HoodLoupe
- ☐ Photo vest
- ☐ Camera backpack (we prefer Clik Elite)
- ☐ Knee pads or gardening mat

**If wind is in the forecast, add:**
- ☐ Extra tripod
- ☐ White sheet or light tent
- ☐ A Wimberley Plamp

**If rain threatens:**
- ☐ Large golf umbrella
- ☐ Rain cover
- ☐ Garbage bag, poncho, or other rain cover for your camera bag
- ☐ Rain jacket and pants
- ☐ Waterproof shoes
- ☐ Hand towel

### Practice "Leave No Trace" Principles

We admit, giving away some of our favorite spots was difficult, as we risk over-use and damage to the places we love and want to protect the most. We trust you will visit and enjoy these locations responsibly. As the old adage goes, "Leave only footprints and take only pictures."

Please practice these "Leave No Trace" principles so that others may see and enjoy these locations for generations to come:

- Do not pick the flowers or destroy any live plants to get your shot. Leave all natural objects as you find them.
- Stay on pre-existing trails when they are present. Do not trample the vegetation.
- Pack it in, pack it out. Carry out all equipment, trash, and food, leaving nothing behind.
- Be respectful and courteous to other visitors you see in the field.
- Prior to visiting, understand any special rules and regulations that apply to the location. Public access rules and restrictions can change.
- Be self-reliant and prepared for extreme weather, natural or man-made hazards, and potential emergency situations.

*Paul photographing a wildflower field at the Grand Canyon. Photo courtesy of Ron Pelton*

# Caution!

## Poisonous Wildflowers

It may be tempting to reach out to stabilize a bloom blowing in the wind, but beware! Although most wildflowers are harmless, some plants contain toxins that make them poisonous to touch or eat. Touching scorpionweed can result in a rash similar to poison ivy. Rubbing against fiddleneck can cause skin irritations. Eating purple nightshade could result in death.

True to "leave no trace" principles, do not pick or eat any flowers you find. If you do come in contact with these flowers, wash exposed areas with soapy water immediately.

*Poisonous scorpionweed. Canon 5D, 100mm macro, ISO 320, f/6.3 @ 1/200 sec. Colleen Miniuk-Sperry*

## Snakes, Scorpions, and Other Wildlife

Poisonous snakes, scorpions, and spiders call the Arizona desert their home. As the weather warms up in the spring, encounters with these elusive, but dangerous, critters are possible. Avoid placing your hands in holes, under rocks, or in other places where they like to rest. Watch your step as you travel along rocky terrain, using hiking poles, snake chaps, and leather boots to protect yourself.

Arizona's diverse environment also supports mammals like deer, elk, coyotes, bobcats and less commonly, bear, mountain lions, and wolves. While hiking, watch for signs of these animals and remain a substantial distance away from any wildlife—or livestock—you encounter.

## Storms

Though rain is a rare event in the desert, prolonged downpours during spring and summer storms can flood normally dry washes with little or no warning. Even if little or no rain exists at your current location, run-off from storms further upstream may drain into your area. If you see or hear a flash flood, seek higher ground at once. If you are driving and come upon a flooded area, don't drive through it no matter how shallow the water appears.

These storms can also produce dangerous lightening and blowing dust, especially during Arizona's monsoon season from the end of June to September. NOAA suggests, "When thunder roars, head indoors!" Take cover immediately in a vehicle or an enclosed building.

## The Arizona-Mexico Border

Some of the locations recommended in this book are in close proximity to the Arizona-Mexico border. At these places, it is possible to see United States Border Patrol agents and/or illegal immigrants. Do not intervene with border patrol activities and report any suspicious activity to authorities immediately.

## Staying Hydrated

Bring and drink at least one to two gallons of water per person per day when exploring warm and dry Arizona, especially if you're visiting from a more cool or humid place. If you feel thirsty, you're already dehydrated.

Indian paintbrush, yellow butter and eggs, purple locoweed, and King's lupine on Schultz Pass near the San Francisco Peaks. Wista 4x5, 120mm, Fuji Velvia 50, f/32 @ 1 sec. Paul Gill

*Wildflowers of*
# NORTHERN ARIZONA

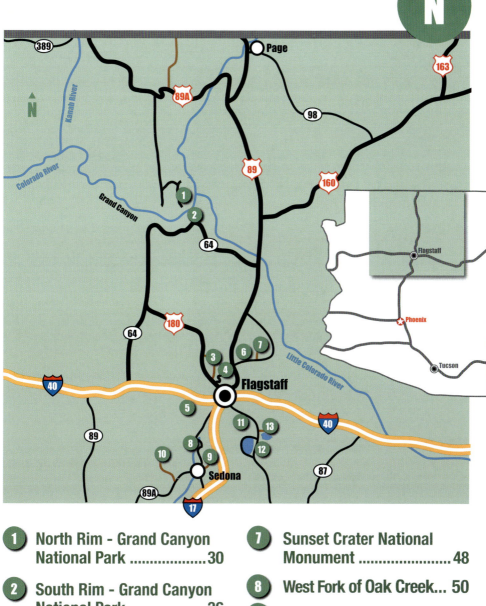

| 1 | North Rim - Grand Canyon National Park ............30 |
| 2 | South Rim - Grand Canyon National Park ............36 |
| 3 | Hart Prairie .................38 |
| 4 | Arizona Snowbowl ..........40 |
| 5 | The Arboretum at Flagstaff ......................42 |
| 6 | Robinson Crater................46 |
| 7 | Sunset Crater National Monument ....................48 |
| 8 | West Fork of Oak Creek... 50 |
| 9 | Schnebly Hill Road ...... 54 |
| 10 | Red Canyon ................. 56 |
| 11 | Upper and Lower Lake Mary.................... 58 |
| 12 | Mormon Lake ...............60 |
| 13 | Ashurst Lake ...............64 |

# NORTH RIM
# Grand Canyon National Park

**NORTHERN ARIZONA**

*Lupine carpets a burn area near Vista Encantada. Wista 4x5, 90mm, Fuji Velvia 100, f/22 @ 1/4 sec. Paul Gill*

**BLOOM TIME**
July to August

**IDEAL TIME OF DAY**
Early afternoon to sunset

**VEHICLE**
Any

**HIKE**
Easy

The North Rim is sometimes called the "quiet side of the Grand Canyon" and for good reason. Only about ten miles (16.1 km) away as the crow—or perhaps more appropriately, the California condor—flies, the North Rim is at least a four-hour drive from the more popular South Rim. However, the extra effort is well worth the trip, especially during July and August when a profusion of high country wildflowers blossom beneath moody monsoon skies on the edge of one of the world's most scenic geological wonders.

On the winding drive to the North Rim, visitors will first see the harsh impacts of the lightning-caused Warm Fire. Since regeneration of the land began immediately after the June 2006 blaze, disturbance wildflowers like Hill's lupine and New Mexican vervain now wriggle their way up through this charred landscape where ponderosa pines and aspens once stood. A **normal lens around 50-80mm** in focal length works best to record Mother Nature's striking juxtaposition.

Before the park entrance, a serene sub-alpine meadow, called DeMotte Park, borders the west side of the road. Here you can find towering larkspur soaking in the sun, aspen fleabane swaying in the shadow of slender aspens, and Rocky Mountain columbine hiding under the cover of conifers. Capture the colorful field with a **wide-angle lens**. Or focus on individual blooms with a **macro lens**. If the trees produce dappled light, use a **diffuser** over your floral bouquet to create more even illumination.

Set out for Cape Royal early in the afternoon, when threatening clouds provide fleeting and ever changing light. Make your first stop at Point Imperial where the unique Kaibab paintbrush, tall goldenrod, and aspen fleabane make for colorful subjects in front of a macro lens. Then continue towards Cape Royal, but watch both sides of the road for abundant patches of skyrockets, Hill's lupine, and goldeneye blooming in the meadows. Dropping your **tripod** low to the ground and using a **telephoto lens** with a wide aperture (e.g. f/2.8 or f/4) can help isolate a single flower among the sea of purple and yellow.

Arrive at Cape Royal at least 45 minutes before sunset to scout for compositions at the fenced overlook and in the surrounding area. Watch your step along the exposed cliffs.

Around the overlook, clusters of broom snakeweed grow with

*Broom snakeweed blooms on Cape Royal with Wotan's Throne in background. Canon 5D, 24-105mm at 32mm, ISO 100, f/11 @ 1/4 sec., polarizer. Colleen Miniuk-Sperry*

determination through small cracks in the white rock, offering photographers a vibrant foreground as the final glow of the day illuminates the monolithic Wotan's Throne in the background. Try a wide-angle lens angled towards the flowers to emphasize their size, placing the flat horizon towards the top third of your frame. Then use a small aperture to maximize your depth of field.

As the sun dips below the horizon, shutter speeds will start to slow, so mount your camera on a sturdy tripod and use a **cable release** to help keep it still. A **polarizer** will cut through some of the haze evident in the canyon, and using a **graduated neutral density filter** over the sky will balance the difference in exposure between the foreground and background.

Situated at 8,000 feet (2,438 m) in elevation, the North Rim sees decidedly cooler weather than the surrounding desert, and afternoon storms frequent this area during the summer months. Dress in layers and pack rain gear for you and your camera when visiting. For your safety, do not venture to the exposed overlooks if lightning is present.

## Tall Goldenrod

*Solidago altissima*
**Blooms:** August to October along roadsides and open meadows at elevations between 2,500 and 8,500 feet (762 and 2,591 m). (Perennial)
**Fun Fact:** Nebraska and Kentucky adopted goldenrod as their official state flower in 1895 and 1926 respectively.

**NORTHERN ARIZONA**

NORTH RIM
# Grand Canyon National Park

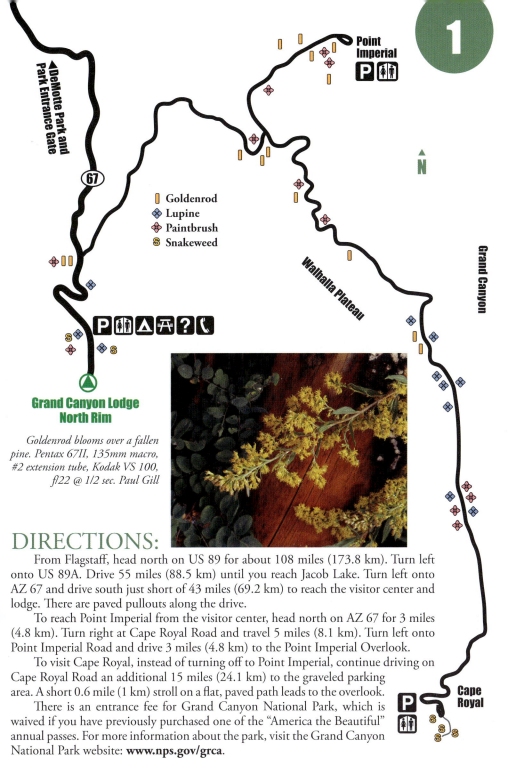

- Goldenrod
- Lupine
- Paintbrush
- Snakeweed

**Grand Canyon Lodge North Rim**

*Goldenrod blooms over a fallen pine. Pentax 67II, 135mm macro, #2 extension tube, Kodak VS 100, f/22 @ 1/2 sec. Paul Gill*

# DIRECTIONS:

From Flagstaff, head north on US 89 for about 108 miles (173.8 km). Turn left onto US 89A. Drive 55 miles (88.5 km) until you reach Jacob Lake. Turn left onto AZ 67 and drive south just short of 43 miles (69.2 km) to reach the visitor center and lodge. There are paved pullouts along the drive.

To reach Point Imperial from the visitor center, head north on AZ 67 for 3 miles (4.8 km). Turn right at Cape Royal Road and travel 5 miles (8.1 km). Turn left onto Point Imperial Road and drive 3 miles (4.8 km) to the Point Imperial Overlook.

To visit Cape Royal, instead of turning off to Point Imperial, continue driving on Cape Royal Road an additional 15 miles (24.1 km) to the graveled parking area. A short 0.6 mile (1 km) stroll on a flat, paved path leads to the overlook.

There is an entrance fee for Grand Canyon National Park, which is waived if you have previously purchased one of the "America the Beautiful" annual passes. For more information about the park, visit the Grand Canyon National Park website: **www.nps.gov/grca**.

*LEFT: Kaibab paintbrush and tall goldenrod bloom on the rim overlooking Point Imperial. Pentax 67II, 55mm, Kodak VS 100, f/32 @ 1/30 sec., polarizer. Paul Gill*

# Landscape Photography Basics

**PHOTO TIP 1**

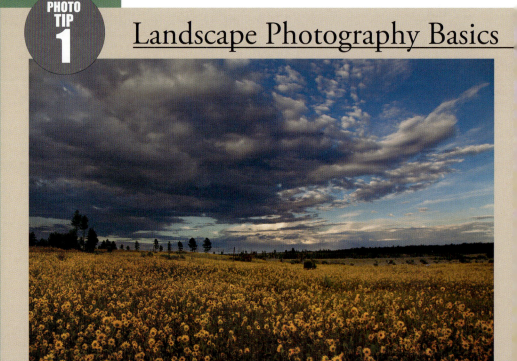

*Using common sunflowers as foreground, a horizon line placed low in the composition emphasizes a dramatic sky. Canon 5DMII, 16-35mm at 24mm, ISO 100, multiple graduated neutral filters in Adobe Photoshop Lightroom 5.7. Paul Gill*

Arizona's awe-inspiring landscape has attracted the attention of photographers since the territorial period and their work has helped share the region's scenic treasures with the rest of the world. Recording unrivaled scenes of carpets of vibrant wildflowers gracing the Earth's floor can be a magical experience. But successfully capturing these grand images can become a struggle when the expansive view in front of you feels busy and visually overwhelming.

Before you press the shutter, let the land speak to you, inspire you, and guide you. To overcome any initial confusion, start by asking yourself, "What is catching my eye in this scene? What do I love about this scene? What's my primary subject?" By answering these questions first, you'll be able to set up a thoughtful picture that your viewers – who are not standing next to you when you make the photograph – can clearly understand and enjoy. Once you have identified a subject, compose your scene following

*A low perspective draws a viewer's attention to the ruby red chuparosa in the foreground at Bartlett Lake. Pentax 67 II, 45mm, Velvia 50, f/8 @ 1/80 sec., three stop graduated neutral density filter. Paul Gill*

the Rule of Thirds (see page 52), taking into consideration what is happening in the sky. Align the horizon with the bottom third of your frame if there are clouds above. Otherwise, highlight the blooming desert or field by placing the horizon towards the top third of your frame and minimizing a less interesting sky.

Getting low and including wildflowers in your foreground will draw attention to individual plants or clusters of blooms among the sea of color while extending your tripod high and tilting the camera down will exaggerate the feeling of expansiveness. Whether you choose a lower or higher perspective, look for naturally occurring lines of flowers that can draw a viewer's eye into the frame and create a sense of depth in your scene.

Break out your wide-angle or tilt-shift lens, preferably 24mm or wider for the broadest view, but don't be afraid to also use a telephoto lens to isolate landscape details in the distance. No matter which lens you select, using a polarizing filter (see page 156) will enrich the beautiful colors across your scene.

To keep everything in your frame in sharp focus, maximize your depth of field by using a smaller aperture such as f/16 or f/22 and focusing on the objects located one-third of the way into your frame, which is roughly equivalent to the hyperfocal distance.

*Under a cloudless sky, tilt the camera down, and focus on the flowers, as done here with a field of Coulter's lupine and Mexican gold poppies near the Silver King Mine Road. Canon 5DMII, 16-35mm at 20mm, ISO 100, f/22 @ 1/4 sec. Paul Gill*

If you are uncertain about depth of field settings, print out depth of field charts (available for free online at **dofmaster.com**) and carry them with you. To confirm your focus in the field, use these charts in conjunction with holding down your camera's depth of field preview button. Pressing this button causes the camera to stop down to your set aperture and shows you how much of the image is in focus once your eyes adjust to the darker scene.

Sunrise and sunset are often the best times to capture a scenic landscape because of the rich, warm, even-toned light and long shadows. In these situations, using smaller apertures will translate into slower shutter speeds, so place your camera on a tripod and use a cable release to minimize camera movement during the exposure. Since your camera will sit on a tripod, consider a less sensitive film speed setting such as an ISO speed of 100 or 200 to optimize image quality.

Remember to check your histogram after each shot. Often times, a colorful sky may appear overexposed or too bright. To help balance the overall exposure of your photograph, place a graduated neutral density filter (see page 190) over the sky in your frame or capture multiple images to blend together later in high dynamic range (HDR) post-processing software.

**NORTHERN ARIZONA**

## SOUTH RIM
# Grand Canyon National Park

*Rabbitbrush at Desert View. Canon 5DMIII, TS-E 17mm, ISO 100, f/22 @ 1/8 sec.
Paul Gill*

**BLOOM TIME**
Late June to early September

**IDEAL TIME OF DAY**
Sunrise and sunset

**VEHICLE**
Any

**HIKE**
Easy

Each summer, the Grand Canyon gets a little grander after fierce monsoon storms arrive and encourage summer wildflowers to sprout along the geological wonder's southern rim. From Mather Point to Desert View, shutterbugs can spot fiery red Indian paintbrush, orange globemallow, towering banana yucca, elegant Apache-plume, and scruffy grizzly bear cactus teetering on the edge of the abyss.

Although carpets of color are not common, the far east end of the park offers the best chance of finding scattered, but abundant blooms. The increase in seasonal moisture persuades the oversized (4- to 5-foot (1.2 to 1.5 m) tall) rabbit brush around the Desert View overlook's paved walkways to sprout a profusion of yellow blooms. At the same time, a collection of more subtle, but equally photogenic, blooms show their colors around Navajo Point.

Because of the variety of flowers you are likely to encounter, pack an assortment of lenses ranging from **wide-angle** (24 mm or wider) to **telephoto** (200mm or longer). Also, bring a **polarizer** to help reduce the haze often visible from the rim. If you plan to venture out at sunrise or sunset, pack **graduated neutral density filters** to help balance the different exposure levels between the land and the sky.

In any season, the grandeur of this scene can be visually overwhelming. Before snapping the shutter, ask yourself what you enjoy about your scene and consider assigning a title to your photograph to direct your photographic efforts.

When including vibrant splashes of color in the foreground of your photographs, utilize a small aperture (such as f/16 or f/22) to extend your depth of field from the flowers in the front to the canyon's distant cliffs in the back. For precise focus point placement, consult the Depth of Field Master tool (**dofmaster.com**) to determine the hyperfocal distance for your camera, lens, and subject distance.

Because monsoon storms can develop quickly, tote rain gear for you and your camera to stay dry in a passing rain shower. Take cover if you spot lightning or hear thunder.

# DIRECTIONS:

From Flagstaff, there are two ways to reach the South Rim:

**To reach the main Grand Canyon Visitor Center and Mather Point:** From downtown Flagstaff, follow Highway 180 to the northwest for approximately 49 miles (78.9 km). At the T-intersection in Valle, turn right to keep following Highway 180 north (also referred to as AZ 64). Continue 24.2 miles (39 km) to reach the park's entrance station. After paying the entrance fee (waived if you have purchased one of the "America the Beautiful" annual passes), proceed an additional 4.5 miles (7.2 km), following the signs to the Grand Canyon Visitor Center and Mather Point. Turn right into the paved parking area. Walk to the northwest to visit Mather Point.

**To reach the park's easternmost entrance and the Desert View area:** From Flagstaff, take US 89 north for about 50 miles (80.5 km). Near Cameron, turn left onto AZ 64. Travel an additional 31 miles (50 km), passing through the park's entrance station. Turn right into the Desert View parking area. Walk north on the paved walkways to the viewpoint.

From Desert View, drive westward an additional 0.6 miles (1 km) to reach Navajo Point.

*Globemallow on the canyon's edge. Canon 5DMIII, TS-E 17mm, ISO100, f/22 @ 1/4 sec. Paul Gill*

## Indian Paintbrush

*Castilleja sp.*
**Blooms:** March to September between 2,000 and 9,500 feet (610 and 2,896 m) in elevation. (Perennial)
**Fun Fact:** Of the 200-plus known species of paintbrush, over a dozen bloom across Arizona and are difficult to distinguish.

37

## NORTHERN ARIZONA

# Hart Prairie

*Sunset warms western sneezeweed, aspens, and the San Francisco Peaks. Wista 4x5, 120mm, Kodak VS 100, f/32 @ 1 sec., two-stop graduated neutral density filter. Paul Gill*

**BLOOM TIME**
July to August

**IDEAL TIME OF DAY**
Sunset

**VEHICLE**
2WD high-clearance; 4WD high-clearance if wet

**HIKE**
Easy

The northern high country of the Grand Canyon State offers a stark contrast to the dry, dusty deserts to the south. The quivering quaking aspens, towering ponderosa pine trees, and lush grassy meadows found in Hart Prairie are more reminiscent of Colorado or Montana landscapes. While the deserts are scorching under the hot summer sun, the monsoon rains of July and August bring this tranquil area to life with plentiful wildflowers.

Western sneezeweed, Arizona gilia, Hill's lupine, and desert paintbrush grow alongside shrubby cinquefoil, swaying aspens, and fallen pine trunks against the picturesque backdrop of the majestic San Francisco Peaks.

Try to arrive at the prairie a couple of hours before sunset in order to discover the magical world of details in the area. Seek out individual flowers and use a **macro lens** and a **close-up filter**, **bellows**, or **extension tubes** to capture delicate patterns, shapes, and lines. If the blooms you find are not in shade, use a **reflector** to redirect light back into the shadowed areas to reduce the contrast with the bright highlights. Or use a **diffuser** to create softer light across the entire scene.

As the sun begins to set, change to a **wide-angle lens** to include not only the beautiful flowers blooming at the aspens' feet in the foreground, but also the volcanic peaks in the background. A small aperture such as f/16 or f/22 will ensure the flowers and the mountains are in focus. A **tripod** and **cable release** will help keep your shot sharp with slower shutter speeds.

After you've captured your image, zoom in on your photograph to make certain your shutter speed is fast enough to freeze the flowers when the wind blows. If the blooms appear blurry, increase your ISO speed setting to a faster speed.

Also, to warm up your scene, consider setting your white balance to Shade or Cloudy. This suggests to your camera that the light is much bluer than it really is, and so the camera adds hints of orange color to the entire image and serves as a warming filter without adding a piece of glass in front of your lens.

Monsoon storms often bring dramatic weather here during this time of year, so use a **graduated neutral density filter** to bring out the clouds while keeping the foreground well-exposed for a moodier picture. To keep yourself and your camera dry during a passing rain shower as you shoot, remember to pack a rain jacket, umbrella, rain cover, and other rain gear.

## DIRECTIONS:

From downtown Flagstaff, drive north on Humphreys Street. Turn left onto US 180 and drive northwest for about 9.5 miles (15.3 km). Turn right onto the signed Forest Road 151 (also known as Hart Prairie Road). Drive about 3.5 miles (5.6 km) on this rocky dirt road. For the next mile (1.6 km), scan both sides of the road for flowers. Pull off on the side of the road or on one of the dirt roads to park.

*Western sneezeweed and Hill's lupine bloom in the aspen forests lining Hart Prairie. Wista 6X9 back on Wista 4x5, 120mm, Fuji Velvia 100, f/32 @ 1/2 sec. Paul Gill*

## Arizona Gilia

*Ipomopsis aggregata var. arizonica*
**Blooms**: May to September in volcanic soil between elevations of 5,000 and 9,000 feet (1,524 and 2,743 m). (Biennial)
**Fun Fact:** Like its cousin, the skyrocket, the Arizona gilia starts blooming in its second year of life.

## NORTHERN ARIZONA
# Arizona Snowbowl

*Paintbrush and lupine along the Humphreys Trail. Canon 5DMIII, TS-E 17mm, ISO 100, f/22 @ 0.3 sec. Paul Gill*

**BLOOM TIME**
July to September

**IDEAL TIME OF DAY**
Late afternoon to sunset

**VEHICLE**
Any

**HIKE**
Moderate

On the slopes of Arizona's tallest mountains, the Arizona Snowbowl is best known as a winter playground for alpine skiers. As the snow melts, though, the warm sunshine of the summer season encourages a vivid floral bouquet to spread along the western flanks of the majestic San Francisco Peaks. From July to September, a short stroll along the Humphreys Trail (which cuts across the eastern side of the ski area) brings wildflower enthusiasts into a tree-lined meadow teeming with Indian paintbrush, Hill's lupine, larkspur, and golden western sneezeweed.

Plan to arrive in the late afternoon and stay through sundown to take advantage of the setting sun's direct and shaping sidelight. Grab your **macro lens**, **reflector**, and **diffuser** to study nature's bounty while the sun sits higher in the sky, but also bring your **wide-angle lens**, **polarizer**, and **graduated neutral density filters** to record the final glow of daylight. Do not forget your **tripod** and **cable release**!

Shutterbugs need only to hike a mere 0.5 miles (0.8 km) of the Humphreys Trail's 5.5-mile (8.9 km) one-way length (which brings you to the summit of Humphreys Peak) before spotting an artist's palette of colors. Though the walk is short, the lower oxygen levels at over 9,000 feet (2,743 m) elevation may make the hike feel laborious. Stay hydrated, take it slow, and stop if you feel dizzy.

From the well-trodden trail, broad vistas of Hart Prairie, Kendrick Peak, and the expansive Coconino Plateau to the west offer scenic backdrops to the wildflowers you find. As you set up, look for multiple visual layers to create a sense of depth in your image. To increase the emphasis on an abundant field of flowers in the mid-ground between your foreground and background objects, raise your tripod higher. To minimize a middle ground with few flowers, lower your tripod instead. As your compositions get wider, watch out for the ski lift overhead.

## DIRECTIONS:

From downtown Flagstaff, follow Highway 180 to the northwest towards the Arizona Snowbowl for approximately 7 miles (11.3 km). After passing mile marker 222, turn right onto Snowbowl Road. Drive the winding 7 miles (11.3 km) to the lower dirt parking lot (which will be the left-most parking area once you reach the ski area). Join the Humphreys Trail on the north end of the parking area.

For more information, visit the Arizona Snowbowl's website at **www.arizonasnowbowl.com**.

☆ Clark Valley Larkspur
✣ Paintbrush
✪ Sacred Datura
◈ Lupine

*Sacred datura blooms on rocky ledges. Canon 5DMIII, 24-105mm, ISO 100, f/8 @ 1/400 sec. Paul Gill*

## Sacred Datura

*Datura meteloides*
**Blooms:** April to November in washes and disturbed soil at elevations in between 1,000 and 6,000 feet (305 and 1,829 m). (Perennial)
**Fun Fact:** Also known as the "moon lily," this poisonous plant's striking white flower opens as the sun sets and closes as the sun rises.

## NORTHERN ARIZONA
# The Arboretum at Flagstaff

*Walkways crisscross different gardens at The Arboretum at Flagstaff. Canon 5DMII, 24-105mm at 32mm, ISO 400, f/11 @ 1/2500 sec., polarizer. Paul Gill*

**BLOOM TIME**
June to August

**IDEAL TIME OF DAY**
Mid-day

**VEHICLE**
Any

**HIKE**
Easy

In 1981, long-time resident Frances McAllister opened her gorgeous private gardens to the public with the founding of The Arboretum at Flagstaff. Since then, guests have enjoyed over 200 acres (81 hectares) of pure visual delight under the towering ponderosa pines with views of the stately San Francisco Peaks in the distance.

A visit to "America's Mountain Garden" offers a perfect midday outing with a **macro lens**, **diffuser**, **reflector**, and **tripod** in hand. Though wildflowers pop up along many of the Arboretum's trails, a stroll through the appropriately named Wildflower Garden, Penstemon Garden, Pollinator Garden, and Sunflower Maze won't disappoint even the most discriminating flower followers. Even during a poor bloom year, many flashy wildflowers common at this elevation, like western yarrow, tobacco-root, desert paintbrush, fireweed, blue flax, and Rocky Mountain columbine, offer reliable color from year to year, thanks to the staff's consistent watering.

The summer spectacle starts as early as June and continues well into August, when free monthly Wildflower Walks provide the opportunity to learn more about the blooms in front of your camera. However, the highlight of the year occurs in July when arguably the largest collection of penstemon species in the United States bloom en masse during the Annual Penstemon Festival.

As you wander through the various gardens, look for an illuminated flower situated against a background in shade as this will draw attention to your primary subject in your photograph. If you have a hard time finding that combination, hold a black or brown board or shirt a foot or two (0.3 to 0.6 m) behind your flower to darken the backdrop. Then use a large aperture such as f/2.8 or f/4 to selectively focus on the flower while blurring the artificial background.

Because afternoon storms occur frequently in summer here, pack a rain jacket, rain pants, umbrella, and rain cover to protect you and your equipment from a sudden rain shower.

*Aspen fleabane, locoweed, and Indian paintbrush intermix with Cooper's goldflower. Canon 5DMII, ISO 100, 24-105mm at 90mm, f/11 @ 1/400 sec. Paul Gill*

# Rocky Mountain Columbine

*Aquilegia caerulea var. pinetorum*
**Blooms**: June to July in moist soil in coniferous forests between 8,000 and 11,000 feet (2,438 and 3,353 m) elevation. (Perennial)
**Fun Fact:** Colorado designated the Rocky Mountain columbine as its official state flower in 1899.

**NORTHERN ARIZONA**

# The Arboretum at Flagstaff

## DIRECTIONS:

From Flagstaff, take I-40 heading west. Take Exit 192 for Flagstaff Ranch Road. After exiting the interstate, turn right onto Flagstaff Ranch Road. Drive less than a half mile (0.8 km), then turn right onto Route 66/I-40 Business Loop. Drive 1 mile (1.6 km), then turn right onto Woody Mountain Road. Drive 3.8 miles (6.1 km) to arrive at the arboretum. The last 2.8 miles (4.5 km) of this stretch are unpaved and sometimes bumpy.

Visitors must pay an entrance fee. For more information, visit The Arboretum at Flagstaff website: www.thearb.org.

*Purple coneflower in the Pollinator Garden. Canon 5DMII, 100mm macro, ISO 400, f/4.0 @ 1/60 sec., diffuser, my mother's hiking shoe used as blue artificial background. Colleen Miniuk-Sperry*

**PHOTO TIP 2**

# Macro Photography Basics

Macro photography opens the door to an enchanting world of details often overlooked in a broader scene. Wildflowers serve as the perfect subject for this type of photography but require different equipment and approach than landscape photography.

A macro lens allows photographers to magnify and get closer to their subjects than other lenses. Some camera manufacturers call this a "micro" lens. Though many lenses claim they have macro-like capabilities, true macro lenses enable 1:1 or 1:2 magnification ratios. These ratios indicate that the photograph will render the subject at full, life-size (1:1) or half size (1:2). Some specialty lenses can magnify subjects up to a 5:1 magnification ratio, or five times larger than life-size! Consult the instruction manual that came with your lens to determine its ratio.

Those without an official macro lens can still

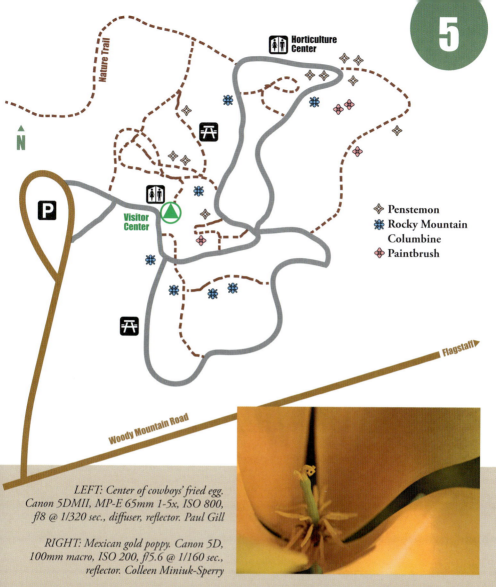

LEFT: Center of cowboys' fried egg. Canon 5DMII, MP-E 65mm 1-5x, ISO 800, f/8 @ 1/320 sec., diffuser, reflector. Paul Gill

RIGHT: Mexican gold poppy. Canon 5D, 100mm macro, ISO 200, f/5.6 @ 1/160 sec., reflector. Colleen Miniuk-Sperry

capture fine detail with a telephoto lens or by using close-up filters, extension tubes, and bellows on a variety of different focal length lenses (see page 216). No matter the lens and accessories you place on your camera, set up on a tripod to keep the camera from shaking and to aid in focusing. Using a focusing rail (see page 130) and manual focus (MF) mode can make it easier to find the precise focus with the shallow depth of field inherent to a macro lens.

As with a landscape scene, start by asking yourself, "What is catching my eye with this flower? Why do I enjoy this bloom? What's my subject?" Set up close to a healthy-looking specimen and determine the detail you'd like to emphasize in your frame, such as the center of the flower or an insect inspecting the bloom. Place this in-focus subject off-center, according to the Rule of Thirds (see page 52).

Then change your aperture setting to a wide aperture such as f/2.8 or f/4. This will blur the background, but check to ensure there are no bright or odd-shaped objects distracting your viewer's eye away from your exquisite flower.

## NORTHERN ARIZONA
# Robinson Crater

*Common sunflowers with the San Francisco Peaks in background. Canon 5DMIII, 16-35mm at 16mm, ISO 100, f/22 @ 1.3 sec., polarizer, three-stop graduated neutral density filter. Paul Gill*

**BLOOM TIME**
August

**IDEAL TIME OF DAY**
Late afternoon to sunset

**VEHICLE**
4WD high-clearance

**HIKE**
Moderate to strenuous

While few photography experiences can match seeing an expansive carpet of blooms in the Arizona landscape, let's be honest: sometimes getting an eye-level perspective of the small, ground-loving flowers can make our backs and knees ache. Hurt no more at Robinson Crater! Though the uphill, trailless trek might make your legs burn, backs and knees will rejoice upon the sight of waist-high, eight-inch (20-cm) diameter common sunflowers blanketing this volcanic remnant's western flank.

Warm up your shutter finger along the first part of the drive, where the flatter section provides easy access to hairy fleabane, wild geranium, and locoweed blooms. When you find a flower of interest, look for side or back lighting on your subject to create the illusion of depth.

Before setting out to explore the sunflowers in the Robinson Crater area, reduce your backpack's load to a **wide-angle lens**, **polarizer**, **graduated neutral density filters**, a **tripod**, and **cable release**. Also, pack a headlamp or flashlight to illuminate your way back to your car after sunset.

Even a short hike puts shutterbugs in the middle of a wildflower wonderland. However, as you near the crater's summit, more prominent views appear of the San Francisco Peaks and Sunset Crater—both of which supply a stunning backdrop. As you compose, ensure the horizon line does not run through the middle of your frame. Emphasize the expansive field of flowers by tilting your camera down.

Afternoon thunderstorms commonly pass through this area. Should you see lightning or hear thunder, retreat to your vehicle immediately.

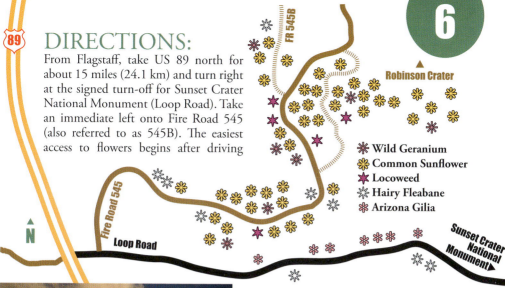

## DIRECTIONS:

From Flagstaff, take US 89 north for about 15 miles (24.1 km) and turn right at the signed turn-off for Sunset Crater National Monument (Loop Road). Take an immediate left onto Fire Road 545 (also referred to as 545B). The easiest access to flowers begins after driving only about 0.5 miles (0.8 km) along this road.

Drive 1.5 miles (2.4 km) from the Loop Road and then turn right onto a small dirt track. Drive approximately 0.4 miles (0.6 km). Pull off the road to park and then begin walking eastward (uphill) towards the blooms.

To reach the highest point (and minimize your uphill walk), drive 2.2 miles (3.5 km) instead from Loop Road. Turn right onto an unnamed dirt road and proceed 0.1 miles (0.2 km). Park at the dead-end and then begin walking southeastward towards the flowers.

Rains from monsoon storms can cause the road to get muddy and a bit rutted so 4WD is recommended.

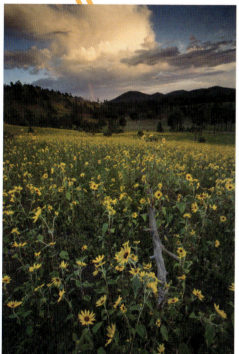

*Distant rainbow at sunset as waist-high common sunflowers sprout in the Robinson Mountain foothills. Canon 5DMIII, 16-35mm at 16mm, ISO 100, f/22 @ 2.5 sec., polarizer. Paul Gill*

## Common Sunflower

*Helianthus annus*
**Blooms:** May to October along roadsides and fields in between 100 and 7,000 feet (31 and 2,134 m) elevation. (Annual)
**Fun Fact:** Kansas adopted the common sunflower as the state flower in 1903.

**NORTHERN ARIZONA**

# Sunset Crater National Monument

*Broom snakeweed blooms in the cinder hills near O'Leary Peak. Canon 5DMIII, TS-E 17mm, ISO 100, f/22 @ 1/20 sec. two-stop graduated neutral density filter. Paul Gill*

**BLOOM TIME**
July to August

**IDEAL TIME OF DAY**
Sunrise and sunset

**VEHICLE**
4WD high-clearance

**HIKE**
Easy

Throughout the eleventh and twelfth centuries, violent caldrons spewed black ash and fiery lava just north of present-day Flagstaff. Today, the tall cinder cones within the Sunset Crater National Monument are no longer active but certainly remind visitors of a more intense time in Arizona's geological history.

Each summer, the fertile volcanic soil provides ideal growing conditions for the elegant Apache-plume, which, in good monsoon years, carpets this eerie moonscape. Among the rugged chunks of hardened lava and powdery ash, delicate white flowers sprout beneath gnarled ponderosa pines. Oversized golden rabbit brush, vibrant Rocky Mountain penstemon, and flashy red Arizona gilia erupt out of the cinders as well. More subtly, the rare flesh-colored Newberry's twinpod flowers also grow in this peculiar, off-the-beaten-path place.

Because of the harsh tonal contrast between the reddish-black landscape and the colorful blooms, sunrise and sunset provide subtle and warm light that is optimal for photographing nature's contradiction. A **wide-angle lens** on a **tripod**, paired with a **polarizer** and a **graduated neutral density filter**, will help record flowers dotting the rolling hills in the foreground with O'Leary Peak or Sunset Crater rising prominently in the background. To maximize your depth of field, remember to use an aperture setting of f/16 or smaller and focus one-third of the way into your frame.

Bring a **macro** or **telephoto lens** to study the elegant blooms up close as well, isolating botanical bunches in front of textured ponderosa pine bark.

Pay close attention to your histogram while photographing here, as a U-shaped graph on your camera's screen indicates a high-contrast scene. To resolve, illuminate the dark shadows on your subject with a **reflector** or use a pop of **off-camera flash**. If your scene is small, a **diffuser** can help turn your histogram into a more desirable bell-shaped curve.

## DIRECTIONS:

From Flagstaff, take US 89 north for about 15 miles (24.1 km) and turn right at the signed turn-off for Sunset Crater National Monument (Loop Road). Continue driving 2 miles (3.2 km) to the entrance station and visitors center.

After paying the entrance fee or showing your "America the Beautiful" annual pass, continue down Loop Road heading east for 5.5 miles (8.9 km) until you see the Cinder Hills Overlook on the right and an unmarked road on the left. Turn left onto this unsigned dirt road (listed as Forest Road 546 on maps). Travel 1.3 miles (2.1 km), dropping into four-wheel drive when crossing occasional patches of deep sand-like cinders. When you see the wildflowers, find a wide spot in the road to park.

For more information, visit the Sunset Crater National Monument website at **www.nps.gov/sucr**.

- Apache-Plume
- Arizona Gilia
- Rabbit Brush
- Broom Snakeweed

*Pink and white Apache-plume under a ponderosa. Pentax 67II, 55-100mm at 55mm, Fuji Velvia 100, f/22 @ 1/2 sec. Paul Gill*

## Apache-Plume

*Fallugia paradoxa*
**Blooms:** April to October near roadsides, dry washes, and dry hillsides between 4,000 and 8,000 feet (1,219 and 2,438 m) elevation. (Perennial)
**Fun Fact:** The nickname for this evergreen shrub is appropriately, "feather duster bush."

**NORTHERN ARIZONA**

# West Fork of Oak Creek

*Wild bergamot growing along the West Fork of Oak Creek. Canon 5D, 24-105mm at 24mm, ISO 400, f/22 @ 0.6 sec. Colleen Miniuk-Sperry*

**BLOOM TIME**
**Late May to August**

**IDEAL TIME OF DAY**
**Early morning**

**VEHICLE**
**Any**

**HIKE**
**Easy**

Soaring red rocks and an idyllic creek inspired famed author Zane Grey to compose his novel, *The Call of the Canyon*, in the 1920s while visiting the Mayhew Lodge at the mouth of Oak Creek Canyon's famous West Fork. Years later, movie director Victor Fleming used this eye-catching canyon as a backdrop for his silent film of the same name.

Although the Mayhew Lodge burned in 1980 and the 2014 Slide Fire damaged much of the forest understory, the scenic canyon still offers photographers, hikers, and nature lovers the chance to stroll through one of Arizona's most beautiful - and popular - riparian areas. Early morning is not only the best time to beat the crowds, but it is also when shade and reflected light within the canyon provide ideal conditions for photographing wildflowers along the peaceful creek.

As you begin your hike, saunter across the bridge where the first

50

blooms, typically the ground-loving purple myrtle and the poisonous sacred datura, come into view. Within a quarter mile (0.4 km), you will pass the remnants of the Mayhew Lodge and quickly understand why prominent politicians and celebrities like President Herbert Hoover, Clark Gable, and Maureen O'Hara spent time here.

An easy, well-defined dirt trail continues into the canyon, meandering much like the creek it follows, for about the next three miles (4.8 km). Several short creek crossings may require some rock hopping along the way. Your **tripod** or hiking poles can serve as a helpful aid in stabilizing your steps across the creek. If you visit the West Fork of Oak Creek any time between May and August, you will see color popping up along both sides of the trail underneath the canopy of pine and deciduous trees beginning after your first creek crossing.

Large carpets are unusual here, but individual and small groupings of mingling wildflowers make highly photogenic subjects for more intimate compositions.

*Cutleaf coneflowers, also called brown-eyed Susans. Canon 5D, 100mm macro, ISO 200, f/2.8 @ 1/25 sec. Colleen Miniuk-Sperry*

Wild bergamot, monkeyflower, desert paintbrush, western wallflower, cutleaf coneflower, and wild geranium are prevalent along the forested trail and among the bracken ferns. Due to the May 2014 Slide Fire, a new blend of wildflowers (like fireweed and Hill's lupine) will sprout to help the forest recover from the wildfire's effects.

Using a **macro** or **telephoto lens** and a wide aperture, isolate blooms against the rust-colored cliffs or reflection pools found in the creek. A **polarizer** will not only reduce the sheen on the flower, but also emphasize the colors and saturation in the petals, the red rocks, and the reflections in the water. If there are no clouds overhead, a **diffuser** can help create softer, more even, light on your intimate scene.

Try to keep your shutter speeds on the fast side though around 1/30th of a second or faster, to freeze a wildflower swaying in the gentle breeze. If you have opened up your aperture to the maximum setting, increase your ISO speed to enable faster shutter speeds.

## Wild Bergamot

*Monarda fistulosa* var. *menthaefolia*
**Blooms:** May to September in moist spruce-fir and pine forests between 5,000 and 9,000 feet (1,524 and 2,743 m) elevation. (Perennial)
**Fun Fact:** Nicknamed "bee balm," some people use wild bergamot in teas to soothe sore throats, coughs, and colds.

**NORTHERN ARIZONA**

# West Fork of Oak Creek

*Myrtle. Canon 5DMII, 24-105mm at 105mm, ISO 400, f/8 @ 1/125 sec. Colleen Miniuk-Sperry*

After exploring the first three miles (4.8 km), the defined path ends and a backcountry route continues through the water into a section called the Narrows. Those prepared to wade through knee- and chest-high water could proceed, but be sure to pack your camera gear in dry bags before doing so.

No matter how far you decide to walk on this trail, you might consider wearing water shoes and packing a separate pair of shoes to leave in your vehicle if you plan to wade in the water. Beware of poison ivy and poison oak along the trail and near the creek. Wearing long pants will help prevent an itchy rash from developing after your visit. Also, bug spray will help deter the pesky mosquitoes.

## PHOTO TIP 3: The Rule of Thirds

Composition refers to the way a photographer organizes and places various objects within the rectangular shape of the frame. The goal is to develop a sense of harmony among the different elements included in the photograph and to create the illusion of three-dimensional depth in a two-dimensional media.

Since the advent of the art, photographers, like other visual artists, have composed according to one of the most well-known guiding principles of composition: the "Rule of Thirds."

Imagine a tic-tac-toe board on top of your frame. Ideally, the most important part of the photograph would fall at one of the four intersection points formed by the two equally spaced invisible vertical lines and two equally spaced invisible horizontal lines. It's not critical that you hit these intersection points with exact precision. This approach simply suggests that your main subject should not fall in the center of the frame.

By following the Rule of Thirds, your photograph will show asymmetrical balance, which tends to create a sense of unity among the

*Calliopsis near Ashurst Lake. Canon 5DMII, 16-35mm at 18mm, ISO 200, f/18 @ 1/13 sec., two-stop graduated neutral density filter. Colleen Miniuk-Sperry*

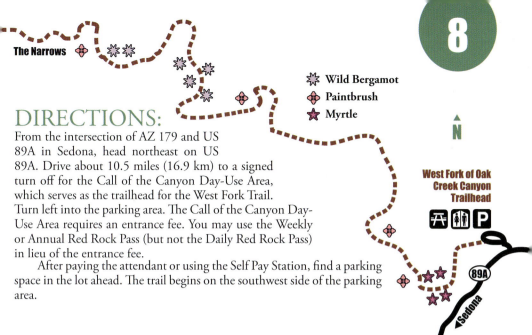

**The Narrows**

* Wild Bergamot
* Paintbrush
* Myrtle

## DIRECTIONS:

From the intersection of AZ 179 and US 89A in Sedona, head northeast on US 89A. Drive about 10.5 miles (16.9 km) to a signed turn off for the Call of the Canyon Day-Use Area, which serves as the trailhead for the West Fork Trail. Turn left into the parking area. The Call of the Canyon Day-Use Area requires an entrance fee. You may use the Weekly or Annual Red Rock Pass (but not the Daily Red Rock Pass) in lieu of the entrance fee.

After paying the attendant or using the Self Pay Station, find a parking space in the lot ahead. The trail begins on the southwest side of the parking area.

*Close-up of yellow salsify. Canon 5DMII, MP-E 65mm 1-5x, ISO 200, f/9 @ 1/160 sec., black mat board as artificial background. Paul Gill*

different interacting parts within a photograph. Symmetrical balance, on the other hand, divides and creates competition among the included elements.

When composing a macro scene of flowers, fill the entire frame with the bloom and place the pistol/stamen off-center. It is not necessary to include the entire flower within your picture, but no matter how much of the flower remains visible, position the middle of the flower near one of the grid's intersection points.

When photographing wildflowers in the landscape, position the camera to capture a grouping of flowers in the foreground, but check to ensure you have not inadvertently placed the horizon line across the middle of the photograph. If this occurs in your composition, choose either the sky or land to accentuate, then tilt your camera up or down respectively to align the horizon with either top or bottom third part of the frame according to the Rule of Thirds.

Some cameras can display grid lines viewable through either the viewfinder or the screen on the back of the camera. These guides are particularly helpful in keeping your subject and horizons in perfect alignment.

## NORTHERN ARIZONA
# Schnebly Hill Road

Arguably one of the most scenic drives in Arizona, Schnebly Hill Road weaves through Bear Wallow Canyon and the picturesque red rocks for which Sedona is so famous. The road's name honors Sedona Schnebly, a homesteader who lived in the area now referred to as the city of Sedona with her husband Theodore in the late 1800s.

Though you may follow the rocky dirt road the entire 12-mile (19.3 km) length, the best blooms occur between the Huckaby Trailhead parking area and the Schnebly Hill Vista – a solid six miles (9.7 km) of terrain to explore – starting in mid-May. A couple weeks later, blooms appear seven to eight miles away (11.3 to 12.9 km) from AZ 179 as you get higher in elevation.

Start by driving to the top of the plateau beyond the Schnebly Hill Vista and into the national forest where a medley of desert paintbrush, sego lily, woodbane phlox, western wallflower, and larkspur await your **macro lens**. Use a **reflector** and **diffuser** to tame harsh contrast found with mid-day light.

About two hours before sunset, head down the canyon towards AZ 179, looking for individual or groups of desert globemallow, Colorado four-o'clock, scarlet bugler, and New Mexico locust flowers to highlight with a macro or **telephoto lens** along the road.

Roughly 30 minutes before sunset, head to one of the west-facing informal overlooks with your **wide-angle lens** to capture postcard-quality photographs of this jaw-dropping scene within Bear Wallow Canyon. If clouds prevail in the sky, the color above could easily match the colorful wildflowers on the ground. A **graduated neutral density filter** can help balance the exposure between the land and sky. Since you'll be photographing in low light, don't forget your **tripod** and **cable release**.

ABOVE: Colorado four o'clocks bloom among an agave along the lower elevations of Schnebly Hill Road. Canon 5D, 24-105mm at 58mm, ISO 250, f/8 @ 1/15 sec.
RIGHT: Desert globemallow along Schnebly Hill Road. Canon 5DMII, 16-35mm at 16mm, ISO 400, three-exposure HDR.
Both by Colleen Miniuk-Sperry

**BLOOM TIME**
Late May to August

**IDEAL TIME OF DAY**
Early afternoon to sunset

**VEHICLE**
2WD high-clearance;
4WD high-clearance if wet

**HIKE**
Easy

- Four O'Clock
- Globemallow
- Paintbrush
- Sego Lily

## DIRECTIONS:

From Sedona, take AZ 179 south past the Tlaquepaque shopping area and across the Oak Creek bridge. At the round-about, turn onto Schnebly Hill Road heading northeast.

If you plan to stop or hike anywhere along Schnebly Hill Road between AZ 179 and the Schnebly Hill Vista, you must have an "America the Beautiful" annual pass or a Red Rock Pass. You can acquire the Red Rock Pass at numerous gas stations, shops, and hotels in Sedona, or at the self-pay station located at the Huckaby Trailhead (located 1 mile (1.6 km) from AZ 179 on the left/north side of Schnebly Hill Road). From the Schnebly Hill Vista to I-17, the road is within the Coconino National Forest where neither pass is necessary for stopping and hiking.

No formal parking areas exist along this route, so look for established pullouts and other wide, safe spots along the road to park.

## Colorado Four O'Clock

*Mirabilis multiflora*
**Blooms:** April to September on roadsides, sandy areas, and mesas in between elevations of 2,500 and 6,500 feet (762 and 1,981 m). (Perennial)
**Fun Fact:** These flowers bloom late in the afternoon – yes, around four o'clock! – and then shrivel up the next morning.

## NORTHERN ARIZONA
# Red Canyon

*Indian paintbrush at Red Canyon. Canon 5DMII, 16-35mm at 16mm, ISO 400, f/16 @ 1/160 sec., two-stop graduated neutral density filter. Colleen Miniuk-Sperry*

**BLOOM TIME**
May

**IDEAL TIME OF DAY**
Late afternoon to sunset

**VEHICLE**
Any

**HIKE**
Easy to moderate

Visitors from all corners of the globe flock to Sedona to soak in the awe-inspiring vistas. With recent developments, it's getting harder and harder to find untouched natural beauty in this impressive—and rightfully so, popular—red rock country. Fortunately, the Red Canyon area still provides an "off-the-beaten-path" opportunity to enjoy not only an abundance of wildflowers blooming each spring but also stunning views of craggy buttes common to the Red Rock-Secret Mountain Wilderness Area.

During the entire month of May, this lesser-known area bursts into a profusion of dazzling color as cream cups, owl clover, blue dicks, white primrose, sego lilies, Indian paintbrush, and strawberry hedgehog cactus bloom simultaneously in good years. Even when winter and spring rains haven't been abundant, individual flowers like Goodding's verbena, desert globemallow, and blackfoot daisy sprout in the reddish rocky dirt, making this a worthwhile outing for close-up photography any time of day.

An ideal visit would start a few hours before sunset to capture individual flowers against Engelmann's prickly pear cactus, alligator junipers, and pinyon pines with your **macro lens**. If your selected blooms are not in the shade, which is hard to come by in this pinyon-juniper woodland, use a **diffuser** to create a patch of more even light on subjects within your frame.

About one hour before sunset, the perfect combination of side light and shadow falls on the towering orange-red cliffs to the north. Break out the **widest angle lens** in your camera bag, a **polarizer**, your **tripod**, and a **cable release**. Then compose such that the wildflowers in the foreground make up two-thirds of your frame, keeping the red rocks as strong middle ground and the sky as your background. To keep the flowers in the foreground and the cliffs in the background in sharp focus, use a small aperture such as f/16 or f/22. Don't forget to try both vertical and horizontal orientations of the same scene!

Evidence of cattle grazing in this area is obvious, so you might bring a lightweight blanket or floor mat to sit on and set your gear upon while you're photographing. Also, since enough photographic opportunities exist up to 30 minutes beyond sunset if colorful clouds grace the sky, bring a headlamp or flashlight to help find your way back in the dark.

## DIRECTIONS:

From the intersection of AZ 89A and AZ 179 in Sedona, travel south on AZ 89A for about 9.6 miles (15.5 km). Turn right onto Forest Road 525 (also called Loy Butte Road on maps) and drive 6 miles (9.7 km). Veer right onto Boynton Canyon when the road splits. Drive an additional 0.7 miles (1.1 km) until you see a barbed wire fence on the east side of the road. There are no formal parking areas, so look for a safe, wide spot along the road to park. Pass through the open gate in the fence and walk along the old jeep trail east for about 15-20 minutes, or about three-quarters of a mile (1.2 km), until you reach the open fields on either side of the path.

An "America the Beautiful" annual pass issued by the National Park Service or a Red Rock Pass is required to visit this site. Purchase the daily Red Rock Pass at one of the many shops, gas stations, or hotels in Sedona before visiting. Also, the dirt roads on this route become impassable to all vehicles after a rain, so check the current road conditions with the Coconino National Forest office before heading out.

For more information, visit the Coconino National Forest website at **www.fs.fed.us/r3/coconino**.

*Blackfoot daisies along the trail. Canon 5DMII, 100mm macro, ISO 400, f/13 @ 1/200 sec. Colleen Miniuk-Sperry*

- Cream Cups
- Paintbrush
- Owl Clover
- Strawberry Hedgehog Cactus

## Cream Cups

*Platystemon californicus*
**Blooms:** March to May in open rocky and sandy areas in between 1,500 and 4,500 feet (457 and 1,372 m) in elevation. (Annual)
**Fun Fact:** Native to Arizona, California, Utah, and Oregon, cream cups are a member of the Poppy family.

## NORTHERN ARIZONA
# Upper and Lower Lake Mary

*Goldeneye carpet the shoreline of Upper Lake Mary. Canon 5DMII, 16-35mm at 35mm, ISO 400, f/11 @ 1/100 sec. Paul Gill*

**BLOOM TIME**
**August**

**IDEAL TIME OF DAY**
**Sunrise and sunset**

**VEHICLE**
**Any**

**HIKE**
**Easy**

In the early 1900s, wealthy lumber baron—and historically prominent Flagstaff resident—Timothy A. Riordan constructed a dam along Walnut Creek in an effort to supply water to the growing town of Flagstaff six miles (9.7 km) to the north. In 1941, a second dam along Upper Lake Mary was built. As a result of these two efforts, two reservoirs formed. Riordan named these twin lakes after his oldest daughter, Mary. Although somewhat confusing, Lower Lake Mary resides to the north of Upper Lake Mary.

Today, the water levels in both pools fluctuate dramatically based on the weather. Following the spring runoff, both lakes can fill. At most other times, though, either or both can dry out such that only the streambed of Walnut Creek remains.

The additional moisture brought on by the summer monsoon season transforms the barren dry lakebeds into a golden visual feast for wildflower enthusiasts. Each August, ribbons of yellow goldeneye, calliopsis, and sunflowers wave in the wind along the eastern and western grassy shorelines and in the section appropriately named "The Narrows" in between the two lakes. Patches of butter and eggs hide beneath the ponderosa pines lining the lakes. Fog often settles in the valley in the morning, creating an ethereal mood for this tranquil scene.

The feeling of wide-open spaces here lends itself well to **wide-angle lenses** ranging from 16mm to 24mm. At sunrise and sunset, emphasize a colorful, stormy sky by using a **graduated neutral density filter** over your lens. Tilt the filter, if necessary, to match the angle of the trees along horizon line.

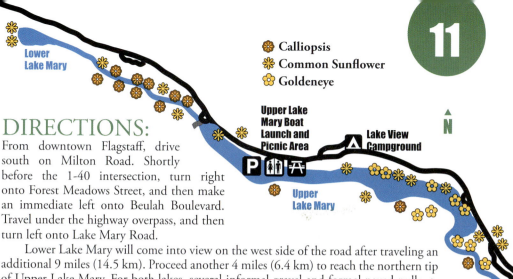

- Calliopsis
- Common Sunflower
- Goldeneye

## DIRECTIONS:

From downtown Flagstaff, drive south on Milton Road. Shortly before the 1-40 intersection, turn right onto Forest Meadows Street, and then make an immediate left onto Beulah Boulevard. Travel under the highway overpass, and then turn left onto Lake Mary Road.

Lower Lake Mary will come into view on the west side of the road after traveling an additional 9 miles (14.5 km). Proceed another 4 miles (6.4 km) to reach the northern tip of Upper Lake Mary. For both lakes, several informal gravel and formal paved pullouts exist along the length of the drive.

With the sun higher in the sky, study individual bloom heads through a **macro** or **telephoto lens**. Create an "instant cloudy day" using a **diffuser** over your smaller scene, taking care to position it such that both your subject and background are evenly illuminated.

During an especially wet monsoon storm season, swimmers and anglers flock to the lake.

Stay north or far south of the day use area (at Upper Lake Mary specifically) to avoid getting people in your shot.

In case of a passing storm, bring rain gear for both you and your camera. If the lake has recently drained, you might find water shoes more comfortable than hiking shoes.

*Common sunflowers appear along the shoreline as calliopsis carpets the dry Lower Lake Mary in the background. Canon 5DMIII, 24-105mm at 24mm, ISO 800, f/22 @ 1/4 sec., two-stop graduated neutral density filter. Paul Gill*

## Butter and Eggs

*Linaria dalmatica*

**Blooms:** From May to September along disturbed areas (like roadsides and fields) at elevations ranging from 5,500 to 7,500 feet (1,676 to 2,286 m). (Perennial)

**Fun Fact:** Originating from the Mediterranean, this perennial herb (which is also called Dalmatian toadflax) is considered a noxious weed in Arizona.

### NORTHERN ARIZONA

# Mormon Lake

*Mormon Lake South Overlook with a mix of goldeneye, calliopsis, and yellow sweet clover. Canon 5DMII, 24-105mm at 105mm, ISO 100, f/22 @ 1/8 sec. Paul Gill*

**BLOOM TIME**
May to September

**IDEAL TIME OF DAY**
Late afternoon to sunset

**VEHICLE**
Any

**HIKE**
Easy

Though little more than a swampy marshland most of the year, Mormon Lake is Arizona's largest naturally occurring lake. Named for the Mormon settlers who traveled to the area in the late 1800s, this location showcases expansive views of high country meadows filled with a vibrant mix of summer wildflowers.

"Petal-peepers" can get a taste of what's to come starting in May, when fields of Rocky Mountain iris turn green lush meadows surrounding Mormon Lake into showy displays of blue, purple, and white. As June comes, desert paintbrush, antelope horns, and New Mexico butterweed sprout in the coniferous forests adjacent to the lake. An even larger display of color arrives in July as monsoon wildflowers like desert globemallow, yellow sweet clover, butter and eggs, and wild geranium bloom along the shore of the picturesque lake.

Visit the low-lying meadow south of the lake a couple hours before sunset to explore the intricate details of singular blooms with a **macro** or **telephoto lens**, using a wide aperture such as f/2.8 or f/4.0 to selectively focus on the most important part of the flower in your photograph. Fill the entire frame with the colorful patterns and tilt your camera using the "Dutch tilt" technique (see page 150) for a more dynamic composition. Shade from a nearby ponderosa pine tree can provide even lighting, but bring a **diffuser** in case you see a picture-perfect flower in direct sun.

As the sun begins to set, point your camera with a **wide-angle lens**

# 12

## DIRECTIONS:

From downtown Flagstaff, drive south on Milton Road. Shortly before the I-40 intersection, turn right onto Forest Meadows Street, and then take an immediate left onto Beulah Boulevard. Travel under the I-40 overpass, and then turn left onto Lake Mary Road. Travel 22 miles (35.4 km) south to the Mormon Lake Overlook on the west side of the road.

Continue along Lake Mary Road, passing a second overlook on the west side with equally impressive views, for an additional 3.9 miles (6.3 km) to reach Forest Road 124C on the east side of the road. Turn left onto this dirt road and immediately look for a dirt track heading towards the open field to the south. Instead of driving on this faint path, pull off the road to park and walk a few hundred yards to the meadow.

and **tripod** north from either of the designated overlooks along Lake Mary Road to capture a cluster of flowers in your foreground leading up to the majestic San Francisco Peaks in the background. A **polarizer** will deepen the blues in the sky overhead, while a **graduated neutral density filter** will help balance a bright sky with shaded foreground.

Because irises (or more properly "irides") like to grow in damp conditions, consider wearing water resistant boots and rain pants to help keep you dry as you carefully navigate through the fields. Add a rain jacket when visiting in July and August to stay dry during a passing monsoon storm. Since you will be in close proximity to standing water, bring along bug spray to prevent mosquito bites.

- Goldeneye
- Rocky Mtn. Iris
- Yellow Sweet Clover
- Common Sunflower
- Paintbrush
- Calliopsis
- Globemallow

*Three Rocky Mountain irises. Canon 5DMII, 100mm macro, ISO 100, f/8 @ 1/100 sec. Paul Gill*

## Rocky Mountain Iris

*Iris missouriensis*
**Blooms:** May to September in moist meadows and forest clearings at elevations in between 6,000 and 9,500 feet (1,829 and 2,896 m). (Perennial)
**Fun Fact:** Because of its appearance, an alternate name for the Rocky Mountain iris is the "Fleur-de-lis."

# Making the Photo 1

# Using All 1,000 Words
By Colleen Miniuk-Sperry

Prairie sunflowers bloom beneath a colorful sky at the Mormon Lake Overlook. Canon 5DMII, 16-35mm at 20mm, ISO 250, f/14 @ 1 sec., four-stop graduated neutral density filter.
Colleen Miniuk-Sperry

Prior to deciding to focus on outdoor photography exclusively, I photographed food commercially for three years after seeing a stock call for "southwestern recipes" from a calendar company more famous for its landscape photography. "Hmmm," I naively said, "that could be fun!"

Though I am no longer a shutterbug of sushi, I do not regret spending those years getting a different flavor of photography. In fact, I believe it has made me a better nature photographer, as I still incorporate many of the techniques learned while photographing food during my outdoor escapades.

One of the most profound learnings I took away from the experience was if a picture is truly worth 1,000 words, then photographers should utilize all 1,000 words to convey our visual messages—not 999 or less! During the extensive set designing process while photographing cuisine, I deliberately and precisely placed every single sesame seed, slice of lime, and sprinkle of cilantro in an exact location. Before snapping the shutter, I studied every corner, the edges of the frame, and the visual relationship between the elements to ensure the scene appeared exactly as the client wished. Every pixel of the image (i.e., all "1,000 words") was intentional.

Although changing moments in nature do not often allow a six to eight hour review of a composition before snapping (as I had when photographing food), we can take a minute to evaluate whether we have intentionally included every part of our image. One of the fastest ways to determine whether the photograph you created represents what you imagined to be at the scene versus what you actually saw is to perform a "border patrol." Scan the edges of your frame in search of distracting objects you did not intend to record (e.g., out of focus branches, bright tones). Do not waste even a few words on things you never intended to be a part of your clear visual message.

Case in point: After spending some productive time in Arizona's high country, I decided to take the leisurely route home via Lake Mary Road and AZ 87 (instead of battling the weekend traffic racing down I-17 from Flagstaff). Although my drive would take me past Lower Lake Mary, Upper Lake Mary, Mormon Lake and other scenic locales, I did not have intentions to photograph along the way.

As I approached Mormon Lake, I noticed the clouds in the sky starting to take on a different, lighter, color as the sun kissed the horizon. The clouds held all the promise of another gorgeous Arizona sunset. I pulled into the next overlook simply to enjoy the moment. Once I parked, however, my eye caught a patch of tall prairie sunflowers reaching to the sky on the north side of the parking lot. I thought the cluster would make a nice photograph. I opened my car door to get a closer look. In that instance, the sky began transforming into intermixing layers of pastel blues and pinks. And I was not ready to photograph the scene!

I ran to the back of my Toyota 4Runner and hastily dug my photography gear out from beneath other suitcases and bags. While unzipping my camera bag, I glanced back at the flowers and developing backdrop. I immediately visualized a composition, one that positioned the flowers in the foreground, a moderate amount of mid-ground, and the distant San Francisco Peaks and colorful clouds as my background. Given this arrangement, I locked my wide-angle lens onto my camera and slung my gear around my neck. I quickly confirmed I had both a battery and memory card in the camera. Then, I grabbed my tripod and four-stop graduated neutral density filter. Running towards the flowers, I set my ISO to 100 and my aperture to f/16 to maximize my depth of field. Within seconds, I was ready to shoot…but did not.

Although the clouds were turning from pastel to fiery, I focused not on blasting away, but rather on what I saw now that I stood in front of the scene. This extra second of concentration allowed me to refine my visualized composition in the photographic frame. I realized I needed to lower my tripod to reduce the size of the less interesting mid-ground (and to make the road less noticeable). I increased my ISO speed to ISO 250 and opened my aperture to f/14 to keep my shutter speed at 1 second since the flowers were wiggling in the light breeze. After waiting a few more seconds for a lull in the wind, I snapped only a few frames (making subtle adjustments in between each photograph) before the color in the sky waned.

Upon the show's conclusion, I flipped through my photographs on the LCD screen to see how I had done. After doing a "border patrol" on the different frames, it became apparent that I did not see the leaves on the bottom left or right of my frame when I photographed. I saw everything else. While these two minor unintentional elements are not likely to ruin the overall impact of the image (or even be noticed by viewers), it served as a reminder to me to continue to slow down and ensure every part of the frame is intentional.

**NORTHERN ARIZONA**

# Ashurst Lake

*Carpets of calliopsis in the fields en route to Ashurst Lake. Canon 5DMII. 17-35mm at 20mm, ISO 100, f/16 @ 1/30 sec. Paul Gill*

**BLOOM TIME**
July to September

**IDEAL TIME OF DAY**
Late afternoon to sunset

**VEHICLE**
Any

**HIKE**
Easy

Like nearby Mormon Lake, Ashurst Lake is one of the few naturally occurring lakes within Arizona. Typically full year-round, this moist environment allows the water-loving water knotweed to grace its shoreline as dramatic monsoon storms race across the high country. As if this unusual flower alone was not enough to draw shutterbugs to this spot, those seeking photogenic carpets of color need to look no further than the meadows surrounding this charming lake.

The summer show begins in July with vibrant pink cylindrical flowers sprouting along the southern edge of the lake near the campground. Simultaneously, in the normally dry grasslands neighboring the water, Engelmann's prickly pear cactus bud their lively yellow flowers.

Towards the end of summer, in August, yellow calliopsis covers the fields for as far as the eye can see. Large swaths provide a vibrant foreground to compliment the equally beautiful backdrop of the silhouetted San Francisco Peaks to the north at sunset.

Arrive late in the afternoon to scout for the water knotweed along the southern shoreline. To keep this elongated bloom in focus as it bobs up and down in the water, use a faster shutter speed and a Wimberley Plamp (see page 84). A **macro** or **telephoto lens** with a wide aperture will help isolate the bloom against the soothing background of blue water.

Before the sun goes down, visit the meadows along Forest Road 82E and point your camera towards the western horizon. Find an individual flower to isolate among the masses with your telephoto lens. The backlight creates a halo around your subject, which will separate it from the background and create the illusion of depth. Make your chosen bloom stand out even more by setting a wide aperture (e.g. f/4 or f/5.6), using the dark volcanic rocks

**Flagstaff**

- ◆ Water Knotweed
- ✸ Calliopsis
- ✦ Paintbrush

# 13

**Ashurst Lake**

**Forked Pines CG**

## DIRECTIONS:

From downtown Flagstaff, drive south on Milton Road. Shortly before the I-40 intersection, turn right onto Forest Meadows Street, and then take an immediate left onto Beulah boulevard. Travel under the I-40 overpass, and then turn left on to Lake Mary Road. Travel 17 miles (27.4 km) south, then turn left onto the well-maintained gravel Forest Road 82E. After driving 1 mile (1.6 km), watch for wildflowers in the fields along this route, parking in a wide spot on the side of the road when you see the blooms.

Forest Road 82E meanders 3.9 miles (6.3 km) to the lake. Turn left onto the dirt road towards the Forked Pine Campground and scan the shoreline once you pass the campground.

or a black artificial background as a backdrop.

As the sun starts to drop behind the ponderosa pines, switch to a **wide-angle lens** and a small aperture such as f/16 or f/22 to capture a stunning sunburst above the field of gold. Limit lens flare by composing your photograph such that the sun is on the top right or left third of your frame and partially obstructed by the trees whether you shoot in a vertical or horizontal orientation. Don't forget to use a **tripod** to stabilize your camera during the slower shutter speeds at sundown.

Because of the difference in light levels between the sky and the land when shooting sunbursts, use a **graduated neutral density filter** over the sky. Or take multiple exposures at the camera's metering settings of 0, then +2 and -2 so you can blend the three resulting images using High Dynamic Range (HDR) post-processing software later.

*Calliopsis blooms among volcanic rock. Canon 5DMII, 16-35mm at 27mm, ISO 200, f/13 @ 1/15 sec. Colleen Miniuk-Sperry*

## Water Knotweed

*Polygonum amphibium*
**Blooms**: July to September in lakes, marshes, and ponds in between 5,000 and 9,000 feet (1,524 and 2,743 m) elevation. (Perennial)
**Fun Fact:** Water knotweed grows in every state in the Union, except for Florida, Georgia, Alabama, and Hawai'i.

A river of magenta-colored owl clover snakes through fields of fiddleneck and Mexican gold poppies at Saddle Mountain. Pentax 67II, 90mm, Fuji Velvia 50, f/32 @ 1/4 sec. Paul Gill

# Wildflowers of WESTERN ARIZONA

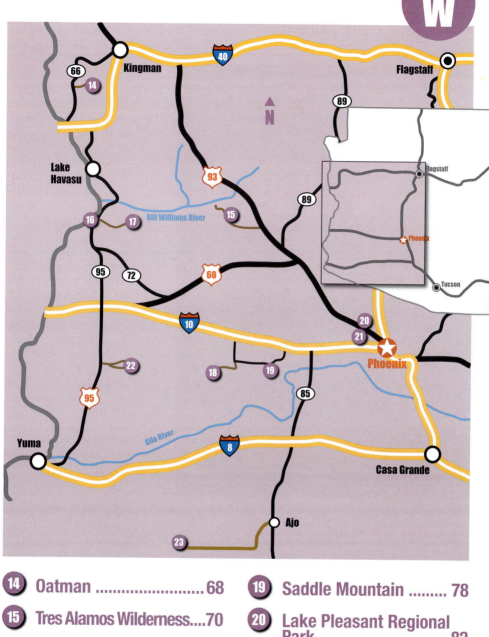

| | | | |
|---|---|---|---|
| **14** | Oatman ........................... 68 | **19** | Saddle Mountain ......... 78 |
| **15** | Tres Alamos Wilderness....70 | **20** | Lake Pleasant Regional Park............................... 82 |
| **16** | Buckskin Mountain State Park ...................... 72 | **21** | White Tank Mountains Regional Park................ 88 |
| **17** | Gibraltar Mountain Wilderness ..................... 74 | **22** | Kofa National Wildlife Refuge............................ 90 |
| **18** | Eagletail Mountains Wilderness ..................... 76 | **23** | Cabeza Prieta National Wildlife Refuge............. 94 |

**WESTERN ARIZONA**

# Oatman

*Poppies carpet the hillsides with Boundary Cone in background. Pentax 67II, 45mm, Fuji Velvia 50 f/22 @ 1/30 sec., polarizer. Paul Gill*

**BLOOM TIME**
**February to April**

**IDEAL TIME OF DAY**
**Late afternoon to sunset**

**VEHICLE**
**Any**

**HIKE**
**Easy**

In the early 1900s, prospectors discovered rich gold veins in the heart of the desolate and appropriately named Black Mountains. Not surprisingly, their discovery quickly transformed a scanty tent camp into a flourishing settlement later known as Oatman. Although mining activities have since declined, those seeking gold today can find a different kind in the mountains located just south of the historic community. After plentiful winter rains, a profusion of radiant golden wildflowers transforms what used to be a boom town into a bloom town.

On the flanks of the rugged Black Mountains, large spreads of yellow cups bloom in concert with Mexican gold poppies, fiddleneck, and brittlebush starting as early as February. An occasional splash of purple Coulter's lupine breaks up the beaming monochromatic display across the dusty desert.

Plan to arrive a couple hours before sunset with **macro**, **telephoto**, and **wide-angle lenses** if you wish to capture open Mexican gold poppies worshipping the sun overhead. Position your **tripod** towards the mouth of the canyon, using the photogenic volcanic plug known as Boundary Cone as your background for the patch of flowers in your foreground.

To help reduce the sharp contrast between the shadows and highlights that occurs in late afternoon light, wait for a cloud to eclipse the sun temporarily before triggering the shutter on a broad landscape scene. If the day is short on clouds, use a **diffuser** or **reflector** to even the light across smaller compositions instead.

As the sun starts to drop towards the western horizon, the poppies close their delicate petals for the night, but the rest of the flowers on the north facing bajada continue to soak up the warm sunset light. Point a wide-angle lens coupled with a **polarizer** to the south to capture the side light draping across on the jagged ridgelines. Because much of the canyon will fall into shade before sunset, a **graduated neutral density filter** can help keep the sky from blowing out while still maintaining details in the foreground.

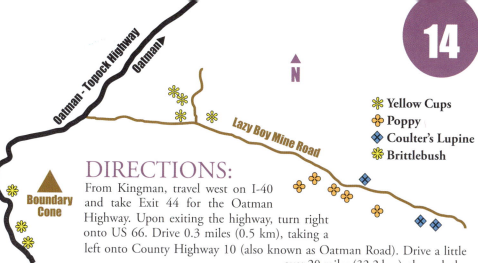

- ❋ Yellow Cups
- ✤ Poppy
- ◆ Coulter's Lupine
- ❋ Brittlebush

## DIRECTIONS:

From Kingman, travel west on I-40 and take Exit 44 for the Oatman Highway. Upon exiting the highway, turn right onto US 66. Drive 0.3 miles (0.5 km), taking a left onto County Highway 10 (also known as Oatman Road). Drive a little over 20 miles (32.2 km), through the town of Oatman, and then veer left onto the Oatman-Topock Highway when the road splits. Continue for another 6.1 miles (9.8 km) and then turn left onto an unmarked dirt road (referred to as Lazy Boy Mine Road on some maps) just north of the large mountain called Boundary Cone. The best flowers are located all along this 2 mile (3.2 km), sometimes bumpy, dirt road. To park, pull off at a wide spot in the road.

*Yellow cups bloom along the Lazy Boy Mine Road. Pentax 67II, 45mm, Velvia 50, f/22 @ 1/4 sec., two-stop graduated neutral density filter. Paul Gill*

## Yellow Cups

*Camissonia brevipes*
**Blooms:** February to May in desert washes and on slopes below 4,500 feet (1,372 m) elevation. (Annual)
**Fun Fact:** Though a member of the evening primrose family, yellow cups start blooming at sunrise, not sunset.

**WESTERN ARIZONA**

# Tres Alamos Wilderness

*Evening light on a blooming Joshua tree. Canon 5DMII, 24-105mm at 32mm, ISO 100, f/11 @ 0.3 sec., polarizer. Paul Gill*

**BLOOM TIME**
**March to April**

**IDEAL TIME OF DAY**
**Sunrise and sunset**

**VEHICLE**
**2WD high-clearance**

**HIKE**
**Easy**

Four deserts span the vast North American continent: the Mojave, the Chihuahuan, the Great Basin, and the Sonoran. Arizona is the only state in the union to host all four. In Tres Alamos Wilderness, visitors see firsthand the collision of two of these deserts, the Mojave and Sonoran, where uniquely-shaped Joshua trees drastically outnumber the stately saguaro cacti.

The gentle slopes along the Black Mountains (not to be confused with the mountains near Oatman with the same name) offer a reliable Joshua tree bloom starting in March. Wildflower carpets aren't common here, but after a healthy soaking by winter rains, owl clover and Mexican gold poppies sprout in patches beneath the majestic trees while brittlebush covers rocky hillsides.

To show the blooming yucca in its environs, back away from your selected subject and use either a **normal lens around 50 to 80mm** or a **telephoto lens** depending on how many Joshua trees you wish to include in your frame. On the other hand, to emphasize the height of the tree-like yucca reaching into the sky, move closer and use a **wide-angle lens**. Create a frame using the blooming branches to help direct a viewer's eye to the distant Joshua trees in the background.

As you set up, check to ensure you don't have any trees or branches merging with each other which can disrupt the feeling of movement throughout the frame. Then try both a vertical and horizontal composition

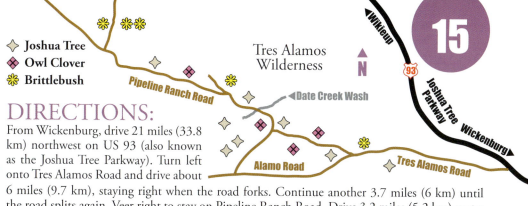

- ✦ Joshua Tree
- ✦ Owl Clover
- ✽ Brittlebush

## DIRECTIONS:

From Wickenburg, drive 21 miles (33.8 km) northwest on US 93 (also known as the Joshua Tree Parkway). Turn left onto Tres Alamos Road and drive about 6 miles (9.7 km), staying right when the road forks. Continue another 3.7 miles (6 km) until the road splits again. Veer right to stay on Pipeline Ranch Road. Drive 3.2 miles (5.2 km) past a ranch and through sandy Date Creek Wash to reach the best flowers.

---

with and without the rounded Sawyer Peak to the north, before moving your tripod to a new scene.

However you decide to set up, a **polarizer** will help saturate the blue sky. If clouds are overhead, also place a **graduated neutral density filter** over the sky in your picture to help keep the sky's exposure consistent with the land.

Some Joshua tree arms extend low enough to allow for close-up photographs. Because the blooms can reach up to four feet (1.2 m) in length, a normal length lens can easily capture the detail of the white cluster of flowers, so leave the macro lens behind.

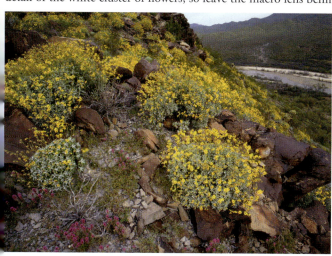

Since sunrise and sunset are the best times to photograph in this remote location, pack a flashlight or headlamp to navigate in the dark. Bring a GPS and a topographic map with you as well, as this is not the easiest place to find with the abundance of small dirt roads crisscrossing through the desert around the wilderness area.

*Brittlebush and owl clover above the swollen Santa Maria River. Wista 4x5, 120mm, Kodak VS 100, f/32 @ 1/2 sec. Paul Gill*

## Joshua Tree

*Yucca brevifolia*
**Blooms:** March to April on rocky plains and hillsides in between 2,000 and 3,500 feet (610 and 1,067 m) elevation. (Perennial)
**Fun Fact:** Though its name suggests otherwise, Joshua trees are not trees; they are an evergreen yucca in the agave family.

**WESTERN ARIZONA**

# Buckskin Mountain State Park

*Coulter's lupine and yellow cups bloom along the Buckskin Loop Trail. Contax 645, 45mm, Fuji Velvia 100, f/32 @ 1/2 sec., polarizer. Colleen Miniuk-Sperry*

**BLOOM TIME**
**March**

**IDEAL TIME OF DAY**
**Sunrise and sunset**

**VEHICLE**
**Any**

**HIKE**
**Strenuous**

Many people head to Arizona's West Coast during the blazingly hot summer months to take a dip in the cool and refreshing Colorado River winding its way through the rugged desert. However, each March, this popular oasis provides surprising opportunities to photograph wildflowers when the rolling hills within the park yield bountiful beavertail cactus, Coulter's lupine, and scorpionweed blooms.

Get started on the moderately strenuous Lightning Bolt Trail before sunrise, taking a right onto the equally difficult Buckskin Loop Trail. The best spot for sunrise is over the pedestrian bridge and up the hill on the ridge across the road. However, as you walk down this well-maintained dirt path, look for wildflowers blooming on either side of the trail before you cross the overpass as this will be the location you'll want to return to after your sunrise shoot.

After crossing the bridge, follow the Buckskin Loop Trail as it meanders uphill to the highest point. A couple of benches provide a welcome respite from the stair-step climb. From these benches, you will also have outstanding scenic views looking north across the Colorado River at California's Whipple Mountains.

A blooming beavertail cactus or a combination of purple Coulter's lupine and scorpionweed adds a splash of color to your foreground as the sun rises and illuminates the craggy Whipple Mountains with warm sidelight. Drop your **tripod** low to the ground and get close to a selected bloom with your **wide-angle lens**, allowing the carpet of nearby flowers to fill your frame. A small aperture such as f/16 or f/22 will help keep you

## DIRECTIONS:

From Parker (along the Colorado River between I-10 and I-40), take AZ 95 north toward Lake Havasu for about 12 miles (19.3 km) before arriving at the entrance to Buckskin Mountain State Park on the left-hand side of the road. The trailhead for the Lightning Bolt Trail, which leads to the Buckskin Loop Trail, is located south of the ranger station.

Buckskin Mountain State Park requires an entrance fee unless you can show a previously-purchased annual pass issued by the Arizona State Parks. After paying at the ranger station or the self-pay station, park in the day use parking area just north of the ranger station unless you plan to camp here overnight.

For more information, visit the Buckskin Mountain State Park website at **www.pr.state.az.us/parks/BUMO/index.html**.

*Backlit beavertail cactus. Nikon N90s, 100mm, Velvia 100, f/8 @ 1/25 sec.*
*Paul Gill*

flowery foreground and distant background in focus.

As the sun rises high in the sky, return the way you came, crossing the bridge and revisiting the area near the intersection with the Lightning Bolt Trail. Along this section, look for healthy flower specimens to capture more close-up details of the blooms through a **macro** or **telephoto lens**. Mesquite trees, paloverde trees, and creosote bushes provide shade and, therefore, more diffused light well-suited for macro work. However, the light trickling through the branches may render uneven patches of highlights and shadows on your floral subjects, so use a **diffuser** to create your own shade as you shoot through the harsher morning light.

As evening approaches, grab a flashlight or headlamp and head back to the same areas you visited in the morning along the Buckskin Loop Trail. But this time, position your camera towards the Buckskin Mountains on the southeastern horizon.

## Beavertail Cactus

*Opuntia basilaris*
**Blooms:** March to May along rocky slopes, washes, and desert flats in between 200 and 4,000 feet (61 and 1,219 m) elevation. (Perennial)
**Fun Fact:** The brownish-grey fruit that appears after the flower blooms is edible and is a favorite treat for javelina.

## WESTERN ARIZONA
# Gibraltar Mountain Wilderness

*Scorpionweed. Wista 6X9 back on Wista 4x5, 120mm, Fuji Velvia 50, f/32 @ 1/2 sec., two-stop graduated neutral density filter.*
*Paul Gill*

**BLOOM TIME**
March to April

**IDEAL TIME OF DAY**
Sunrise and sunset

**VEHICLE**
Any

**HIKE**
Easy

When it came to the Gibraltar Mountain Wilderness, it's almost as if Mother Nature couldn't decide on how to design this piece of land. She started with a textured carpet of Sonoran Desert vegetation in the lowlands coupled with a dark, rugged volcanic backdrop and then added a bed of rough volcanic tuff complimented by a splash of oddly shaped eroded beige sandstone to round out the strange geological motif. But in November 1990, the United States Congress knew exactly what to do with this extraordinarily diverse piece of land: designate it a wilderness area.

In this rarely visited area east of Parker, Mother Nature brings home fresh flowers every day in March and April to put the final and most captivating touch on her unusual décor in this wilderness. Considered a scorpionweed mecca, the lower lands also host extensive brittlebush, bluestem pricklepoppies (also known as the "cowboys' fried egg"), and ocotillo blooms while dune primrose rises out of the sandy, rolling foothills beneath the park's namesake Gibraltar Mountains.

The low light at sunrise and sunset highlights a stronger tonal contrast between the colorful flowers and the green hills than what you would see mid-day, so arrive at the break of day with your **wide-angle lens**, **polarizer**, **graduated neutral density filter**, **tripod**, and **cable release**. Because you'll have easy access to your vehicle, also pack a **macro** or **telephoto lens** to study the roadside blooms when the sun distances itself from the horizon. Look for vertical and horizontal compositions that include the desert scenery or the unusual rock formations. Get low, but avoid rolling around on the ground. Scorpionweed may give those who come in contact with it bloom a nasty skin irritation, so bring along extra water and soap to rinse your boots and hands off after your outing.

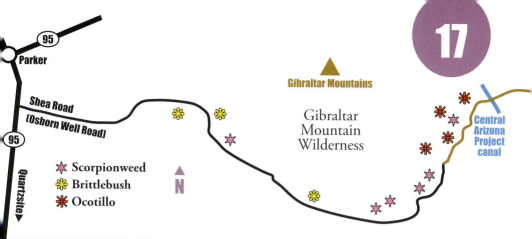

## DIRECTIONS:

From downtown Parker (along the Colorado River between I-10 and I-40), head southeast toward Quartzite on AZ 95. After about 2 miles (3.2 km), turn left (east) onto Shea Road (also known as Osborne Well Road). After driving 10 miles (16.1 km) on this paved road, start scanning the north side for wildflowers over the next 3 miles (4.8 km). When you find a promising patch of flowers, locate a safe spot to pull over on the side of the road.

*Brittlebush and scorpionweed in morning light. Wista 4x5, 120mm, Fuji Velvia 100, f/32 @ 1 sec., two-stop graduated neutral density filter. Paul Gill*

## Scorpionweed

*Phacelia crenulata*
**Blooms:** February to May along roadsides, sandy washes, and desert plains below 4,000 feet (1,219 m) elevation. (Annual)
**Fun Fact:** Touching scorpionweed can result in an itchy rash similar to one you might get when rubbing against poison ivy.

**WESTERN ARIZONA**

# Eagletail Mountains Wilderness

*Pre-dawn light casts a blue tint over a landscape covered in owl clover (compare to the cover shot, which was made three days later at sunrise in the same area). Wista 4x5, 90mm, Kodak VS 100, f/32 @ 2 sec. Paul Gill*

If you looked up "remote" in the dictionary, an entry referring to the Eagletail Mountains Wilderness would likely exist. Established by the Arizona Desert Wilderness Act in 1990 (the same act that also designated the Gibraltar, Table Top, and Tres Alamos wilderness areas), the saw-toothed stones in the shape of an eagle's tail could easily serve as the main attraction in these 100,000 acres (40,469 hectares) of untouched, isolated Sonoran Desert. That is, until one of the rarest, and arguably the most spectacular, spring blooms in Arizona arrives.

When all the variables for a once-in-a-decade show magically come together, carpets of owl clover stretch across this dry land to celebrate the change in season. The last significant bloom occurred in 2005, when these magenta flowers appeared in hordes from the Eagletail Mountains in the south, across the Saddle Mountain area (see page 78) and extending north to Alamo Lake.

Patches of bladderpod mustard, Mexican gold poppy, Coulter's lupine, and fiddleneck create a rainbow of color in front of the rugged volcanic spires, sporadically interrupting the blanket of showy owl clover.

When this spectacle happens, bring every piece of photography gear you own to fully explore the expansive nature of this bloom! Because of its rare occurrence, consider visits at sunrise over multiple days throughout March and April when it happens.

With a **wide-angle lens, polarizer, graduated neutral density filter, tripod,** and **cable release**, compose looking north to capture the best sidelight on the area's namesake, Eagletail Peak, and Double Eagle Peak. As the sun rises, replace the wide-angle lens with a **telephoto lens** and zoom in on a patch of flowers compressed against the peaks by lowering your **tripod** to the ground. Or use a **macro lens** to study individual blooms swimming in a sea of wildflowers. Shade is tough to come by here, so also bring a **diffuser** to help create a cloudy day if one doesn't exist overhead.

**BLOOM TIME**
March to April

**IDEAL TIME OF DAY**
Sunrise

**VEHICLE**
2WD high-clearance

**HIKE**
Easy

Because of this location's remoteness, you might also consider packing extra **camera batteries**, **memory cards**, food, and ample drinking water, as modern services are non-existent until you drive an hour to Tonopah.

## DIRECTIONS:

From Phoenix, take I-10 west towards Los Angeles. Take Exit 81 for Salome Road and turn left onto Salome Road. After crossing over the highway overpass, take a right onto Salome Road and drive 0.5 miles (0.8 km) before making a left onto Harquahala Valley Road. Drive south on this paved road for 11.1 miles (17.9km) to Baseline Road. Turn right onto Baseline Road and travel 3.9 miles (6.3km) before turning left onto the 547th Avenue (a well-maintained dirt road) and driving an additional mile (1.6 km). Veer right to stay on 547th Avenue when it intersects with Eagletail Road.

Travel south on 547th Avenue for 0.3 miles (0.5 km) until you see a cattle pen on the west side of the road. Turn right on this unmarked, unnamed dirt road—opening and closing the gate as you pass through to public BLM land. Drive 1.1 miles (1.8 km) until the road splits. Both roads lead to excellent blooms.

*Owl clover, fiddleneck, and Mexican gold poppies photographed mid-day under cloud cover. Pentax 67II, 75mm, Fuji Velvia 100, f/22 @ 1/8 sec., warming polarizer. Paul Gill*

## Owl Clover

*Orthocarpus purpurascens*
**Blooms:** Late February to May in open deserts at elevations in between 1,500 to 4,500 feet (457 to 1,372 m). (Annual)
**Fun Fact:** The nickname for owl clover is "escobita," which means "little broom" in Spanish.

## WESTERN ARIZONA
# Saddle Mountain

*Owl clover and Mexican gold poppies bloom together on the west side of the mountain. Wista 4x5, 210mm, Fuji Velvia 50, f/32 @ 1/4 sec. Paul Gill*

**BLOOM TIME**
March to April

**IDEAL TIME OF DAY**
Sunrise and sunset

**VEHICLE**
2WD high-clearance

**HIKE**
Easy

One glance at Saddle Mountain and you will have no questions about where the name came from. Rugged volcanic remnants rise sharply out of the desert plain, creating the illusion of a western horse saddle complete with a horn, a seat, and a cantle. Not to be confused with the Saddle Mountain Wilderness Area near the Grand Canyon, this location 40 miles (64.4 km) west of Phoenix is home to one of Arizona's most prolific displays of spring color…but only in a good year.

Though massive carpets of pinkish-purple owl clover and yellow bladderpod mustard stretching endlessly into the horizon are possible, an unforgettable display of this sort only occurs once or twice a decade. The last notable bloom occurred here in 2005. So when the Tonopah area has received above-average winter rain, grab your camera and hop in the saddle!

In addition to owl clover and bladderpod mustard, you will also find fiddleneck, scorpionweed, Coulter's lupine, blue dicks, and lesser yellow throat gilia waiting in the desert plains below the craggy peaks. Yellow-orange Mexican gold poppies make an appearance along the north facing slopes of Saddle Mountain and in the rocky washes nearby.

Shoot sunrise from the north side of the peak, turning your camera to the south. Shoot sunset from the west side, looking east.

**Wide-angle lenses** best record the expansive nature of this landscape. Since the blooms are low to the ground, lower your **tripod** to get eye-level with the flowers to include the sweeping swath of color in your foreground. Remember to use a small aperture and focus one-third of the way into your frame—a quick way to approximate the hyperfocal distance—to ensure everything from your foreground to the background is in sharp focus. A **polarizer** and **graduated neutral density filter** will help darken and saturate the color of the sky.

Though sunrise and sunset provide optimal lighting for the grand scene, pack a **macro** and **telephoto lens** as well. This equipment, in addition to a **reflector** and **diffuser**, will enable you to record the minute details of individual or small groups of intermingling flowers when the sun is higher in the sky.

Owl clover and fiddleneck carpet the flatlands west of Saddle Mountain. Wista 4x5, 120mm, Kodak VS 100, f/32 @ 1/8 sec., two-stop graduated neutral density filter. Paul Gill

## Fiddleneck

*Amsinckia intermedia*
**Blooms:** March to May in disturbed areas like fields and roadsides at elevations below 4,000 feet (1,219 m) elevation. (Annual)
**Fun Fact:** Fiddleneck's rough and bristly hairs can irritate bare skin when touched.

**WESTERN ARIZONA**

# Saddle Mountain

*Carpet of owl clover. Wista 4x5, 210mm, Kodak VS 100, f/32 @ 1/8 sec. Paul Gill*

## DIRECTIONS:

From Phoenix, drive on I-10 west towards Los Angeles for about 50 miles (80.5 km) and take Exit 94 towards Tonopah. After exiting the highway, turn left onto 411th Avenue. Drive south 2.8 miles (4.5 km) until the road T's at Salome Highway. Turn right onto Salome Highway and drive 5.2 miles (8.4 km) before turning left onto Courthouse Road. A number of unmarked dirt roads turn left into the Saddle Mountain area.

For the best sunrise spot, drive 1.1 miles (1.8 km) on Courthouse Road. Turn left on an unmarked dirt road and drive another mile (1.6 km), staying on the main track and crossing a number of dry, rocky washes. Turn left and drive 0.4 miles (0.6 km) until the road ends. Park here and walk south.

To reach the best sunset spot, continue driving straight on Courthouse Road for another 2.4 miles (3.9 km) before turning left onto 481st Avenue. Drive 1 mile (1.6 km) on this dirt road, and then turn left onto Van Buren Street. Park along the road.

**PHOTO TIP 4**

## Where's the Light?

Our eyes do not see the world the same way our camera does. While humans naturally see three dimensions, our camera only sees two. Because our camera cannot see depth, photographers need to create the illusion of this third dimension in their pictures by paying attention to which direction the natural light falls on their subject. Whether you are photographing a small macro or a broad landscape scene, look for either side or back light to help produce the feeling of depth within your frame.

Side light illuminates the subject from the side, where the shadow appears next to an object. This type of light allows the camera to capture the visual contrast between the highlights and shadows in order to produce a sense of shape and form.

Back light occurs when the sun lights the subject from behind, causing a bright halo around an object. This glow separates the subject from the background, creating the appearance of depth in the scene. When shooting backlit

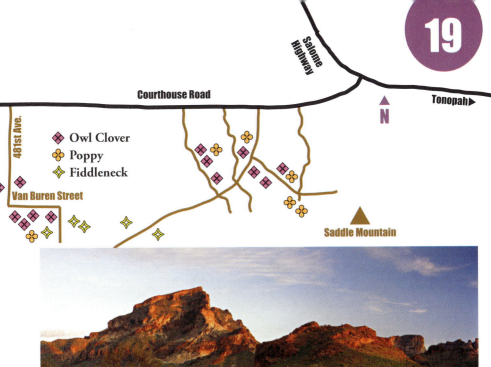

*ABOVE: Side light illuminates Saddle Mountain. Contax 645, 45mm, Fuji Velvia 100, f/22 @ 1 sec., three-stop graduated neutral density filter. LEFT: Backlighting creates a halo around owl clover. Canon 5D, 100-400mm at 400mm, ISO 160, f/5 @ 1/250 sec. Both by Colleen Miniuk-Sperry*

blooms, be sure to use a sun shade, your hand, or a hat held between your camera lens and the sun to prevent lens flare from unintentionally occurring in your photograph.

Generally, the two types of light to avoid when photographing wildflowers are top light and front light. Since the shadows are not visible to your camera, flowers may appear flat and shapeless when the sun illuminates the bloom from the front or the top, which occurs mid-day.

To get a better idea of the light direction and how high the sun will be in the sky for your composition before heading out on your photo shoot, consult the Photographer's Ephemeris (**www.photoephemeris.com**) and use the Sunlight feature on Google Earth. Once you arrive in the field, carefully observe and position yourself based on the direction of the light falling on your subject.

**WESTERN ARIZONA**

# Lake Pleasant Regional Park

*Hillside of Coulter's lupine, Mexican gold poppy, chuparosa, and brittlebush. Wista 4x5, 90mm, Velvia 100, f/32 @ 1/4 sec.*
*Paul Gill*

**BLOOM TIME**
March to April

**IDEAL TIME OF DAY**
Late afternoon to sunset

**VEHICLE**
Any

**HIKE**
Moderate

Lake Pleasant formed in the late 1920s, when the newly constructed Waddell Dam caused the once free-flowing Agua Fria River to pool into a reservoir. After the nine-year construction project concluded in 1993, the New Waddell Dam replaced the historic dam, enlarging the lake's surface area and creating a recreational hotspot near Phoenix. Now a part of the Lake Pleasant Regional Park, the area attracts flocks of outdoor enthusiasts year round. Come spring, color-chasers should head to the Pipeline Canyon Trail on the east side to view a beautiful blanket of intermingling wildflowers.

Though this well-maintained, but somewhat rocky, trail runs about two miles (3.2 km) in length, you only need to walk about a mile (1.6 km) round-trip from the southern trailhead to see the best blooms on the hillsides surrounding this rugged canyon.

Start your afternoon outing by walking a half mile (0.8 km) to Pipeline Cove with **wide-angle**, **macro**, and **telephoto lenses**, **polarizer**, **reflector**, **diffuser**, **tripod**, and **cable release**. Include a headlamp or flashlight in your camera bag since you may return to the trailhead in the dark following your shoot.

As you descend, both sides of the path will, in good years, show off a profusion of wildflowers, including Mexican gold poppies, Coulter's lupine, and desert globemallow. The desert terrain rises above the trail on the side in spots, enabling both wide-angle and macro compositions of wildflowers reaching to the blue sky. If you position your camera towards the sun, prevent unwanted lens flare from ruining your picture by attaching your lens' sun shade or simply holding your hand between the sun and your lens.

At Pipeline Cove, a floating bridge provides a safe crossing and access to prime real estate for owl clover. Choose a macro or telephoto lens to isolate individual blooms or a collection of flowers on the eastern side of the trail. An occasional saguaro cactus or teddy bear cholla creates limited shade, so your best bet is to use your diffuser and reflector to balance harsh

*Late afternoon light highlights Mexican gold poppies before they close for the night. Canon 5D, 24-105mm at 56mm, ISO 100, f/11 @ 1/8 sec. Paul Gill*

shadows in your mid-day compositions.

Plan to retrace your steps back towards the southern trailhead about an hour before sunset, allowing more time if you plan to make stops to photograph on your way back up the hill. The west-facing slopes along this portion of the path soak up the afternoon sun through the last light of the day. Although the poppies will have started to close for the evening, look for a broader composition through a wide-angle lens to show the patterns of colors scattered across the desert floor. If you're facing north or south, a polarizer will help saturate the blue sky and enrich the colorful blooms.

## Desert Marigold

*Baileya multiradiata*
**Blooms:** March to October on rocky roadsides, slopes, and sandy areas below 5,000 feet (1,524 m) elevation. (Annual)
**Fun Fact:** The desert marigold's nickname is the "paper daisy" since its flower petals become more paper-like after blooming.

**WESTERN ARIZONA**

# Lake Pleasant Regional Park

**PHOTO TIP 5**

## Make Friends with the Wind

*Sponsored by Wimberley, Inc., www.tripodhead.com*

During spring and summer, breezy winds whirl across Arizona. Although these sweeping streams of air indicate the start of an exciting new blooming season, they also can make photographing wildflowers nothing short of a frustrating endeavor.

While even the slightest breeze can make you want to pack up and head home, consider these ways to successfully deal with the wind:

- Use the fastest shutter speed you can to give yourself the best chance of freezing motion.
- Increase your ISO speed setting to enable your sensor to be more sensitive to light. By increasing your ISO speed, you'll be able to use faster shutter speeds for a given aperture.
- Set your camera to continuous shoot mode, and then wait for a lull in the wind. As soon as you feel the wind die down for even a split second, blast away!
- With your camera on a tripod, capture two photos of the same scene. First, capture one at a fast enough ISO speed setting to freeze the blooms, and then another at a slow ISO speed to record low noise. In post-processing, paint the frozen flowers into the low noise image by blending the two layers.

## DIRECTIONS:

From Phoenix, take I-17 north towards Flagstaff. On the outskirts of Phoenix, take Exit 223B for AZ 74/Carefree Highway. After exiting the highway, turn right (west) onto AZ 74/Carefree Highway. Travel westward for about 11.5 miles (18.5 km), and then turn right onto Castle Hot Springs Road, heading north for another 2.3 miles (3.7 km). Turn right at the park entrance.

After paying the entrance fee or showing your Maricopa County Parks and Recreation Annual Pass, continue straight on North Park Road for about 1.5 miles (2.4 km) until it ends in a parking area. The well-marked southern Pipeline Canyon Trailhead is on the north end of the parking area.

For more information, visit the Lake Pleasant Regional Park website at **www.maricopa.gov/parks/lake_pleasant/default.aspx**.

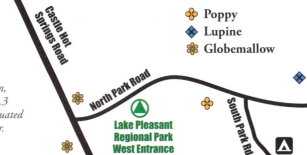

LEFT:
Mexican gold poppies at sunset on west-facing hill. Canon 5DMII, 16-35mm at 35mm, ISO 100, f/20 @ 0.3 sec., three-stop graduated neutral density filter.
Paul Gill

- Use a Wimberley Plamp to stabilize your flower during the exposure.
- Create a wind block by placing your camera backpack upwind from your subject. Or drape a sheet over a tripod or use a light tent to shelter your subject from the breeze.
- Use a camera flash set to second curtain sync (where the flash occurs at the end of the exposure) to freeze a moving subject.
- Zoom out and compose a wider view of your scene, which will allow the flower to move within your frame. Then, crop the image into a tighter composition during post-processing.
- Don't try to freeze the motion. Instead, slow your shutter speed to 1/30th of a second or less to convey blurred action and to show a sense of the moving wind in your photograph.

*Colleen uses a Wimberley Plamp to hold a butter and eggs bloom in place on a windy day at Mormon Lake. Photo courtesy of Jacqueline Miniuk*

# Making the Photo 2

## A Bug's View
By Paul Gill

*Low-angle view of Mexican gold poppies. Canon 5DMIII, 16-35mm at 16mm, ISO 1000, f/22 @ 1/800 sec. Paul Gill*

After spending the morning working my macro lens in a field of flowers, concentrating on the insects and the miniature world around me, the thought suddenly occurred to me, "What is the view from the bug's perspective?"

With strong back lighting, I wanted to show the translucence of the petals. I also wanted to create a sunburst on the edge of the Mexican gold poppy by partially hiding the sun to enhance the rays from the sunburst.

With this vision in mind, I set a small aperture (i.e. f/22), which causes more pronounced sun rays and not one big hazy, white ball. The edges of the diaphragm blades in the lens disperse the light and cause diffraction, resulting in the sun rendering in a star-like form.

Since manufacturers vary the shape of the shutter blades, certain lenses make better sunbursts than others. It seems older lenses do a better job because the newer lenses have curved edges to help prevent diffraction that causes softness at small apertures. When you are out in the field, take a few shots to see if you have a good "sunburst" lens.

Also, I exposed the scene at 1/200th of a second at an ISO speed equal to 400 due to the slight wind. I intentionally underexposed by one stop to help create the sunstar. During my post-processing activities in Adobe Lightroom at home, I darkened the blue channel and lightened the yellow one for more contrast. I also removed some lens flare.

To create a similar scene, take off your macro lens and grab your largest wide-angle lens. Plug in your cable release. Next, set a small aperture (e.g. f/16 or f/22) for greatest effect.

Find a photogenic grouping of tall flowers (preferably one foot (0.3 m) or higher). Then, place a cloth (or even this book!) on the ground underneath them and lay your camera down facing up. Take an approximate measurement from the lens to the flowers, and then pick the camera up and manually set your focus at that measured distance. Replace the camera in its prone position and make an exposure. To make this process easier, use a swing-out LED screen (if available on your camera) or a right-angle viewfinder that attaches to your eye piece. Or, better yet, utilize an external camera monitoring app that works with your smart phone.

Now comes the hard part - the work-intensive process of composing and focusing until you get exactly what you want. In fact, the images shown on these two pages are just two of about 50 attempts in the same location. Move around to find a great composition. Adjust your focus and exposure as needed. Voilà! "A bug's view" in mid-day light!

The image on the right of the bee hovering above a Mexican gold poppy took multiple exposures to capture him in the correct position. The trick to stopping the movement of the wings is to use a high ISO (such as ISO 1000) and a fast exposure (such as 1/800th of a second). As with most macro photography, making an image from a bug's point of view takes lots of patience and time, but the final image is a new way of seeing the world of wildflowers.

Some words of caution regarding this technique: when shooting into the sun at low angles, consider using your Live View mode (if available) to compose. However, do so sparingly, as some say this can damage the camera's sensor. Also, avoid looking directly at the sun as this can be hazardous to your eyes.

*A bee hovers above a Mexican gold poppy. Canon 5DMIII, 16-35mm, ISO 1000, f/22 @ 1/800 sec.*
*Paul Gill*

**WESTERN ARIZONA**

# White Tank Mountain Regional Park

*Littleleaf paloverde trees bloom on the Goat Camp Trail. Super Graphic 4x5, 120mm, Fuji Velvia 50, f/11 @ 1/250 sec. Paul Gill*

**BLOOM TIME**
**March to May**

**IDEAL TIME OF DAY**
**Sunrise; late afternoon**

**VEHICLE**
**Any**

**HIKE**
**Easy**

Considering its proximity to the Phoenix metropolitan area, White Tank Mountain Regional Park offers a convenient escape away from the hustle and bustle of city life nearby. Leave all your stress behind as you pass through the entrance gate when it opens at 6:00 a.m. Arriving early enables you to take advantage of the morning light adorning the untouched beauty of the Sonoran Desert against the backdrop of the park's namesake, the White Tank Mountains.

Starting in March, a collection of desert wildflowers sprout from the normally barren desert floor. Mexican gold poppies, Coulter's lupine, owl clover, ocotillo, and fiddleneck paint the hillsides of the easy Waterfall Trail. Pack a **wide-angle lens**, **polarizer**, and **tripod** for your short 0.9 mile (1.5 km) stroll into the scenic canyon.

As April approaches, golden brittlebush blooms cover the rolling foothills, but vibrant pink blooms from the strawberry hedgehog cactus try to divert your attention. To photograph a group of these showy cactus flowers, position your camera and tripod directly over the cactus, pointing a **normal lens of 50mm or 80mm** downward for an overhead perspective. Align your camera's lens parallel with the petals of the flowers so you can capture consistent depth of field across the bloom.

Perhaps the best show comes when the littleleaf paloverde blooms throughout May. Photograph from a lower vantage point, using a wide-angle lens and composing so the golden blossoms appear in front of the blue sky. A polarizer will enrich this photogenic color combination.

The saguaro cactus also partakes in the annual spring festivities starting in May. The easy Mule Deer Trail leads to stately stands of picturesque saguaros as well as unobstructed views of the Four Peaks Mountains almost 70 miles (112.7 km) across town to the east. Use a **telephoto lens** to compress blooming saguaro cacti in your foreground against silhouetted distant peaks. Remove all filters from your lens and use a sun shade or hold your hand over your lens to prevent lens flare.

By late afternoon, the sun dips behind the mountains and shadow takes over the desert floor, which provides the perfect even lighting conditions to capture close-up shots with a **macro lens** before you pack up and head home.

## DIRECTIONS:

From downtown Phoenix, travel westward on I-10 to Exit 124 for AZ 303 Loop. Upon exiting the highway, turn right onto the AZ 303 Loop. Drive north about 7 miles (11.3 km) to Olive Avenue. Turn left onto Olive Avenue and drive west an additional 4 miles (6.4 km) to the park entrance.

The park charges an entry fee unless you have a Maricopa County Parks and Recreation Annual Pass. For more information, visit the White Tank Mountain Regional Park website at **www.maricopa.gov/parks/white_tank/default.aspx**.

Brittlebush bloom at sunset along White Tank Mountain Road. Canon 5DMIII, 16-35mm at 17mm, ISO 100, f/22 at 8.0 sec., five-stop graduated neutral density filter. Paul Gill

## Littleleaf Paloverde

*Cercidium microphyllum*
**Blooms:** March to May on arid hillsides, mesas, and plains at elevations in between 500 and 4,000 feet (152 and 1,219 m) elevation. (Perennial)
**Fun Fact:** Designated as the state tree for Arizona, the word "paloverde" means "green stick" in Spanish.

**WESTERN ARIZONA**

# Kofa National Wildlife Refuge

*Bladderpod mustard blooms beside ocotillo on the Kofa Queen Road as the Kofa Mountains glow at sunset. Pentax 67II, 55mm, Kodak VS 100, f/32 @ 1/30 sec., two-stop graduated neutral density filter. Paul Gill*

**BLOOM TIME**
**March**

**IDEAL TIME OF DAY**
**Early morning; sunset**

**VEHICLE**
**2WD high-clearance**

**HIKE**
**Moderate**

The name "Kofa" derives from the historic King of Arizona gold mine, whose discovery in the late 1800s led to a small gold rush and an accompanying boom town that survived for several decades. In 1939, this same area became the Kofa National Wildlife Refuge, protecting 664,000 acres (268,711 hectares) of prime desert bighorn sheep habitat in the heart of the Sonoran Desert.

Today, not only do bighorn sheep and other wildlife thrive here, but also a handful of California palm trees – the only native palm growing in Arizona. Come March, spring wildflowers add a touch of color in the canyon where these extraordinary trees grow.

The moderately strenuous half-mile (0.8 km) Palm Canyon Trail provides a glimpse of these rare palms hiding in narrow ravines and reveals fiery red chuparosa, golden brittlebush, and purple Arizona lupine along the way. The more adventurous can bushwhack and climb up a narrow slot canyon located on the east side of the main canyon to see the trees up close, but be prepared for a nerve-wracking 20-foot (6.1-m) scramble up a rocky cliff face.

Pack a **short telephoto lens (80-150mm)** if you plan to photograph from the trail. If you decide to hike up to the palms, bring a **wide-angle lens** instead, though a **tilt-shift lens** will keep the tall trees from converging in your photograph. Either way, do not forget the **tripod** and **cable release**.

Because of the orientation of the cliffs, this area will be in shadow most of the morning, providing excellent diffused and even lighting in which to photograph the blooms in the foreground against the backdrop of cliffs and palms.

About two hours before sunset, head to neighboring Kofa Queen Canyon to capture interspersed patches of bladderpod mustard, desert marigold, and scorpionweed against glowing cliffs and oddly-shaped spires during the last light of the day. With your wide-angle lens on your camera, search for blooming ocotillo, teddy bear cholla, and brittlebush intermixing with the colorful wildflowers. Slower shutter speeds as the sun sets demand the use of a tripod and cable release to keep the camera from moving and images sharp. A **graduated neutral density filter** as well as a **polarizer** will ensure your scene is properly exposed and nicely saturated.

Although it is sometimes a challenge in the surprisingly cluttered desert, keep your compositions simple and clean by scanning the edge of your frame for out-of-focus and unwanted objects (branches, leaves, etc.) before you snap the shutter.

*Red chuparosa bloom between large boulders at the base of the California palm trees in Palm Canyon. Canon 5DMII, TS-E 24mm, ISO 100, f/8 @ 1/25 sec. Paul Gill*

## Chuparosa

*Justicia californica*
**Blooms:** Throughout the year, along rocky slopes and desert washes in between 1,000 and 2,500 feet (305 and 762 m) elevation. (Perennial)
**Fun Fact:** Popular with flying pollinators like birds and butterflies, the word "chuparosa" means "hummingbird" in Spanish.

**WESTERN ARIZONA**

# Kofa National Wildlife Refuge

## DIRECTIONS:

The Kofa National Wildlife Refuge is located along US 95 between Yuma and Quartzite. From I-10 and Quartzite, take US 95 south for a little over 19 miles (30.6 km) to the signed turnoff for Palm Canyon in the Kofa National Wildlife Refuge. Turn left onto the dirt, but well-maintained, Palm Canyon Road.

From Yuma and I-8, head north on US 95 for approximately 64 miles (103 km) to the Palm Canyon turn-off.

To visit Kofa Queen Canyon, drive 3.4 miles (5.5 km) on Palm Canyon Road, then turn left onto the dirt Kofa Queen Canyon Road (labeled on the map provided by the

*Backlit ocotillo in front of Kofa Queen Canyon cliffs. Canon 5DMII, 16-35mm at 30mm, ISO 100, three exposure HDR. Paul Gill*

### PHOTO TIP 6

## How Low Can You Go?

*Sponsored by Hoodman Corporation, www.hoodmanusa.com*

Have you ever wondered what it would be like to see the world from an ant's perspective? Now here's your chance! While photographing a flower from a ground-loving insect's viewpoint takes some effort on your part, unique views and photographs await those photographers willing to change their perspectives a few inches.

Unless the flower is jutting out from higher ground, you will need to get on your knees or even on your stomach to be level with the bloom. Knee pads, a kneeling gardening pad, or a floor mat from a home improvement store will cushion you from the hard and rocky ground.

Drop your tripod as low as you can. Contorting yourself

*Dewdrops on Mexican gold poppy buds. Canon 5DMII, MP-E 65mm 1-5x, ISO 500, f/3.2 @ 1/1000 sec. Paul Gill*

refuge as Junction 19). Drive a little more than 8 miles (12.9 km) along this narrow high-clearance road until it dead ends and you reach a small parking and camping area with pit toilets.

To visit Palm Canyon, stay straight on Palm Canyon Road for another 3.7 miles (6 km) instead of turning off onto Kofa Queen Canyon Road. The road will end at the Palm Canyon Trail trailhead, where ample parking is available.

For more information, visit the Kofa National Wildlife Refuge website at **www.fws.gov/southwest/refuges/arizona/kofa/index.html**.

*Backlit Mexican gold poppy. Canon 5D, 100mm macro, ISO 125, f/7.1 @ 1/640 sec. Colleen Miniuk-Sperry*

to look through the viewfinder is an option – albeit a potentially painful one. You may find it more comfortable to enable the Live View function (if available on your camera model) to help you see the composition of your photograph on the larger screen on the back of your camera. Placing a Hoodman HoodLoupe over the camera's screen while previewing your image in Live View mode will allow closer inspection before clicking the shutter.

Position yourself so the sun illuminates the flower from the side or behind to create the illusion of shape. If the contrast is great, fill the shadows with light bounced off a reflector or a touch of on-camera fill flash.

Then look for patterns, lines, and shapes to create a well-balanced composition, making sure the center of interest does not fall in the middle of the frame. Subtle shifts in your camera's position can make a major difference in finding the precise placement, so be patient and keep moving your tripod around until you see the perfect arrangement.

To isolate those beautiful patterns, use a wide open aperture to create a short depth of field. If you are utilizing a tripod, use a less sensitive ISO speed such as ISO 100 or 200. Your shutter speed setting won't matter too much unless it is windy outside (see page 84).

**WESTERN ARIZONA**

# Cabeza Prieta National Wildlife Refuge

*Desert primrose bloom at sunset. Sierra Pintas background. Canon 5DMIII, 16-35mm at 23mm, f/22 @ 15 sec., ISO 100, three-stop graduated neutral density filter. Paul Gill*

**BLOOM TIME**
Late February to March

**IDEAL TIME OF DAY**
Sunrise and sunset

**VEHICLE**
4WD high-clearance

**HIKE**
Moderate

Following the dedicated efforts by Arizona Boy Scouts to protect the bighorn sheep in this remote area, this enormous stretch of pristine desert wilderness became the Cabeza Prieta National Wildlife Refuge in 1975. Today, thanks to these conservation efforts, not only will visitors find abundant wildlife but also an abundance of wildflowers miraculously sprouting from the sand dunes—specifically near the southwestern base of the Sierra Pinta Mountains in the Tule Desert—following ample winter rains.

In the deafening silence common to the rugged 860,000 acres, (348,210 hectares) photographers can almost hear the pepperweed, desert primrose, Mexican gold poppy, and lupine swaying in the gentle breeze near the Pinta Dunes.

Because of its remoteness and the diversity of photography opportunities, bring a broad range of lenses (including **wide-angle**, **telephoto**, and **macro**), a sturdy **tripod**, and a **cable release**. To tame the harsh desert sun over smaller scenes, also lug along a **reflector** and **diffuser**. Since no services exist (except for very basic ones in Ajo), also remember to pack **extra batteries** and **memory cards**. Finally, since rising temperatures trigger early morning and late afternoon breezes, pack a **Wimberley Plamp** to use with smaller scenes. No matter your composition, use faster ISO and shutter speeds to freeze the flowers in your frame.

Most of the refuge, including this area, closes from March 15 to July 15 to protect the Sonoran pronghorn fawning season. By then, the flowers are typically burned out by the rising spring temperatures.

# DIRECTIONS:

Prior to traveling to this location, pick up a free required visitor permit at one of the permitting agencies (visit **www.fws.gov/refuge/Cabeza_Prieta** for locations). Prior to entering the area, visitors are required to validate their permit at one of the four kiosks located at each of the park's access points.

The easiest entry is from Ajo. Travel southeast on Highway 85 for 1.9 miles (3.1 km). Turn right onto Bates Well Road (also known as Darby Well Road), which turns into the unpaved, sandy El Camino del Diablo. Follow the main track for around 50 miles (80.5 km) crossing through a section of the Organ Pipe Cactus National Monument en route. Find an existing pullout to park your vehicle and walk north towards the dunes for about 1 mile (1.6 km).

Only experienced drivers in high clearance, four-wheel drive vehicles should attempt this route. Since emergency and towing services are unavailable here, pack an extra spare tire and other emergency gear. For your safety, do not venture to this location alone, but groups of five or more vehicles require an additional Special Use Permit.

Primitive camping is available at one of three designated, but unimproved, campgrounds within the refuge. No water or services are available.

Due to its proximity with Mexico, illegal immigration activity occurs in this area. You will likely see numerous United States Border Patrol trucks and all-terrain vehicles during your visit. Report any suspicious activity to law enforcement officials immediately.

Because of past and current military activity, unexploded ordnance remain in the area. If you find one, do not touch it. Report its location to the refuge's staff immediately.

*Desert primrose and verbena. Canon 5DMIII, 100mm macro, ISO 400, f/8 @ 1/250 sec. Paul Gill*

## Desert Primrose

*Oenothera deltoides*
**Blooms:** In open sandy areas below 2,500 feet (762 m) from February to May. (Annual)
**Fun Fact:** Also called "dune evening primrose," wide-spread blooms of this white delicate flower often yields fields of what appears to be tissue paper strewn across the desert.

**Making the Photo 3**

# Preconception and Discovery
By Paul Gill

Before I arrive at a place, I like to have some kind of initial idea or concept. When I first started as a graphic designer and painter, preconceiving what I wanted to create was essential to success. Sometimes sketching an idea helped to start the creative process. Nature photography, however, is very different. We work in the moment with changing light. We also move through our subject matter to find compositions, always looking for sparks of inspiration from shape and light.

Before I visit a location for the first time, I like to use a few visualization tools such as the Photographer's Ephemeris and Google Earth to see where and when the best light will appear. This gives me an idea of where to look for images while I am on site. Then, I tend to create imagery in my head before I even set foot on a location. This can be a great creative exercise and it helps motivate me, but that is where my visualizations end.

When on location and the light is right, I change into discovery mode. I stick all my preconceptions in the back of my head while using my eyes to find shape, line, and light to create on the spot. It is very important to give the preconceived notion space and allow it to evolve in the field – even at the cost of the initial idea becoming completely lost.

The Pinta Dunes area in Cabeza Prieta National Wildlife Refuge (see page 94) is known for carpets of sand verbena and dune evening primrose starting in February. With this in mind, I was convinced I could find wildflowers intermixing with saguaro cacti and sand dunes.

When I arrived, though, I was able to make images with those things in my frame—but not all together as I originally thought. Although I had designed some photographs in my mind, at the Pinta Dunes, I let those ideas slip away.

At first, I tried a long lens to compress the saguaros and sand dunes together, but I felt too much space existed between them. When I saw this scene, the sand dune ridges and how they flowed around the globes of pepperweed attracted me first to this composition. Normally with a cloudless sky, I would minimize the blue horizon, but I wanted the saguaros in the background to show "Arizona" so I included a small amount of sky.

Minutes before sunset, the strong side lighting highlighted a small ridge. I quickly arranged it in my foreground so that its natural line would lead the eye into the image and create a lovely serpentine-like movement across the image. I initially placed the highlighted area in the front of the image on the left to allow it to point into the image. However, a strong, prevalent lens flare occurred so I decided instead to center it. The details in the sand would have disappeared in an instant (as the wind rearranged the sand ridges).

With a wide-angle lens at 24mm, I set the aperture at f/22 to gain the most depth of field possible with that lens. An ISO 100 setting and an exposure of 1/4 seconds resulted in a little movement from the wind but it was acceptable to me. I also used a hard two-stop graduated neutral density filter positioned in alignment with the horizon to keep the bright sky from blowing out.

The final image of pepperweed and sand dune ripples was nothing like what I had preconceived. While creating potential photographs in my mind helps me prepare prior to a photography outing, the process of discovery while on location can reveal fresh ideas which could never have been imagined.

*Pepperweed bloom in the Pinta Dunes at sunset. Canon 5DMIII, 16-35mm at 16mm, ISO 100, f/22 @ 25mm 1/4 sec., two-stop graduated neutral density filter. Paul Gill*

*Last light on field of Coulter's lupine on the hillsides near Silver King Mine Road. Canon 5DMII, 100-400mm at 310mm, ISO 100, f/11 @ 1/4 sec. Paul Gill*

## *Wildflowers of* CENTRAL ARIZONA

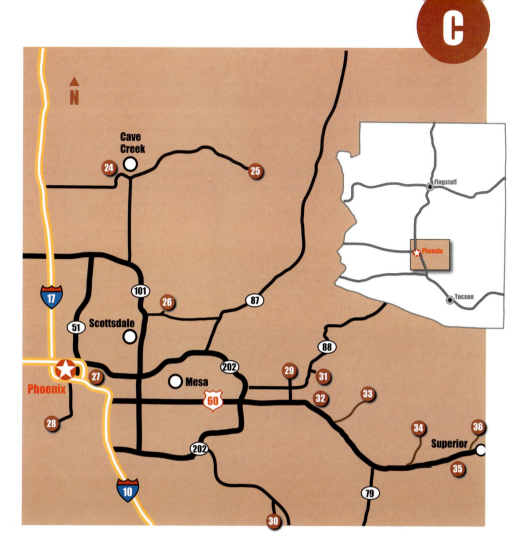

- **24** Go John Trail ............... 100
- **25** Bartlett Lake ............... 102
- **26** Lost Dog Wash Trail .... 108
- **27** Desert Botanical Garden ...................... 110
- **28** South Mountain Park .... 114
- **29** Pass Mountain Trail ...... 116
- **30** San Tan Mountain Regional Park ............. 118
- **31** Lost Dutchman State Park ........................... 120
- **32** Silly Mountain ............. 124
- **33** Peralta Road ................ 126
- **34** Hewitt Canyon ........... 128
- **35** Boyce Thompson Arboretum .................. 132
- **36** Silver King Mine Road ........................... 134

### CENTRAL ARIZONA

# Go John Trail

*Engelmann's prickly pear cactus bloom among saguaros. Canon 5D, 24-105mm at 24mm, ISO 100, f/11 @ 1/40 sec. Paul Gill*

**BLOOM TIME**
March to May

**IDEAL TIME OF DAY**
Early morning; late afternoon to sunset

**VEHICLE**
Any

**HIKE**
Moderate

Oddly enough, the biggest payoff along the Go John Trail is not the intermingling Coulter's lupine, chia, fairy duster, and desert globemallow lining this popular route. Instead, prolific carpets of Mexican gold poppies reward flower followers on the northernmost part of this trail within the Cave Creek Regional Park, indicating John shouldn't be the only one to go to this spot come spring.

After a spectacular bloom show throughout March, speckles of vibrant pink strawberry hedgehog cactus and yellow Engelmann's prickly pear cactus start to peek out in April on rocky hillsides covered with golden brittlebush. Oversized saguaro cacti, which bloom in May, strike photogenic poses throughout the desert foothills.

Because of the initial steep uphill climb, your legs will thank you for limiting your camera gear to a **wide-angle lens**, **polarizer**, **graduated neutral density filter**, **tripod**, and **cable release**. That's all the equipment you'll need to capture grand landscape pictures of the Sonoran Desert in bloom starting late afternoon. Point your set-up north or northeast to use Black Mesa or Continental Mountain, respectively, as a scenic backdrop. Stay on the north side of the mountain through sunset for the richest light, but remember to bring a headlamp or flashlight to help you return to the trailhead.

While March and April typically see tolerable day time temperatures, the weather starts to warm dramatically in May. As the desert heats up, it's best to begin your photographic outing early in the morning when the cactus flowers are open, bringing extra drinking water and hiking poles to thwart any surprise encounters with a rattlesnake sunning itself.

Since the same mix of flowers bloom along the entire length of the footpath (though not in the same quantities), pack a **macro lens**, **diffuser**, and **reflector** only if you have been working out at the gym regularly or plan to visit mid-day and stay close to the trailhead.

# 24

## DIRECTIONS:

From Phoenix, head north on I-17 towards Flagstaff. On the outskirts of Phoenix, take Exit 223A and turn right onto the Carefree Highway. Drive east about 7 miles (11.3 km) to 32nd Street, where you will turn left and travel north to the Cave Creek Regional Park entrance.

After paying the entrance fee or showing your Maricopa County Parks and Recreation Annual Pass, continue straight on the park road, which is now Cave Creek Parkway, for about 1.5 miles (2.4 km) beyond the entrance station. Turn left at the trailhead sign and drive straight until you see the parking area for the Go John Trailhead at the northernmost point of this loop.

For the best flowers, head north from the parking lot on the Go John Trail, taking the left-hand side of the loop trail. Hike on this well maintained dirt path for about 2.5 miles (4 km) until you reach the northernmost edge of the trail. The best blooms typically occur within a mile (1.6 km) after crossing the intersection with the Spur Cross Trail.

For more information, visit the Cave Creek Regional Park website at **www.maricopa.gov/parks/cave_creek**.

*Mexican gold poppies bloom on low, flat, and gently-sloping hillsides. Canon 5D, 24-105mm at 36mm, ISO 100, f/11 @ 1/80 sec. Paul Gill*

## Chia

*Salvia columbariae*
**Blooms:** March to May along sandy washes and desert slopes below 3,500 feet (1,067 m) elevation. (Annual)
**Fun Fact:** The funny looking chia plant is a member of the mint family but smells like a skunk.

**CENTRAL ARIZONA**

# Bartlett Lake

*Mexican gold poppy, scorpionweed, Coulter's lupine, chuparosa, and brittlebush paint the hillside above Bartlett Lake. Wista 4x5, 90mm, Fuji Velvia 50, f/32 @ 1/2 sec., two-stop graduated neutral density filter. Paul Gill*

**BLOOM TIME**
**March to April**

**IDEAL TIME OF DAY**
**Sunrise to late morning; sunset**

**VEHICLE**
**Any**

**HIKE**
**Easy**

Bartlett Lake originally appeared on maps in 1939 after the Salt River Project erected the first dam on the scenic Verde River. Though the desert oasis attracts outdoor enthusiasts throughout the year, the biggest draw for shutterbugs and "petal-peepers" come springtime isn't the water, but rather the extensive assortment of wildflowers and the occasional rare white poppy sprouting in the hills to the west of the lake.

Peaking typically around the second or third week in March, this area offers a fairly reliable crop year after year, even when the rest of the Phoenix area is experiencing an average or below average bloom. The mix of flowers found here changes depending on the timing and quantity of seasonal rains. Some years the purple Coulter's lupine dominates, while in other years, a mix of striking gold and white poppies appear en masse instead. On rare occasions, the late-blooming yellow brittlebush and ruby red chuparosa will bloom alongside the existing flowers to create a photogenic blend of hues.

Best viewed in dawn's early light, the hillsides northwest of the saddle offer the best variety of blooms. Put on a headlamp or use a flashlight to illuminate your path as you weave your way through the trail-less terrain, taking care to not crush tightly packed patches of delicate wildflowers. As the sun rises, a **wide-angle lens**, **polarizer**, **graduated neutral density filter**, **tripod**, and **cable release** will help you capture the expansive sea of color across the Sonoran Desert.

Work through the morning, keeping your compositions simple and tight as the sun gets higher in the sky. Use an artificial background (see page 136) if you can't find a clean backdrop in the busy landscape. Though a few mesquite trees and saguaro cactus produce limited shade, bring a **diffuser** to create the effects of an instant cloudy day over the bloom of your choice.

Once your shoot concludes, drive another 1.2 miles (1.9 km) north along Service Road 459 and park in a wide spot off the road. Rare albino Mexican gold poppies can turn the desert floor white here. If you are lucky enough to see a bunch, use a **macro lens** and get as low to the ground as possible to emphasize the height of this anomaly in nature.

The Lower Rattlesnake Cove area has covered picnic tables, bathrooms, and an unbeatable view of Bartlett Lake, making it an ideal location to take a break during the mid-day heat.

*A crested saguaro surrounded by yellow brittlebush and red chuparosa on the FR42 Trail. Canon 5DMII, 16-35mm at 16mm, ISO 100, f/22 @ 1/20 sec. Paul Gill*

For sunset, plan on returning to the saddle area where the best place to park your tripod is on the southeast side of the saddle. Looking south, Bartlett Lake sparkles in the setting sun while saguaro cactus, wildflowers, and other desert plants provide the perfect foreground when using a wide-angle lens. Try both vertical and horizontal orientations, making sure to get a part of the lake in the background. Ambitious and experienced hikers might consider climbing to the top of the hill for a more aerial-like perspective.

# Albino Mexican Gold Poppy

*Eschscholzia mexicana*
**Blooms:** Mid-February to March on rocky slopes and plains below 4,500 feet (1,372 m) elevation. (Annual)
**Fun Fact:** In rare circumstances, the Mexican gold poppy flower mutates into an albino white spectacle.

**CENTRAL ARIZONA**

# Bartlett Lake

*Mexican gold poppies, scorpionweed, and lupine. Canon 5DMIII, TS-E 17mm, ISO 100, f/22 @ 1/40 sec., polarizer. Paul Gill*

## DIRECTIONS:

From Scottsdale, travel north on Pima Road from the AZ 101 Loop for about 12 miles (19.3 km) before turning right onto Cave Creek Road. Drive for 4.2 miles (6.8 km) and then turn right onto Service Road 205 (referred to as Bartlett Dam Road on some maps).

Just a few hundred feet after turning onto Bartlett Dam Road, you will encounter a ranger station on the left. Access to Bartlett Lake requires a Tonto National Forest Pass (or "Tonto Pass") which you can purchase at the ranger station (or at the Bartlett Lake Marina). After purchasing a pass (or if you have one already), continue east along Bartlett Dam Road for about 13 miles (21 km).

Before you arrive at the Bartlett Lake Marina, turn left on North Bartlett Dam Road/Service Road 459 heading towards Rattlesnake Cove. If you pull into the Bartlett

**PHOTO TIP 7**

## Reflect the Light

Sometimes the natural light in the middle of the day is too harsh, too direct, and too bright to make phenomenal photographs, especially of expansive scenic landscapes. Human eyes have the ability to see a broad spectrum of light, but the camera records a much smaller dynamic range of about five to six stops of light. Because of this, the camera will "see" a mid-day scene as "contrasty" – bright white highlights coupled with dark black shadows and not a lot of mid-tones in between.

Using a reflector can help reduce this stark contrast across a smaller scene and create more pleasing light on your subjects during the middle of the day. A reflector is any reflective surface used to redirect the natural light back into a scene. Commercially-made reflectors have different colored surfaces, but gold and white are the most useful for photographing wildflowers.

As the name suggests, gold provides golden orange tones, as it modifies the reflected natural light so the scene feels warmer in color. A white reflector reflects the existing color of the natural light into the scene, producing the most neutral-toned light.

No matter which color you choose, hold the reflector with the reflective surface towards the sun and guide the light onto your subject. You might have to subtly turn the reflector back and forth until the reflected light hits your subject exactly as you desire.

# 25

*Fairy duster bloom. Canon 5DMII, MP-E 65mm 1-5x, ISO 1200, f/13 @ 1/250 sec. Paul Gill*

Lake Marina, you have gone too far.

Continue along North Bartlett Lake Road, past the Lower Rattlesnake Cove/FR459A turnoff, and up the hill. Park where the shoulder widens at the top of the saddle, where the best flowers bloom in close proximity to the road.

- Albino Poppy
- Poppy
- Lupine
- Brittlebush
- Chuparosa

*The flowers of antelope horns look blue and dull under diffused light. Positioning a gold reflector to the left of the camera adds a warm touch of reflected sunlight to these same blooms. Canon 5DMII, 100mm macro, ISO 400, f/7.1 @ 1/100 sec., reflector (right photo), diffuser. Both by Colleen Miniuk-Sperry*

## Making the Photo 4

# Working the Scene

By Colleen Miniuk-Sperry

For most photographers, it is difficult (if not impossible) to deliver a perfect vision after merely snapping the first frame. To explore and polish one's ever-evolving visual message in a new location or a familiar setting, consider the scene or subject from a multitude of angles, using a variety of lenses, and tapping into different lighting conditions.

Of all the locations to find wildflowers, oftentimes Bartlett Lake offers the most abundant (and most diverse) mix of blooms each spring. A couple years ago, as I strolled around the rolling hills to the west of Bartlett Lake, what impressed me most were the mingling lupine and cream cups. I decided to communicate through my photograph a story of abundance and diversity in lieu of a simple portrait of a single flower.

Carefully observing and surveying the area, I found one slender, but vibrant, lupine bloom rising out of the sea of white. After moments of evaluating this particular scene, I developed a visualized composition. The only trouble? At 10:00 a. m., a clear blue sky prevailed overhead and thus, the sun harshly illuminated the entire area. I could not help but feel like I had arrived at the "right place" to make a meaningful image but seemingly not the "right time."

However, I was determined to make the best image I could given the lighting circumstances. I made multiple frames to confirm my composition (photo #1 to the right). I knew the scene would appear overwhelmingly bright—so much so that the lupine would melt into the scene.

I tried softening natural light with my 22" diameter diffuser (photo #2). Despite moving the diffuser around through additional frames, the results on my LCD proved that my diffuser was not large enough to cover my foreground and background simultaneously. The dark subject against a light background drew attention to the background, not my primary subject! Because the brightest part of the frame draws the viewer's immediate attention, I sought an illuminated subject against a dark background.

To address the overly bright background, I asked my husband to position himself such that his shadow covered the background area visible in my composition (photo #3). Problem solved! Well, almost...the middle ground remained overly bright and distracting. I used my diffuser to aid in darkening the rest of the scene (photo #4). I also lowered my tripod slightly to take advantage of my husband's shadow. I decided that the diffuser did not create a dramatic enough shadow.

I set the diffuser aside. With a cable release in hand, I stood next to my husband so that my shadow filled the middle ground. This "manually-intensive" intervention resulted in photo #5. Had I given up after my first frame, I would not be able to share my visual message concerning a celebration of the diverse blooms in the Arizona desert.

Far too frequently photographers walk away from photographs, dismissed by the unrealistic notion of perfect conditions. If you are willing to work the scene and tango with the conditions presented to you, it is possible that every moment lends itself to "the right place at the right time."

*To reach the final vision of the lupine intermixing with the cream cups (photo #5), I needed to explore the scene through multiple iterations. Canon 5DMII, 100mm macro, ISO 200, f/9 @ 1/160th sec. Colleen Miniuk-Sperry*

**CENTRAL ARIZONA**

# Lost Dog Wash Trail

*Strawberry hedgehog cactus overtaken by purple scorpionweed. Canon 5DMIII, 24-105mm at 105mm, ISO 100, f/22 @ 1/13 sec. Paul Gill*

**BLOOM TIME**
**March to April**

**IDEAL TIME OF DAY**
**Early to late morning**

**VEHICLE**
**Any**

**HIKE**
**Moderate**

What started off in 1994 as a small five-square-mile (12.9-square km) park in Scottsdale has now blossomed into one of America's largest urban preserves. Now encompassing approximately 47 square miles (121.7-square km), the McDowell Sonoran Preserve protects some of Arizona's most pristine Sonoran Desert scenery. As if to celebrate this feat annually each March, an abundance of wildflowers arise from its rolling hillsides.

Although all of the preserve's maintained, well-signed dirt trails transport you quickly away from city life, the Lost Dog Wash Trailhead on the southern end of the park offers the best flower viewing opportunities.

Start hiking northward along the Lost Dog Wash Trail (an old jeep trail). Within the first mile (1.6 km)—especially near the Lost Dog Wash—Mexican gold poppies, scorpionweed, odora, blue dick, buckwheat, and creosote bush sprout and show off their vivid colors. After abundant rains, ocotillo flaunts its red flower tips while strawberry hedgehog and pincushion cacti reveal their pink blooms.

A **wide-angle** or **normal lens** paired with a **polarizer** will help you record this vivacious landscape. To study individual or small groups of intermingling wildflowers, add a **macro** or **telephoto lens**, **diffuser**, and **reflector** to your camera backpack. In either case, a **tripod** and **cable release** will help keep your camera steady during exposures.

For a more remote experience, venture onto the Ringtail Trail (about a half mile (0.8 km) from the trailhead) or the Old Jeep Trail (1.7 miles (2.7

# 26

## DIRECTIONS:

From Scottsdale, travel east on Shea Boulevard from the AZ 101 Loop for 4.4 miles (7.1 km). Turn left onto 124th Street. Drive an additional 1.1 miles (1.8 km). At the roundabout, stay straight to reach the well-maintained, dirt Lost Dog Wash Trailhead parking lot. The trail begins on the northeast side of the parking area.

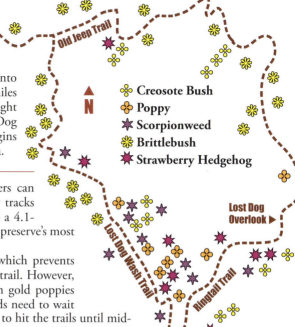

km) from the trailhead). Intrepid hikers can combine these two steeper and rockier tracks with the Lost Dog Wash Trail to create a 4.1-mile (6.6 km) loop through some of the preserve's most remote areas.

The park's gate opens at sunrise, which prevents experiencing the day's first light on the trail. However, shutterbugs anxious to see the Mexican gold poppies unfolded from their tight overnight buds need to wait to hit the trails until mid-morning (after 9 a.m.) anyhow. Very little shade exists—save for a few paloverde and mesquite trees—so bring a wide-brimmed hat, sunscreen, and plenty of drinking water for your outing.

Also, watch for mountain bikers on the trail, especially during busy weekends.

*Mexican gold poppies, purple scorpionweed, and lupine bloom around washes. Canon 5DMIII, TS-E 17mm, ISO 100, f/22 @ 1/30 sec., two-stop graduated neutral density filter. Paul Gill*

## Creosote Bush

*Larrea tridentata*
**Blooms:** Primarily from March to April (some bloom year-round) below 4,500 feet (1,372 m) on dry desert flats and hillsides. (Evergreen)
**Fun Fact:** Creosote bush grows in three of the four American deserts: in the Sonoran, Mojave, and Chihuahuan (not in the Great Basin).

**CENTRAL ARIZONA**

# Desert Botanical Garden

*Lone Mexican gold poppy in the Ottosen Entrance Garden. Canon 5D, 100mm macro, ISO 400, f/5 @ 1/1600 sec. Colleen Miniuk-Sperry*

**BLOOM TIME**
**March to June**

**IDEAL TIME OF DAY**
**Early morning to late afternoon**

**VEHICLE**
**Any**

**HIKE**
**Easy**

Established in the 1930s in an attempt to "Save the Desert," the Desert Botanical Garden today is a world-class venue celebrating the unique plants found in the southwestern United States. Arguably, the garden offers the most bountiful close-up compositions of wildflowers and cactus blooms in Arizona throughout the spring and summer months.

Though the entire garden offers photographic opportunities galore, you won't have to walk much past the Ottosen Entrance Plaza to see flower boxes overflowing and intermingling with a plethora of blooming cacti. Strawberry hedgehog cacti as well as annuals and perennials like desert bluebells, Mexican gold poppies, Goodding's verbena, Parry's penstemon, and chocolate flower immediately grab your attention.

Don't miss the cornucopia of flowers also waiting along the Harriet K. Maxwell Desert Wildflower Trail on the western edge of the garden. This short loop trail winds through two acres (0.8 hectares) of colorful desert terrain.

If there is still time in the day, visit the Cactus Gallery off the Desert Discovery Loop Trail to see an impressive collection of unique cactus species showing off their blooms.

Throughout the gardens, interpretive signs reveal the names of the flowers and cacti in front of you, so remember to take a quick snap of the sign to help later identify the species you're photographing.

No matter where you are in the garden, this is a premier location for close-up work, especially on a cloudy day, so pack your **macro lens**, **diffuser**, **reflector**, **tripod**, and **cable release**. Watch for clean backgrounds free of branches or stems from other plants and use an artificial background (see page 136) if needed. Pay attention to how the light is falling on your subject, looking for side or back light to create the illusion of shape. Use a reflector or diffuser to reduce contrast on your selected bloom. An **off-**

*Strawberry hedgehog cactus in bloom along the Harriet K. Maxwell Desert Wildflower Trail. Canon 5DMII, 100-400mm at 310mm, ISO 125, f/5.6 @ 1/160 sec., diffuser. Colleen Miniuk-Sperry*

## CENTRAL ARIZONA
# Desert Botanical Garden

*A variety of native and non-native cacti bloom in the Cactus Gallery along the Desert Discovery Loop Trail. Canon 5DMII, 16-35mm at 16mm, ISO 200, f/22 @ 1/30 sec., polarizer. Colleen Miniuk-Sperry*

**camera flash** can add a kiss of light to your flower if it's in shade.

Though the gardens are visually stunning, it isn't the place for shooting broad scenic landscape shots so leave the wide-angle lens at home.

Despite a prolific wildflower and cactus bloom in March and April, the most exciting time to visit the Desert Botanical Garden is in late June, when the garden's late closing time and Garden Flashlight Tours allows visitors to photograph numerous species of night-blooming cacti. True to their name, these unique cacti produce their flowers at night before closing and wilting the following morning.

To successfully photograph this phenomenon, pack a macro and/or **telephoto lens** and a tripod and cable release which will help keep your camera steady during the long exposures you'll experience shooting under the night sky. Also remember to bring a flashlight or headlamp, not only to help you see the trail, but also to illuminate and 'paint' the blooms with light.

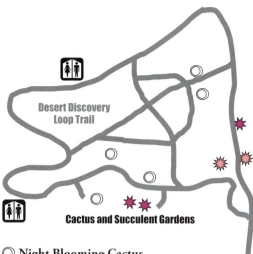

# DIRECTIONS:

From downtown Phoenix, follow I-10 east towards Tucson. Take Exit 147A to merge onto AZ 202. Drive 4 miles (6.4 km), and then take Exit 4 for Van Buren Street. Turn left at Van Buren Street and drive just short of 1 mile (1.6 km) before turning left onto Galvin Parkway. Travel a little more than a half mile (0.8 km) to a traffic roundabout. Take the first exit/right at the roundabout into the Desert Botanical Garden and follow signs to the parking lot.

Visitors must pay an entrance fee. For more information, visit **www.dbg.org**.

*Claret cup cactus in bloom. Canon 5DMII, 100mm macro, ISO 250, f/3.5 @ 1/200 sec., diffuser, reflector, off-camera flash, Omni-Bounce. Colleen Miniuk-Sperry*

## Torch Cactus

*Echinopsis candicans*
**Blooms:** In South America (native) and gardens across the United States (non-native) in sandy or rocky soil. (Perennial)
**Fun Fact:** This night-blooming cactus is one of over 120 different species within the Echinopsis genus.

**CENTRAL ARIZONA**

# South Mountain Park

*Strawberry hedgehog cactus and brittlebush bloom together on the Bajada Trail. Super Graphic 4x5, 120mm, Fuji Velvia 50, f/32 @ 1/50 sec. Paul Gill*

**BLOOM TIME**
March to June

**IDEAL TIME OF DAY**
Early morning; late afternoon to sunset

**VEHICLE**
Any

**HIKE**
Easy

Often referred to as the United States' largest municipal park, the South Mountain Park provides a 16,000-plus-acre (6,475-hectares) natural retreat in the middle of the busy metropolis of Phoenix. When you stroll through desert flats and across rocky hillsides covered in brilliant wildflowers, any stress from city life will melt away as fast as the urban sprawl vanishes in your rear view mirror.

After a wet winter, the normally inhospitable desert transforms into a plush carpet of color as Mexican gold poppies, owl clover, fiddleneck, wild heliotrope, Coulter's lupine, blue dicks, and narrow-leaved popcorn flower line the Bajada Trail beginning in March. This trail traditionally offers the most reliable display of flowers within the park.

As April approaches, strawberry hedgehog cacti put on one of the showiest cactus displays in Arizona as dazzling gold brittlebush adds color to the pristine Sonoran Desert. The event comes to an end in June after an explosion of morning-loving saguaro cactus blooms.

Those wishing to photograph broader landscape compositions should hit the trail mid-afternoon while the poppies are still soaking up the sun. Put the **wide-angle lens**, **polarizer**, **graduated neutral density filter**, **tripod**, and **cable release** in your pack and hike down the easy Bajada Trail looking for a patch of flowers with a southwesterly view of Butterfly Peak in the distant Sierra Estrella range down the valley. Bring a flashlight and headlamp to illuminate the way back to your vehicle should you decide to photograph this area through sunset.

Smaller compositions focused on the juxtapositions between soft, delicate flowers and sharp cacti are plentiful any time of day with a **macro** or **telephoto lens** though the cactus blooms look freshest in the morning. Since shade is rare here, also bring a **diffuser** and **reflector** to help control the contrast on your subjects.

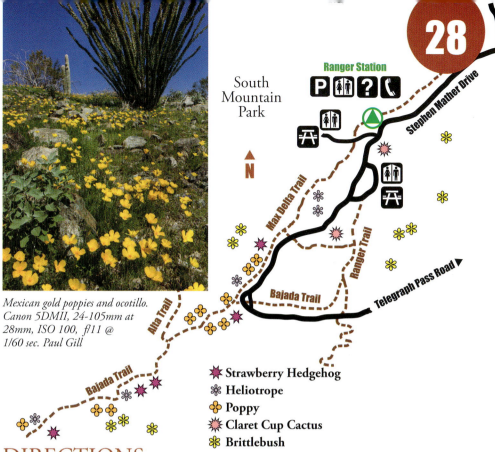

*Mexican gold poppies and ocotillo. Canon 5DMII, 24-105mm at 28mm, ISO 100, f/11 @ 1/60 sec. Paul Gill*

- ✹ **Strawberry Hedgehog**
- ✽ **Heliotrope**
- ✿ **Poppy**
- ✺ **Claret Cup Cactus**
- ✽ **Brittlebush**

# DIRECTIONS:

From downtown Phoenix, follow Central Avenue south to the entrance of South Mountain Park.

For those traveling on I-17, note that there is no exit for Central Avenue. Instead, take Exit 195B for 7th Street. Turn south onto 7th Street and drive about 4.5 miles (7.2 km) to Dobbins Road. Turn right onto Dobbins Road and travel a half mile (0.8 km) before turning left onto Central Avenue. After about 1.5 miles (2.4 km), you will enter the park.

Once in the park, proceed straight on Central Avenue (which becomes Stephen Mather Drive) passing the various picnic areas. Where the road starts to make a hairpin turn up the mountain, there is a turnoff and small parking area for the San Juan Road (closed to vehicular traffic). Park here and walk west to find the Bajada Trail near the closed gate to San Juan Road.

For more information, visit the South Mountain Park website at **phoenix.gov/parks/trails/locations/south/index.html**.

## Strawberry Hedgehog Cactus

*Echinocereus engelmannii*
**Blooms:** March to April on rocky flats and hillsides below elevations of 5,000 feet (1,524 m). (Perennial)
**Fun Fact:** Humans and desert animals alike enjoy eating the sweet-tasting, strawberry-flavored edible fruit of this cactus.

## CENTRAL ARIZONA
# Pass Mountain Trail

*Brittlebush grows up to four feet (1.2 m) tall along the Pass Mountain Trail. Canon 5DMII, TS-E 24mm, ISO 100, f/11 @ 1/20 sec. Paul Gill*

**BLOOM TIME**
March to May

**IDEAL TIME OF DAY**
Sunrise to late morning

**VEHICLE**
Any

**HIKE**
Moderate

If you are wild about wildflowers, then don't pass up the opportunity to photograph along the Pass Mountain Trail, where classic Sonoran Desert scenery, breathtaking views of the Goldfield and Superstition mountains, and a medley of spring wildflowers await.

In March, a profusion of Mexican gold poppies, scorpionweed, and white tackstem cover the ground along the trail after nourishing winter rains. Fairy duster, blue dicks, Coulter's lupine, chia, chuparosa, filaree, and desert globemallow also bloom in abundance. Come April, brittlebush sprouts its yellow flowers toward the sky and by May, Engelmann's prickly pear, strawberry hedgehog, and saguaro cacti join the spring chorus.

To maximize your photographic opportunities, set out on the trail about 30 minutes before sunrise, using a flashlight or headlamp to help you navigate in the dark. As the sun rises, look for healthy blooms along the steep east-facing hillsides.

Once you find the perfect floral foreground, set up your **tripod**, pointing your camera to the north to photograph the Goldfield Mountains or to the southeast to capture the Superstition Mountains. No matter which direction you face, try a **wide-angle lens** and set a small aperture for the broadest depth of field. Then compose such that the palette of color takes up most of your frame. If there is sky in your composition, place a **polarizer** and **graduated neutral density filter** on your lens to ensure the richest color and proper exposure. Before you snap the shutter, scan the edges of your frame to ensure unwanted branches or out of focus flowers are not in your picture, unless you intend to capture your scene with a small depth of field.

As the sun gets higher in the sky, make your compositions smaller, looking for individual flowers to study through a **macro** or **telephoto lens** before retracing your steps back to your vehicle.

## DIRECTIONS:

From Phoenix, take US 60 east towards Apache Junction. Take Exit 190A for AZ 202 Loop heading north and drive about 3 miles (4.8 km) on AZ 202 Loop to Exit 26 for Brown Road. After exiting the highway, turn right onto Brown Road and head east for about 4 miles (6.4 km). When you reach Meridan Road, turn left and drive about 2 miles (3.2 km) north until Meridan Road ends in a dirt parking area on the left hand side of the road.

To reach the best blooms, follow the well worn unnamed trail for a few hundred yards to the northwest until this path crosses a wash and then intersects with the Pass Mountain Trail. Veer right at this intersection and hike a little less than 1.5 miles (2.4 km) along the Pass Mountain Trail to a horseshoe-shaped valley before the trail starts to climb more dramatically into the Goldfield Mountains.

*A field of Mexican gold poppies bloom in the desert along the Pass Mountain Trail. Pentax 67II, 55mm, Kodak VS 100, f/32 @ 1/100 sec., polarizer. Paul Gill*

# White Tackstem

*Calycoseris wrightii*

**Blooms:** March to May on sandy mesas, plains, and hillsides in between 500 and 4,000 feet (152 and 1,219 m) elevation. (Annual)
**Fun Fact:** White tackstem shows minuscule tack-shaped glands on its flower base, unlike the similar desert-chicory flower.

**CENTRAL ARIZONA**

# San Tan Mountain Regional Park

*A wide-angle lens exaggerates the height of a blooming saguaro cactus. Canon 5DMII, 16-35mm at 16mm, ISO 100, f/22 @ 1/80 sec., reflector. Paul Gill*

**BLOOM TIME**
March to May

**IDEAL TIME OF DAY**
Sunrise and sunset

**VEHICLE**
Any

**HIKE**
Moderate

If you are seeking a quiet refuge far from civilization to explore classic Sonoran Desert scenery intermixed with an abundance of spring wildflowers, then a visit to the San Tan Mountain Regional Park is your answer. Though wildflowers pop up along many of the park's trails, the easy-going Moonlight Trail and the more difficult San Tan Trail often offer the most abundant blooms against spectacular backdrops.

Though the Moonlight Trail's name may suggest otherwise, the best time to photograph during March and early April is sunrise. Arrive at the entrance gate precisely at 6 a. m., when the park opens, and hit this trail immediately to photograph the blooming Mexican gold poppies, Coulter's lupine, blue dicks, and desert globemallow. A view north towards the rocky Goldmine Mountains or south towards the rugged San Tan Mountains won't disappoint when using a **wide-angle lens**. Also bring along a **tripod**, **cable release**, **polarizer**, and **graduated neutral density filter**. If there is room in your backpack, slip a **macro lens**, **diffuser**, and **reflector** in to extend your photo shoot beyond first light.

Once you've wrapped up your morning session, brush up on your knowledge of desert wildflowers by joining one of the park's wildflower hikes with a park ranger on select mornings throughout March and April. Cameras welcomed!

In late April and May, come at sunset instead, where ideal light illuminates the spring color along the longer San Tan Trail as the day ends. A profusion of white ratany blooms next to saguaro cactus, littleleaf paloverde, and strawberry hedgehog cactus. If you venture far from the trailhead, pack a headlamp or flashlight to find your way back to your vehicle.

Phillips Road

Entrance

- ☆ White Ratany
- ◆ Lupine
- ✻ Brittlebush
- ✺ Saguaro Cactus

## DIRECTIONS:

From downtown Phoenix, drive east on I-10 towards Tucson to Exit 161 for Pecos Road/AZ 202 Loop, veering left to follow AZ 202 Loop eastward. Drive 12.8 miles (20.6 km) to Exit 42 for Val Vista Drive. Turn right onto Val Vista and drive south for about 4.7 miles (7.6 km). Turn left onto Riggs Road and drive 7 miles (11.3 km), turning right when the road ends at Ellsworth Road.

Travel south on Ellsworth Road for 1.3 miles (2.1 km), which will turn into Hunt Highway. Once on Hunt Highway heading east, travel an additional 1.1 miles (1.8 km) and then turn right onto Thompson Road. Drive 2.2 miles (3.5 km) and then turn right onto Phillips Road. Head west about 1 mile (1.6 km) to the San Tan Mountain Regional Park entrance. Ample parking is available just beyond the entrance gate. The trailhead for both the Moonlight and San Tan trails is located on the western side of the parking area.

Visitors must have a Maricopa County Parks and Recreation Annual Pass or pay an entrance fee. For more information, visit the San Tan Mountain Regional Park's website at **www.maricopa.gov/parks/santan**.

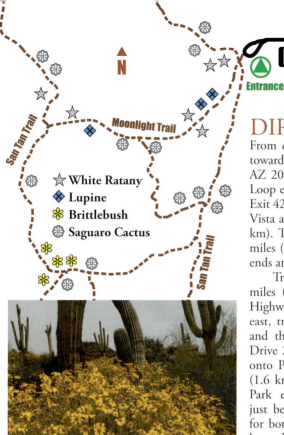

*Brittlebush blooms among saguaro cactus. Canon 5DMII, 24-105mm at 24 mm, ISO 100, f/22 @ 1/10 sec. Paul Gill*

## Desert Globemallow

*Sphaeralcea ambigua*
**Blooms:** Year-round along roadsides, sandy washes, and desert flats below 3,500 feet (1,067 m). (Perennial)
**Fun Fact:** Known also as "sore eye poppy," the leaves of a desert globemallow are an eye irritant.

**CENTRAL ARIZONA**

# Lost Dutchman State Park

*Yellow brittlebush cover the foothills along the Jacob's Crosscut Trail. Canon 5DMII, 24-105mm at 24mm, ISO 100, f/11 @ 1/60 sec.
Paul Gill*

**BLOOM TIME**
March to April

**IDEAL TIME OF DAY**
Early afternoon to sunset

**VEHICLE**
Any

**HIKE**
Moderate

Deep in the Superstition Mountains, there's gold. Legend holds that Jacob Waltz, known as "The Dutchman," knew of an abundant gold deposit hidden somewhere in the depths of these rugged desert mountains. Despite a deathbed confession in 1891 and the existence of a crude map, the location of his mine remains a mystery. The lure of lost treasure has drawn people to this area ever since.

Named for the mysterious character, the Lost Dutchman State Park does contain abundant gold—just not the metallic kind. Each spring, the expansive fields of bright wildflowers along the Jacob's Crosscut Trail will have you shouting "there's gold in them thar hills!"

Blankets of Mexican gold poppies start in mid-March, but much more than golden flowers thrive here. Blooming alongside the peppy poppies are Coulter's lupine, scorpionweed, fiddleneck, chuparosa, fairy duster, and desert globemallow which intermingle with the poppies on the undulating hillsides to create a photogenic kaleidoscope of color. The wildflower bloom often continues into early April, when the bright yellow brittlebush begins to shine.

Come early afternoon to focus on smaller, more intimate, scenes of individual or smaller groupings of intermixed wildflowers with a **macro lens**, **tripod**, and **cable release**. Since the harsh desert environment surrounds you, look for opportunities to create juxtaposition between the

*Single bloom of desert globemallow. Canon 5DMII, 100mm macro, two 12mm extension tubes stacked, ISO 800, f/6.3 @ 1/60 sec. Colleen Miniuk-Sperry*

colorful delicate wildflowers and the prickly cactus found along this trail.

When the poppies close up as the sun goes down, turn your focus to broader perspectives of the floral designs in front of the glowing and towering Superstitions Mountains to capture one of Arizona's most iconic wildflower photographs. Use a **wide-angle lens** and a **polarizer**, which will deepen the blue sky behind the monoliths. Experiment with vertical and horizontal compositions, using the wildflowers intermixed with a saguaro cactus or jumping cholla cactus in your foreground.

Because the rising sun behind the Superstition Mountains creates a substantial shadow across most of the park, reserve mornings along the trail for macro photography using an **off-camera flash** to create shadow and shape in the shade.

## Mexican Gold Poppy

*Eschscholzia mexicana*
**Bloom:** Mid-February to May on rocky slopes and plains below 4,500 feet (1,372 m) elevation. (Annual)
**Fun Fact:** This flower only opens its delicate petals once exposed to full sunlight and then closes when the sun goes down.

**CENTRAL ARIZONA**

# Lost Dutchman State Park

*Mexican gold poppies and brittlebush along the Siphon Draw Trail. Wista 4x5, 120mm, Fuji Velvia 50, f/32 @ 1/2 sec. Paul Gill*

## DIRECTIONS:

From Phoenix, follow US 60 east towards Apache Junction. Take Exit 196 for AZ 88/Idaho Road and turn left onto Idaho Road. Drive about 2.5 miles (4 km), and then veer right onto AZ 88/Apache Trail. Drive approximately 5 miles (8.1 km) to the entrance of Lost Dutchman State Park. Turn right into the park and pay your entrance fee or show your Arizona State Parks Annual Pass. Then head towards the Cholla Day Use Area on the northeast side of the park.

For the best flowers, take Treasure Loop Trail (trail #56 on the park map) out of the southeast side of the parking lot. After about 0.5 miles (0.8 km), this trail intersects with Jacob's Crosscut Trail (trail #58). Turn right onto Jacob's Crosscut Trail and look for wildflowers along the 0.85 miles (1.4 km) hike to the Siphon Draw Trail (trail #53). Hikers can also access Jacob's Crosscut Trail from the west by walking the Siphon Draw Trail about a half mile (0.8 km) out of the campground.

Visit the Lost Dutchman State Park website for more information: **www.pr.state.az.us/parks/lodu/index.html**.

**PHOTO TIP 8**

## Create an Instant Cloudy Day

On average, Arizona enjoys over 300 days of sunshine a year. While this all but guarantees a beautiful day to explore spring's bounty, a cloudless day can create harsh lighting conditions that are difficult for your camera to record. Fortunately, you can create an "instant cloudy day" over a smaller scene with a diffuser.

A diffuser is any semi-transparent material that scatters, and subsequently softens, the light. This accessory helps tame the stark contrast between bright highlights and deep shadow, mimicking the quality of light seen on an overcast day.

You can purchase a commercial diffuser that consists of translucent material stretched across a frame. Collapsible versions (similar to car window shades) are handy when photographing in remote areas. If a store-bought diffuser is not available, consider using a white bed sheet, piece of paper, or a thin t-shirt instead to serve as your instant cloudy day. Or, consider purchasing a light tent to place over your smaller scene.

To create this effect, hold the diffuser between the sun and your subject. As you position it, ensure you use a large enough diffuser to cover the entire frame. An extra tripod, a nearby tree, or a friend can help hold the diffuser in place as you are shooting.

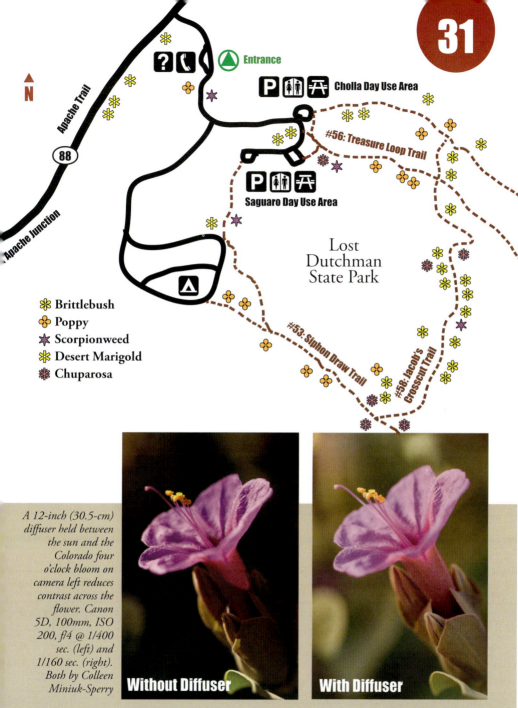

*A 12-inch (30.5-cm) diffuser held between the sun and the Colorado four o'clock bloom on camera left reduces contrast across the flower. Canon 5D, 100mm, ISO 200, f/4 @ 1/400 sec. (left) and 1/160 sec. (right). Both by Colleen Miniuk-Sperry*

If you are on your own, plug a cable release into your camera to free a hand up to hold the diffuser.

Though diffusers and reflectors both aim to solve similar challenges of reducing the contrast seen with direct mid-day light, select a diffuser when you seek to record greater color saturation with your subject.

**CENTRAL ARIZONA**

# Silly Mountain

*Brittlebush and saguaros on the southern flanks of Silly Mountain. Canon 5DMII, 16-35mm at 30mm, ISO 160, f/16 @ 0.6 sec., three-stop graduated neutral density filter. Colleen Miniuk-Sperry*

**BLOOM TIME**
**March to April**

**IDEAL TIME OF DAY**
**Early afternoon to sunset**

**VEHICLE**
**Any**

**HIKE**
**Moderate**

Regardless of whether Pinal County road grader Harry Calwalader intended to call the hill or just the road up the hill "silly," the name Silly Mountain stuck. A fire in 1994 and years of careless off-road vehicle usage make the mountain look scarred for most of the year. But this ugly duckling turns into a most beautiful swan in the spring. As soon as the first week of April arrives, the only thing silly about Silly Mountain is the ridiculously laughable amount of brittlebush that graces this otherwise barren hill along Highway 60.

To capture the best blooms, come early in the afternoon and start your outing with a hike along the Brittlebush Trail, an easy 0.4 mile (0.6 km) hike one way to the north side of the hill. **Macro** and **telephoto lenses** will prove most beneficial to isolate the individual flowers that make up the full brittlebush.

Then retrace your steps back to the Old Mine Trail, a more difficult, albeit shorter, trail than the Brittlebush Trail. Where the Brittlebush and Old Mine trails intersect, veer left (west) onto the Old Mine Trail to explore the southern part of the mountain. Along this trail, you'll see the best mix of blooms and saguaro cactus. Turn to a **wide-angle lens** and broad depth of field as the sun starts to set to capture brittlebush in the foreground with the seemingly endless expanse of color and desert scenery in the background. Continue walking west until you reach the High Point Trail, where you'll

## DIRECTIONS:

From Phoenix, take US 60 east past Apache Junction. Because you cannot access Silly Mountain Road from southbound US 60, pass Exit 198 and then drive just short of 2 miles (3.2 km) to Mountain View Road on the north side of the highway. Turn left onto Mountain View Road and travel 0.2 miles (0.3 km) before turning right onto 32nd Avenue. Proceed for another 0.2 miles (0.3 km) and then turn right onto Silly Mountain Road. Before you meet up with US 60 again, look for the gravel parking areas on both sides of the road. The trails start on the east side of Silly Mountain Road.

❋ Brittlebush
⊛ Saguaro Cactus
❋ Desert Marigold
❃ Creosote Bush

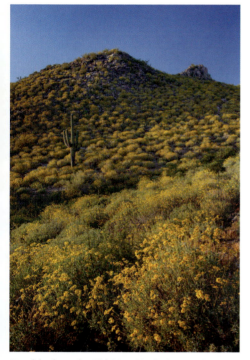

*Brittlebush on the Old Mine Trail. Canon 5DMII, 24-105mm at 28mm, ISO 100, f/11 @ 1/30 sec. Paul Gill*

turn left and walk a quick 100 yards (91.4 m) to see the best blooms and views at sunset.

Surprisingly, the vibrant brittlebush has a tendency to look flat and dull at last light in photographs, so try shooting the blooms with side light, at least a 45-degree angle from the sun, to give the brittlebush shape and dimension in your picture.

Remember to pack a **tripod** and **cable release** to stabilize your camera at sunset. Don't forget a headlamp or flashlight as well for your short trek back to the parking area in the dark.

## Brittlebush

*Encelia farinosa*
**Blooms:** November to May along rocky slopes, sandy washes, and desert flats below 3,000 feet (914 m) elevation. (Perennial)
**Fun Fact:** Brittlebush is also known as "incienso," a Spanish word meaning "incense."

**CENTRAL ARIZONA**

# Peralta Road

*Yellow brittlebush and white flat-top buckwheat besides the Peralta Cliffs near the Peralta Trailhead. Canon 5DMII, 16-35mm at 24mm, ISO 100, f/22 @ 1/30 sec., polarizer. Paul Gill*

**BLOOM TIME**
**March to May**

**IDEAL TIME OF DAY**
**Sunrise to late morning**

**VEHICLE**
**Any**

**HIKE**
**Easy**

Legend suggests that the Peralta family from Mexico established a gold mine in the vast and desolate Superstition Mountains in the mid-1800s. Though Apaches allegedly killed the family in the Peralta Massacre, a relative supposedly shared the gold mine's location with Jacob Waltz years later. Known as "the Dutchman," Waltz found and stashed large quantities of the valuable yellow nuggets in what became known as the mysterious "Lost Dutchman's Mine."

Thanks to these tales, the Peralta name goes hand in hand with the Superstition Mountains, as do the spectacular spring wildflowers that can bloom for months along the Peralta Road up to the Peralta Trailhead with stunning views of the Peralta Cliffs.

In the undulating hills beside the volcanic ramparts of the Superstition Mountains, Mexican gold poppies, Coulter's lupine, scorpionweed, owl clover, and blue dicks kick off the annual spring show in March. Then brittlebush, flat-top buckwheat, ocotillo, and pincushion cactus blossom along the hillsides in April. Finally, the saguaro cactus, littleleaf paloverde, and ironwood sprout their flowers in May before the hot sun scorches the desert in June.

Because rugged cliffs border this area to the west, the photographic opportunities are best at sunrise through late morning before the sun disappears behind the rock monolith. If wildflowers cover large swaths of the desert, start by extending your **tripod**, then tilt a **wide-angle** or **tilt-shift lens** down towards the carpets. Minimize or eliminate the sky to enhance the focus on the flowers. If your composition includes the sky, add a **polarizer** and a **graduated neutral density filter** in front of your lens to help retain the saturated colors in the sky.

As the sun rises higher, look for individual blooms or clusters of intermingling flowers to photograph with a **macro lens** and a **diffuser** or **reflector**.

- Pincushion Cactus
- Brittlebush
- Strawberry Hedgehog Cactus
- Buckwheat
- Saguaro Cactus

## DIRECTIONS:

From Phoenix, take US 60 east towards Apache Junction and Gold Canyon. Turn left onto Peralta Road (also called Forest Service Road 77) at the Peralta Trailhead sign between mileposts 204 & 205. The paved Peralta Road will weave through a housing development and past the Peralta Elementary School for 1 mile (1.6 km). After the school, the road turns into a winding washboard dirt road.

The best blooms begin on the north side of the road once you have driven 1.5 miles (2.4 km) from the school and continue for 5 additional miles (8.1 km) until you reach the Peralta Trailhead.

*Brittlebush and jumping cholla at sunrise. Wista 4x5, 90mm, Fuji Velvia 100, f/32 @ 1/2 sec., two-stop graduated neutral density filter. Paul Gill*

## Pincushion Cactus

*Mammillaria microcarpa*
**Blooms:** April to August in dry gravel desert in shaded areas below 4,500 feet (1,372 m) elevation. (Perennial)
**Fun Fact:** Almost 200 different species of pincushion cactus exist worldwide.

**CENTRAL ARIZONA**

# Hewitt Canyon

*Sunset over Hewitt Canyon. Canon 5D, 24-105mm at 24mm, ISO 100, f/22 @ 1/8 sec., three-stop graduated neutral density filter. Paul Gill*

**BLOOM TIME**
**March to May**

**IDEAL TIME OF DAY**
**Sunrise and sunset**

**VEHICLE**
**2WD high-clearance**

**HIKE**
**Moderate**

Tucked in the southern edge of the vast and rugged Superstition Mountain Wilderness in the Tonto National Forest, Hewitt Station once served as a stop along the Magma Arizona Railroad where copper and occasionally cattle made their way out of Superior en route to the larger Phoenix & Eastern railroad at Magma (30 miles (48.3 km) to the southwest) where the copper continued on to the smelter at Hayden. If you're willing to venture off the beaten path, Hewitt Canyon is the place to visit today when searching for brilliant wildflowers.

Start well before the sun rises to capture the unnamed cliffs surrounding Hewitt Canyon as the day starts. Bring a **wide-angle lens** and a **graduated neutral density filter**, as the landscape in your foreground will be in shadow as the rugged rocks in the background soak up the golden morning sun when you're facing north.

As the sun gets higher in the sky, travel past Hewitt Canyon through the sinuous wash and proceed up the hill for 0.2 miles (0.3 km). When you see a 50-foot (15.2-m) patch of asphalt in the road, stop and let your eyes follow the wash up to the Hewitt Canyon Arch concealed by the rocky amphitheater behind it.

Find a pullout on the right hand side of the road and hike up to the arch to explore the multitude of wildflowers and brittlebush bursting with colors around this often overlooked geological feature. Getting behind the arch on the west side makes for a wonderful backlit sunrise shoot with a wide-angle lens—so long as you can find the arch in the dark with a headlamp or flashlight!

During the day, look for saguaro-lined washes and hillsides showing off Mexican gold poppies, Coulter's lupine, blue dicks, and chia intermixed with Engelmann's prickly pear cactus. The tall rock ledges along the road occasionally play host to a line of flowers, making it easy to photograph underneath isolated blooms with a **polarizer** against a saturated blue sky.

As evening nears, head back to the south end of Hewitt Canyon to photograph the west-facing Byous Butte basking in the light of sunset with carpets of wildflowers in your foreground. The flanks of this monolith see an abundant Mexican gold poppy bloom from March to April, but it's a steep climb without trails to get the best views.

Revisit this same area in May with a wide-angle, **macro**, and **telephoto lens**, where saguaro cactus, ironwood, littleleaf paloverde, and Engelmann's prickly pear cactus put on their own vibrant show of spring.

Because of the extensive photo opportunities no matter what month you visit, pack a lunch to enjoy among the wildflowers since modern services in Gold Canyon are located about an hour's drive away.

*Mexican gold poppies open in morning sun among a hillside of Coulter's lupine. Pentax 67II, 55mm, Kodak VS 100, f/32 @ 1/30 sec., polarizer. Paul Gill*

## Blue Dicks

*Dichelostemma pulchellum*
**Blooms:** February to May on open mesas, slopes and plains below 5,000 feet (1,524 m) elevation. (Perennial)
**Fun Fact:** The tall blue dicks flower is a member of the lily family.

**CENTRAL ARIZONA**

# Hewitt Canyon

## DIRECTIONS:

From Phoenix, take US 60 east towards Superior. Drive about 1.5 miles (2.4 km) past Florence Junction (where US 60 and AZ 79 meet) and then turn left onto Queen Valley Road right before the old railroad crossing. Drive a little less than 2 miles (3.2 km) on the paved Queen Valley Road, and then veer right onto Hewitt Station Road (referred to as Forest Road 357 on maps).

Drive about 3 miles (4.8 km) on this gravel road until you see the sign for the Woodbury and Rogers Trough Trailhead. At the sign, turn left onto Hewitt Canyon Road (called Forest Road 172 on maps), a dirt road, where you will immediately cross the usually dry Queen Creek.

After a heavy rainfall, however, the creek may be impassable due to high waters.

The best flowers typically bloom along the Hewitt Canyon Road 2 to 3 additional rocky and rough miles (3.2 to 4.8 km) into Hewitt Canyon beyond Queen Creek.

*Mexican gold poppies stay open until the last light of the day. Canon 5DMII, 16-35mm at 16mm, ISO 100, f/22 @ 1/2 sec. Paul Gill*

**PHOTO TIP 9**

## Focus With Precision

Sponsored by Hoodman Corporation, **www.hoodmanusa.com**

When using a macro lens, a lens with an extension tube attached, a close-up diopter, or bellows, focusing can be an exercise in futility whether you attempt to hand hold your camera or move your tripod around. Using focusing rails can help achieve precise focus when working up close and personal with minuscule floral scenes.

A single axis focusing rail will move the camera towards and away from your subject. A focusing rail with two axes is also capable of moving from side to side. Having multiple adjustments can help tremendously when attempting to focus.

Set up your tripod so your camera's lens is within six to eight inches (15 to 20 cm) of your subject, closer if you are using extension tubes, a close-up filter, or bellows. Then, patiently move the focusing rail back and forth until your subject comes into focus.

Unless the autofocus (AF) functionality on your camera allows you to move the focus

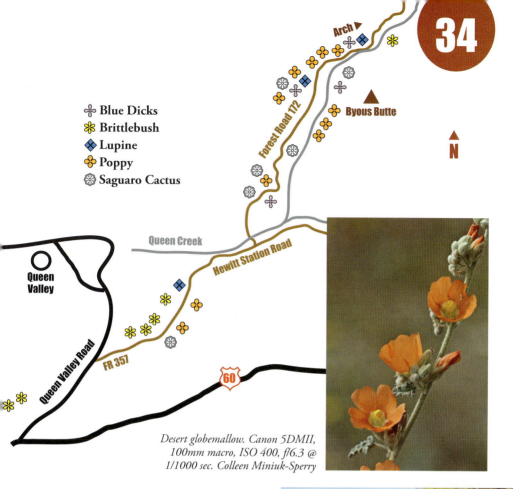

*Desert globemallow. Canon 5DMII, 100mm macro, ISO 400, f/6.3 @ 1/1000 sec. Colleen Miniuk-Sperry*

point to different areas besides the center part of your frame, use Manual focus to hone in on your subject. Using the Live View mode (if available on your camera model) in conjunction with a **Hoodman HoodLoupe** will help you review your image's sharpness more precisely on your camera's large LCD screen instead of through the small viewfinder.

As soon as you think your flower is in focus, capture an image. Then reevaluate the focus by zooming in on your photo on your camera's screen, making tiny changes to the focus using the rail adjustments and snapping another frame. By capturing multiple images, not only are you covering your bases, but you also can later stack these multiple exposures in post-processing software like Helicon Focus or Zerene Stacker to extend the depth of field.

*To precisely focus on a blanketflower at Boyce Thompson Arboretum, Colleen uses a focusing rail to subtly adjust her Canon 5DMII and 65mm 1:5X lens into the perfect position. Paul Gill*

**CENTRAL ARIZONA**

# Boyce Thompson Arboretum

ABOVE: The Demonstration Garden comes alive with color. Canon 5DMII, 24-105mm at 73mm, ISO 100, f/22 @ 1/4 sec. RIGHT: One desert marigold blooms between golden barrel cacti. Canon 5DMII, 24-105mm at 24mm, ISO 100, f/16 @ 0.6 sec. Both by Paul Gill

**BLOOM TIME**
March to June

**IDEAL TIME OF DAY**
Early morning to late afternoon

**VEHICLE**
Any

**HIKE**
Easy

Established in the early 1920s, the Boyce Thompson Arboretum claims the title as the oldest and largest botanical garden in Arizona. The longstanding goal of the facility is to both showcase amazing desert plants of the world and to help educate the public on the ecology of arid lands and plants both native and not native to Arizona. Today, this scenic 300+ acre (121+ hectares) sanctuary nestled below the rugged Picketpost Mountain serves as home to over 800 species of cactus, not to mention picturesque wildflower blooms starting in March.

After entering the park, head towards the Cactus and Succulent Garden on an easy and wide gravel walking path. On the northwest-most corner of this garden, you'll find the Boyce Thompson hedgehog cactus showing off vibrant magenta flowers in mid-April through May. Simultaneously, Engelmann's prickly pear blooms dominate as the earlier wildflowers start to fade in hot temperatures.

Continue to follow the path towards Ayer Lake and the overlook near the Picketpost House, scanning both sides of the path for blooming wildflowers. Mexican gold poppies, desert marigold, scorpionweed, Coulter's lupine, blue dicks, fiddleneck, Parry's penstemon, and desert globemallow—to name just a few—blossom along the trail.

Finally, take a spin through the Desert Garden within the larger Demonstration Garden, where you can typically see an explosion of wildflowers and cactus blooms side by side. Come May and June, the garden and nearby meadow fills with Mexican hat, blanketflower, and yellow columbine.

## DIRECTIONS:

From Phoenix, take US 60 east towards Superior. Look for the signed entrance on the right side of the road near milepost 223 shortly before reaching Superior. If you travel into Superior, you've gone too far east.

The Boyce Thompson Arboretum charges an entrance fee, unless you possess an Arizona State Parks Annual Pass. For more information, visit the Boyce Thompson Arboretum's website at **arboretum.ag.arizona.edu**.

---

No matter your subject matter, look for side light, back light or shade as you set up your compositions. If the sky is clear of clouds and the sun is directly lighting your subject, use a **diffuser** to soften the contrast between the bright highlights and dark shadows.

Keep your compositions simple and backgrounds clean of any distracting elements as it's easy to get visually overwhelmed with all the beautiful plants here. A **macro** or **telephoto lens** can help you hone in on your specific center of interest, while an artificial background (see page 136) can serve to keep your backdrop uncluttered.

To learn more about the flowers you photograph in the arboretum, join one of the guided wildflower walks during March and April.

## Boyce Thompson Hedgehog Cactus

*Echinocereus boyce-thompsonii*
**Blooms:** March to April in rocky and gravelly soils below 5,000 feet (1,524 m) elevation. (Perennial)
**Fun Fact:** This cactus was first identified as a new cactus species in the Boyce Thompson Arboretum.

**CENTRAL ARIZONA**

# Silver King Mine Road

*Late light illuminates Mexican gold poppies and Coulter's lupine on the hillside above Silver King Mine Road. Canon 5DMII, 16-35mm at 20mm, ISO 100, f/22 @ 1/4 sec., two- and three-stop graduated neutral density filters stacked. Paul Gill*

**BLOOM TIME**
**March to April**

**IDEAL TIME OF DAY**
**Sunset**

**VEHICLE**
**2WD high-clearance**

**HIKE**
**Strenuous**

In 1875, a group of prospectors found a rich silver vein in the rolling desert hills north of present-day Superior. After they registered their claim, a large mining operation and associated boom camp quickly sprang up at the site. The famous Silver King Mine was born. The mine was a major producer for over a decade, but by the early 1900s, declining silver prices and the removal of the richest ore had turned the camp into a ghost town and brought regular mining operations to a close (although some sporadic work has continued there ever since). As of this writing, the mine is currently inactive, and so Coulter's lupine—not silver—is king in the Silver King Mine area. Each spring, as bare hillsides come alive in March, it is often the premier spot for lupine blooms in central Arizona.

Getting to the Silver King Mine area takes some effort, but even if you don't travel the full distance, worthwhile blooms grace both sides of the jeep trail leading to your final destination. As you get closer to the mine, look to the south-facing hillsides for splashes of orange and purple indicating patches of photogenic Coulter's lupine and Mexican gold poppies intermixing.

Try to be on-site an hour or two before sunset to scout for the best

*Coulter's lupine carpet the steep hillsides at sunset. Canon 5DMII, TS-E 24mm, ISO 100, three-exposure HDR. Paul Gill*

flowers. With the sun higher in the sky, first look for intimate arrangements of patterns of colors among the large swaths of flowers on the hillsides using a **telephoto** or **macro lens**. Bring a **diffuser**, a **reflector**, and plenty of water as there are few trees in the area to provide shade for you or your compositions.

To photograph broad landscapes of the evening's last light kissing the fields of wildflowers, use a **wide-angle lens**, **polarizer**, **graduated neutral density filters**, and **tripod**. As you compose the scene, keep your tripod low to the ground to emphasize the fields of flowers in the foreground and scenic hills in the background, which will minimize the somewhat uninteresting and bare middle ground.

If you venture far from your vehicle, consider bringing along a flashlight or headlamp to illuminate your way after sunset.

## Coulter's Lupine

*Lupinus sparsiflorus*
**Blooms:** January to May on mesas, desert slopes, and roadsides below 3,000 feet (914 m) elevation. (Perennial)
**Fun Fact:** Lupine derives its name from the Latin word "lupin" meaning "wolf."

**CENTRAL ARIZONA**

# Silver King Mine Road

*Mexican gold poppies and Coulter's lupine. Canon 5DMII, 16-35mm at 22mm, ISO 100, f/22 @ 1/100 sec., polarizer. Paul Gill*

**PHOTO TIP 10**

## Bring Your Own Background

Nature often provides perfect backdrops for photographing individual wildflowers. But sometimes, despite employing a selective focus through a wide aperture, bright areas or odd shapes in the background detract from the beautiful bloom.

A quick solution to cleaning up your background is to position an artificial backdrop behind your subject. Draping a shirt, sheet, or poster board over an extra tripod or held in place by a helpful friend can keep your background free of unwanted and distracting objects.

Black is a common color to use, but natural greens, browns, and blues occurring in nature or even an old photograph you have of the desert can also serve as an effective backdrop to your flower.

When using an artificial background, remember to set your camera to a wide aperture such as f/4 or f/5.6 to render a short depth of field. Then, position the background far enough away from the primary subject—usually a foot or two (0.3 to 0.6 m)—so that the background is blurred enough to obscure its actual identity. The distance needed will vary based on the lens you are shooting with, the aperture set, and your camera's distance from your subject, so don't be afraid to experiment with your background's placement while out in the field.

## DIRECTIONS:

From Phoenix, take US 60 east towards Superior. Before you enter the town of Superior, turn left onto Silver King Mine Road (the turnoff is directly across the highway from the tiny Superior Municipal Airport). Drive down this dirt road past the industrial operations on the left hand side of the road. After about 0.7 miles (1.1 km), you will come to a fork in the road. Stay to the right, traveling past the substation located on the left. Travel for about another 2.9 miles (4.7 km), staying on the main track. Park near the corral. On foot, follow the old jeep trail across the wash and along the hillside for about 1 to 2 miles (1.6 to 3.2 km).

For alternative access, you can continue driving approximately another 0.5 miles (0.8 km) beyond the corral. Park along the road when you spot flowers in the hills to the northwest.

NOTE: The site of the actual Silver King Mine itself (located further up the Silver King Mine Road) is on private property and should be not be visited without permission from the owners.

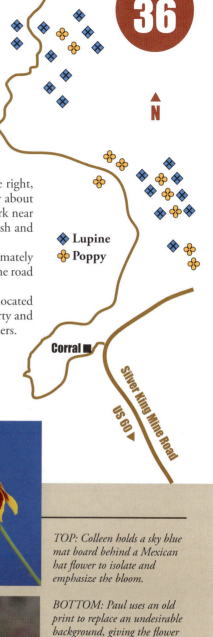

TOP: Colleen holds a sky blue mat board behind a Mexican hat flower to isolate and emphasize the bloom.

BOTTOM: Paul uses an old print to replace an undesirable background, giving the flower a more natural-looking background.

## Making the Photo 5
# Tilting for the Near-Far Technique
By Paul Gill

When I started working in landscape photography, my biggest influence was David Muench, known as the "Father of Near-Far Photography." At that time, I used a wooden 4x5 field camera, which allowed me to adjust the focal plane by tilting and shifting both the lens and film planes to the left and right as well as up and down.

Today, tilt-shift lenses (also known as perspective control lenses) work similarly to change an image's perspective by moving the angle of the lens relative to the sensor. These adjustments not only increase the apparent size of foreground objects (a photographer can tilt the camera and lens to exaggerate this even more so), but they can also help prevent the convergence effect typically seen with wide-angle lenses.

*Same bloom head shot with a 16-35mm at 16mm, ISO 100, f/11 at 1/20 sec. Paul Gill*

The secret to using a tilt-shift lens is to first find your composition. Then, tilt the camera while tilting the lens in order to change the perspective to polish the composition the way you like. This often takes multiple movements to fine tune. Check the image in Live View mode (if available on your camera) with a Hoodman HoodLoupe to ensure everything is in focus.

For example, starting in early May each year, I get excited to shoot the saguaro cactus bloom. I have spent years scouting old growth, sagging arm saguaros across Arizona, and I pay my favorites an early morning visit to catch the bloom heads soaking up the best light. I like to use a pair of binoculars to find a cactus with abundant flowers. Then, I hike to the saguaro and use the crown of blooms for a foreground. May and early morning is not only the best time for saguaro bloom but also for rattlesnakes. Bring a walking stick and a flashlight when you are hiking to your next great saguaro bloom shot.

I made the image on the left off the Happy Camp Road south of the Silver King Mine (see page 134). I wanted to exaggerate the size of the saguaro buds and blooms in the foreground. To do so, I used a 17mm tilt-shift lens to bring the foreground seemingly closer to the camera as well as to straighten the saguaro cacti in the background. I also used a warm reflector to bounce the light back into the main flower.

As I composed, I wanted space between the different visual elements so the flow from the main subject to the saguaro arms and back would lead the eye around the image in a constant serpentine loop. I love the play between the arms coming into the frame and the crown of the flowers. Unfortunately, I had a cliff behind me and couldn't back up enough to get the bloom on the right in the frame without moving and losing the background saguaro on the left.

At home, in Adobe Lightroom, I adjusted the image to render a little more tilt. I wish I had returned the next morning to see if even more blooms appeared. Nonetheless, always capture an image when you see one in case you do not get a second chance. In addition, snap multiple frames. The photograph above resulted from the same bloom head on the same morning with a different lens. While I prefer the composition on the left, I still enjoy the dynamic lines and framing in the above photograph.

LEFT: Saguaro bloom in foreground Canon 5DMIII, TS-E 17mm, ISO 100, f/22 @ 1/13 sec., reflector. Paul Gill

*Pink water knotweed floats on Luna Lake in the White Mountains. Canon 5DMII, TS-E 24mm, ISO 100, f/11 @ 0.3 sec., two-stop graduated neutral density filter positioned above flower tops, two-stop graduated neutral density filter positioned at horizon line. Paul Gill*

# Wildflowers of
# EASTERN ARIZONA

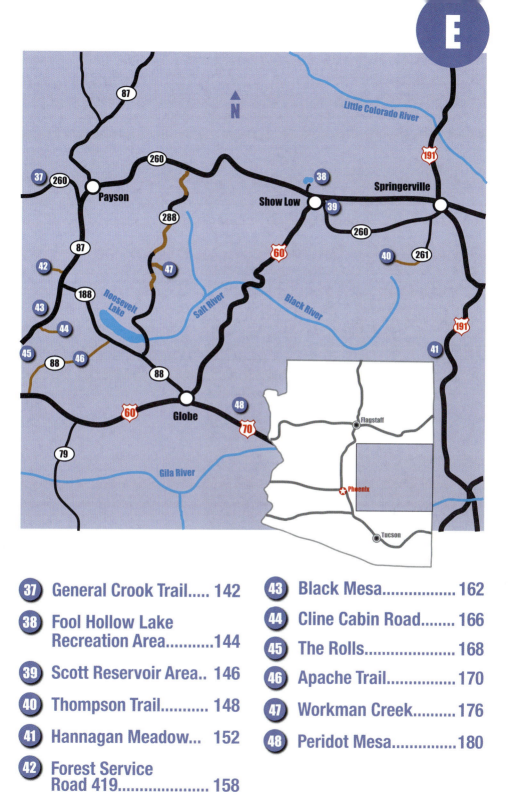

| | | | |
|---|---|---|---|
| ③⑦ | General Crook Trail..... 142 | ④③ | Black Mesa................. 162 |
| ③⑧ | Fool Hollow Lake Recreation Area...........144 | ④④ | Cline Cabin Road........ 166 |
| ③⑨ | Scott Reservoir Area.. 146 | ④⑤ | The Rolls..................... 168 |
| ④⓪ | Thompson Trail........... 148 | ④⑥ | Apache Trail................ 170 |
| ④① | Hannagan Meadow... 152 | ④⑦ | Workman Creek.......... 176 |
| ④② | Forest Service Road 419..................... 158 | ④⑧ | Peridot Mesa...............180 |

**EASTERN ARIZONA**

# General Crook Trail

◀ **Camp Verde**

Named after one of the United States Army's most respected generals during the nineteenth century Apache Wars, the General Crook Trail traces the southern meandering edge of the Colorado Plateau. Whether General George Crook stopped to smell the flowers during his expeditions along the Mogollon Rim is debatable. But wildflower enthusiasts will certainly want to retrace this historic icon's footsteps come spring and summer.

In the wavy Buckskin Hills, where the upper Sonoran Desert meets the pinyon-juniper woodland, the Engelmann's prickly pear cacti kick off the wildflower bloom throughout April and May. Across the same grassy meadows, a reliable crop of Parry's century plants blooms each year from July to August. Though an individual plant only produces a single stalk within its lifetime, sister plants from the same mother often shoot their floral display simultaneously towards the puffy cumulous clouds overhead.

*Parry's century plants along the General Crook Trail. Wista 4x5, 120mm, Kodak VS 100, f/32 @ 1 sec., warming polarizer, two-stop graduated neutral density filter. Paul Gill*

A vertical composition with a **wide-angle lens** and a broad depth of field such as f/16 or f/22 seems like an obvious choice to focus on a grouping of these remarkable blooms, but also study the far reaching vistas with a more tranquil horizontal treatment. Because of the lower light and the smaller aperture, stabilize your camera by placing it on a **tripod**. If you are lucky enough to see dramatic skies and rainbows, use a **polarizer** and **graduated neutral density filter** in front of your lens. As you rotate the polarizer, look through your viewfinder to ensure you are intensifying the rainbow, not eliminating it.

Unless you bring a ladder, the century plant blooms will be out of reach for any significant close-up photography, so bring a **telephoto lens** to zoom in from a distance. Reserve your **macro lens**, **diffuser**, and **reflector** for close up studies of desert paintbrush or annual goldeneye along the road.

On your summer visit, bring rain gear for you and your camera, but stay away from the open fields if lightning is present.

**BLOOM TIME**
April to May; July to August

**IDEAL TIME OF DAY**
Sunrise to sunset

**VEHICLE**
Any

**HIKE**
Easy

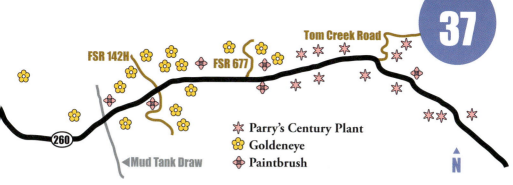

## DIRECTIONS:

From Camp Verde (along I-17 between Phoenix and Flagstaff), take AZ 260 (General Crook Trail) east for about 23.4 miles (37.7 km) to Forest Service Road 677. Turn left and park along this dirt road.

Goldfield wildflowers carpet the open plains in early October after bountiful monsoon rains. Canon 5DMIII, 16-35mm at 27mm, ISO 100, f/11 @ 1/20 sec. Paul Gill

## Parry's Century Plant

*Agave parryi*
**Blooms:** June to August in dry rocky soil in between 4,500 and 8,000 feet (1,372 and 2,438 m) elevation. (Perennial)
**Fun Fact:** The Parry's century plant shoots up a single flowering stalk after about 25 years. Once the plant blooms, the agave dies.

**EASTERN ARIZONA**

# Fool Hollow Lake Recreation Area

*Calliopsis wildflowers carpet the eastern shoreline after monsoon rains. Canon 5DMIII, TS-E 17mm, ISO 100, f/22 @ 0.5 sec., two-stop graduated neutral density filter. Paul Gill*

**BLOOM TIME**
June to September

**IDEAL TIME OF DAY**
Sunrise and sunset

**VEHICLE**
Any

**HIKE**
Easy

In the late 1800s, Mormon settlers, led by two brothers, Wesley Adair and Thomas Jefferson Adair Jr., established a small community called "Adairville" northwest of Show Low. Though productive in their farming efforts, limited water supply caused many of the original pioneers to quickly move to more sustainable lands in the surrounding area. However, one member of the Adair family stayed—an idea some locals purportedly called foolish. Residents then named Adairville "Fool Hollow." Then, in 1957, the Arizona Game and Fish Department constructed a dam at the confluence of Show Low Creek and Fool Hollow Wash — creating Fool Hollow Lake and erasing the town site.

For those searching for wildflowers, go ahead and be foolish! Head to this lake's scenic eastern shoreline to see a colorful assortment of calliopsis, woolly paintbrush, lupine, aspen fleabane, bluestem pricklepoppy, New Mexican vervain, milkweed, penstemon, and water knotweed.

Guided by a headlamp or flashlight, stroll along the dirt walking path at least 30 minutes before sunrise (or one hour before sunset).

Bring along a **wide-angle** to **normal lens**, **polarizer**, and **graduated neutral density filters**. A **tripod** and **cable release** will help keep your camera still during your low light exposures.

To emphasize the foreground, get close and low to the flowers. Maintain a sharp depth of field throughout your frame by setting a small aperture (e.g. f/16 or f/22) and focusing on the hyperfocal distance for your lens and subject distance (see page 23).

Since the monsoon season often brings passing afternoon showers, pack rain gear for you and your equipment. Also, pack bug spray and wear long pants to prevent getting bitten by mosquitoes.

## DIRECTIONS:

From Show Low, follow Highway 77 (also referred to as Deuce of Clubs and AZ 60) to the southwest. Turn right onto AZ 260. Drive 1.9 miles (3.1 km) and then turn right onto Old Linden Road. Continue an additional 0.6 miles (1 km). Turn left after spotting the large sign for the Fool Hollow Lake Recreation Area. Travel an additional 0.8 miles (1.3 km) until you reach the parking area on the left hand side of the road. The walking trail begins on the east side of the parking lot.

The park charges an entrance fee. For more information, visit **azstateparks.com/parks/FOHO/index.html.**

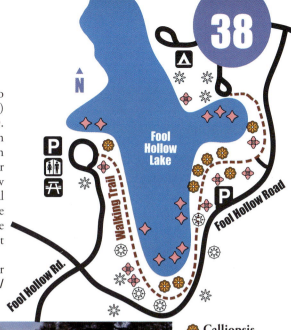

- Calliopsis
- Knotweed
- Fleabane
- Paintbrush
- Pricklepoppy

*Red woolly paintbrush sprouts along the eastern side of the trail after monsoon rains. Canon 5DMIII, TS-E 17mm, ISO 100, f/22 @ 0.5 sec., two-stop graduated neutral density filter. Paul Gill*

## Calliopsis

*Coreopsis tinctoria*
**Blooms:** July to October in moist, disturbed areas like roadsides and meadows around elevations of 6,000 to 7,000 feet (1,829 to 2,134 m). (Annual)
**Fun Fact:** In 1991, Florida designated flowers from the genus Coreopsis as the state's official wildflower.

**EASTERN ARIZONA**

# Scott Reservoir Area

*Annual goldeneye at sunset with monsoon rains and lightning on the horizon. Canon 5DMIII, 16-35mm at 27mm, ISO 100, f/22 @ 15 sec., two-stop graduated neutral density filter. Paul Gill*

**BLOOM TIME**
**August to September**

**IDEAL TIME OF DAY**
**Sunset**

**VEHICLE**
**Any**

**HIKE**
**Easy**

In the early 1900s, Anna Christina Hansen and her husband, Robert Scott, built a small home with two chimneys in the pinyon pine and juniper forest north of the small modern community of Lakeside. Then, in 1928, when officials dammed nearby Porter Creek, they named the resulting lake "Scott Reservoir" to honor his presence in the area. Today, the expansive meadows near the lake boast carpets of wildflowers once monsoon season commences.

From the west of Scott Reservoir to the north of Porter Mountain Road, blooms from goldenrod, common mullein, bull thistle, aspen fleabane, and woolly paintbrush create a flashy spectacle starting in August. In September, yellow annual goldeneye transforms these same fields into an endless sea of gold.

Arrive at least one to two hours prior to sunset to allow ample time to scout the area. When the sun sits high in the sky, explore individual blooms or small clusters of intermingling flowers with a **macro** or **telephoto lens**. Use a **diffuser** and/or **reflector** as needed to reduce the contrasts between highlights and shadows in your scene.

A **wide-angle lens** can help convey a broad perspective of this vast landscape alive with color. Should the sky overhead display its own multi-hued glow at sunset, place a **graduated neutral density filter** over your lens to balance your exposure. Due to the low light—and consequently slower shutter speeds—use a **tripod** and **cable release** to keep your camera still.

## DIRECTIONS:

From Show Low, follow AZ 260 south for 8.2 miles (13.2 km). Turn left onto Porter Mountain Road. Continue 1.6 miles (2.6 km) and then turn left onto Juniper Drive which is a well-maintained dirt road. Continue driving 0.7 miles (1.1 km), following the road through a residential area and as it curves to the northwest. Park in the dirt parking lot.

To ward off mosquitoes prevalent here (mainly in August), wear long pants and apply bug spray before heading out. Also, bring rain gear for both you and your camera gear in case of a passing monsoon shower. Should you see lighting in the area, retreat to your vehicle immediately.

*Annual goldeneye blooms beneath a moody sky at sunset. Canon 5DMIII, 16-35mm at 16mm, ISO 100, f/11 @ 1/4 sec., two-stop graduated neutral density filter. Paul Gill*

## Annual Goldeneye

*Heliomeris longifolia var. annua*
**Blooms:** Along roadsides, fields, and hills in between 2,500 and 7,000 feet (762 and 2,134 m) from May to October. (Annual)
**Fun Fact:** This vibrant yellow flower is a member of the sunflower family and is native to Nevada, Utah, Texas, New Mexico, and Arizona.

## EASTERN ARIZONA

# Thompson Trail

*The West Fork of the Black River flows through fields of western sneezeweed. Canon 5DMII, 16-35mm at 20mm, ISO 100, f/11 @ 1/10 sec. Paul Gill*

**BLOOM TIME**
July to August

**IDEAL TIME OF DAY**
Early morning

**VEHICLE**
Any

**HIKE**
Moderate

If Hannagan Meadow (see page 152) wins the award for being the most idyllic place in Arizona, then it beats the Thompson Trail by only the narrowest of margins. This flat, historic railroad grade meandering through a forested canyon in the White Mountains enraptures wildflower enthusiasts looking to explore lush green meadows filled with summer wildflowers along the zigzagging West Fork of the Black River.

Though the 2011 Wallow Fire created a mix of burned hillsides and unscathed forests, much of the verdant river bed remained intact. Come July and August, the grassy fields along this serene stream welcome large swaths of yellow western sneezeweed, aspen fleabane, red firecracker penstemon, and Mogollon Indian paintbrush. Those areas affected by the wildfire should feature additional and plentiful disturbance wildflowers for another two to three years.

A **wide-angle lens**, coupled with a small aperture of f/16 or f/22, will help record a composition inclusive of both the field of summer blooms and the picturesque bends in the river. To create the feeling of depth in your photograph, position your camera such that the snaking West Fork leads a viewer's eye into the frame from either the right or left bottom corner.

Though the trail does not cross the creek, you might consider wearing water shoes to wade across it and subsequently capture the best angle for the pink New Mexican checkermallow which blooms prolifically along the banks. Before venturing in the water, add a wide-angle or **normal lens (from 16-50mm)** onto your camera and place the set-up on a **tripod**.

In addition, put a **polarizer** on your lens which will not only help eliminate or enhance the reflection in the water (depending on the effect you desire), but will also slow your shutter speed down to create soft, cotton-like water in your images. Keep a careful watch on your exposure time if morning winds are sweeping through the canyon and increase your ISO speed if you notice blurry flowers when reviewing on your camera's playback screen.

If getting your feet wet doesn't appeal to you, an abundance of photogenic wildflowers positioned perfectly for a **macro lens** await in the many dry meadows along this leisurely stroll. In case clouds aren't overhead, pack a **diffuser** to create even shade across your close-up scene.

Afternoon storms tend to roll through this area consistently during the monsoon season, so keep your eyes on the sky for lightning and rain. To protect yourself and your camera from a dousing, either conclude your outing before the skies threaten or pack rain protection for you and your gear to extend your shoot.

*New Mexican checkermallow blooms along the Black River. Canon 5DMII, TS-E 24mm, ISO 100, f/22 @ 1/8 sec., polarizer. Paul Gill*

# New Mexican Checkermallow

*Sidalcea neomexicana*
**Blooms:** June to September in between 5,000 and 9,500 feet (1,524 and 2,896 m) elevation along streams and in moist meadows. (Perennial)
**Fun Fact:** Because the New Mexican checkermallow also grows in salt flats, its nickname is "alkali pink."

**EASTERN ARIZONA**

# Thompson Trail

Pink fireweed blooms next to a fallen burnt aspen along the Thompson Trail. Fireweed will normally grow and bloom for years after a fire. Canon 5DMIII, 24-105mm at 105mm, ISO 100, f/9 @ 1/60 sec. Paul Gill

PHOTO TIP 11

## The Dutch Tilt

Wildflowers often reach high into the sky. While repeating vertical lines may create an interesting pattern, sometimes photographing a single or a group of blooms standing tall can cause a scene to be static and maybe a little boring. To make the composition more dynamic, use the Dutch tilt!

Best applied in wildflower photography when the horizon is not visible, the photographer intentionally slants the camera a few degrees to the right or left while composing. This popular cinematography technique turns static vertical or horizontal lines into more dynamic diagonal lines, making for a more pleasing composition.

When you experiment with this trick, keep the intersection points of the Rule of Thirds (see page 52) in mind and place your subject such that you create a line between two kitty-corner points. Also, try capturing a frame with your camera tilted in each direction, as a subject might look better when you slant your camera towards one side or the other depending on the arrangement of the flowers in your frame.

## DIRECTIONS:

From downtown Show Low, head east on AZ 260 and drive 35.7 miles (57.5 km). Turn right onto AZ 273 towards the Sunrise Ski Resort and travel an additional 14.4 miles (23.2 km) on this paved road. Turn right onto the signed Forest Road 116 and drive 4 miles (6.4 km) on this maintained dirt road to the Thompson Trailhead parking lot. After parking, access the trailhead on the south side of the road. The best flowers occur in the meadow at the trailhead and within the first 2 miles (3.2 km) along the trail.

For the most updated information, visit the Apache-Sitgreaves National Forest website at: **www.fs.usda.gov/asnf**.

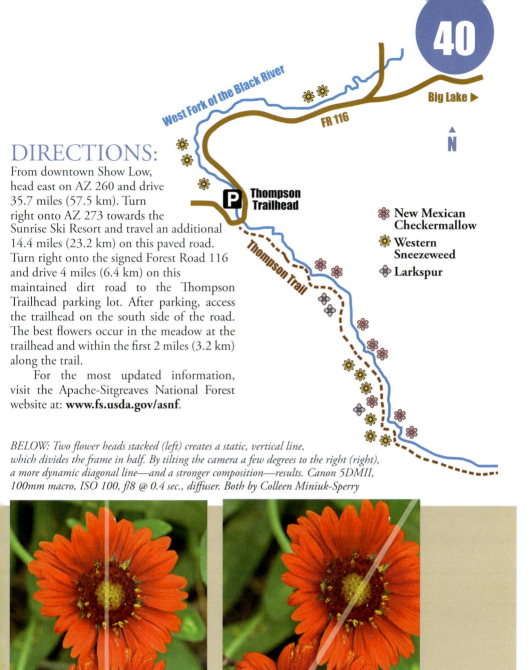

BELOW: *Two flower heads stacked (left) creates a static, vertical line, which divides the frame in half. By tilting the camera a few degrees to the right (right), a more dynamic diagonal line—and a stronger composition—results. Canon 5DMII, 100mm macro, ISO 100, f/8 @ 0.4 sec., diffuser. Both by Colleen Miniuk-Sperry*

**EASTERN ARIZONA**

# Hannagan Meadow

ABOVE: *Butterfly on western sneezeweed. Canon 5DMII, 24-105mm at 105mm, ISO 400, f/4 @ 1/500 sec.* RIGHT: *Fields of western sneezeweed and Douglas fir. Canon 5DMII, TS-E 24mm, ISO 100, f/11 @ 1/80 sec. Both by Paul Gill*

**BLOOM TIME**
May to August

**IDEAL TIME OF DAY**
Late afternoon to sunset

**VEHICLE**
Any

**HIKE**
Easy

Though blessed with an abundance of breathtaking places, few spots in the Grand Canyon State are as idyllic as Hannagan Meadow. As tall grasses, mature ponderosa pine trees, and quaking aspens sway together in the gentle summer breezes of the White Mountains, a profusion of picturesque summer wildflowers will have you skipping through the pristine meadow during your picture-perfect photography outing.

At over 9,000 feet (2,743 m) elevation, the floral festivities begin in May with one of the highest wildflower displays in the state as blue and white Rocky Mountain iris dot the grassland. Wild rose and King's lupine join in during June, followed by yellow western sneezeweed with a mixture of narrowleaf penstemon, Mogollon Indian paintbrush, and the rare purple Gunnison mariposa lilies once the monsoon rains start in July.

Effortless access means your vehicle will not be very far away, so pack all your camera gear—including **wide-angle**, **telephoto**, and **macro lenses**, **tripod**, and **cable release**—to record the wildflower celebration.

A photogenic wooden fence surrounds the meadow, offering an effective leading line when placed in the bottom of either the right or left hand corner of your photograph. As you compose, ensure the fence line leads your eye somewhere interesting, like a patch of flowers or the pine forest in the distance, and not out of the frame. The fence will appear as if it is extending into infinity when using a wide-angle lens set to capture a broad depth of field at f/16 or f/22.

Wait patiently for wispy clouds to cover the sun and reduce the harsh mid-day contrast before snapping the shutter. A **polarizer** can also help reduce the glare on the blooms and increase saturation in the field, flowers, and sky.

The fence posts can also provide a clean, natural-looking dark

**EASTERN ARIZONA**

# Hannagan Meadow

*Western sneezeweed surrounds a wooden fence at Hannagan Meadow. Canon 5DMII, TS-E 24mm, ISO 100, f/22 @ 0.3 sec. Paul Gill*

background when photographing a cluster of blooms low to the ground with a macro lens and a short depth of field. Use a **reflector** to highlight an individual bloom or a **diffuser** to soften the light on the entire scene during a cloudless day.

Once you've explored Hannagan Meadow, take a quick spin down either Forest Service Road 576 or 564 where prolific wildflower blooms fill long meadows ringed by stands of aspens and pines. Take special note of the spots where the May 2011 Wallow Fire burned the forest along the way. These areas should eventually display copious amounts of disturbance wildflowers as the affected lands recover.

# 41

## DIRECTIONS:

Hannagan Meadow is located along US 191 about 47 miles (75.6 km) south of Springerville and 71 miles (114.3 km) north of Clifton-Morenci. The meadows are located on the east side of the road directly across from the Hannagan Meadow Lodge. Pull off the road to park. Or drive 0.3 miles (0.5

❋ Western Sneezeweed
✤ Paintbrush
◇ Rocky Mountain Iris

km) south of the lodge, turning left onto Forest Service Road 29A for the Steeple Mesa/Foote Creek Trailhead. Park along the dirt road and walk north into the meadow.

To reach the additional fields, turn west on Forest Service Road 576 located 0.2 miles (0.3 km) north of the lodge and drive west on this well-maintained dirt road for about 2 miles (3.2 km) to reach the flowers.

The turn off for Forest Service Road 564 is located about 0.9 miles (1.5 km) further north of the turn off for 576. Turn west onto this bumpy dirt road and travel 1.1 miles (1.8 km) until just beyond the hairpin curve. Find a wide spot in the road to safely park.

*Indian paintbrush and western sneezeweed grow among the aspen trees and ferns. Canon 5DMII, TS-E 24mm, ISO 100, f/11 @ 1/2 sec. Paul Gill*

## Western Sneezeweed

*Dugaldia hoopesii*
**Blooms:** June to September in mountain meadows and pine forests between 7,000 and 11,000 feet (2,134 and 3,353 m) elevation. (Perennial)
**Fun Fact:** Nicknamed "owl-claws," this showy flower is poisonous to cattle, deer, and other ruminants.

# Polarizer Magic

*Sponsored by Singh-Ray,* **www.singh-ray.com**

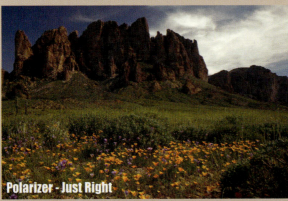

Have you ever looked at a scene while wearing sunglasses and decided to take the glasses off to get a better look—only to find the scene appeared better with the sunglasses? If so, you've experienced the effects of a polarizer through polarized sunglasses!

A polarizing filter for your camera acts like those sunglasses. A polarizer attaches to the front of your lens and filters out reflected light our unaided eye sees as glare from non-metallic, polarizing surfaces. To accomplish this, most modern cameras (post-1970s) require a circular polarizer, rather than a linear one.

A polarizer can benefit your work in multiple ways. First, it helps reduce atmospheric haze and reflected glare that might appear in your natural scene. Second, this filter can intensify the color saturation—most notably a blue sky. Third and lastly, a polarizer can enhance or eliminate unwanted reflections in water or off of wildflowers.

After placing it on your lens, rotate the polarizer, turning it slowly to see a visible effect on the amount of haze, color saturation, and reflections. Where you leave the polarizer during your rotation is a personal preference, but watch for over-polarization where the sky becomes unrealistically dark blue. At high elevations, it is possible to turn the sky almost black!

At Lost Dutchman State Park, the sky and cliffs appear richer in color after the polarizer is applied. Whether the polarization is "just right" or "too strong" is a matter of personal taste. Canon 5D, 24-105mm at 32mm, ISO 200, f/16 @ 1/25 sec., polarizer in bottom two photos. All by Colleen Miniuk-Sperry

**No Polarizer**     **Polarizer**

*Using a polarizer while shooting a macro perspective of a flower can reduce the glare occurring on the petals. However, because the polarizer reduces the amount of light passing through your lens, make sure you have a fast enough shutter speed to freeze a moving bloom. If you need a faster shutter speed, increase your ISO speed. Canon 5D, 100mm macro, ISO 200, f/16 @ 1/25 sec., polarizer (right). Both by Paul Gill*

If you don't see the effect of the polarizer in your viewfinder before your shoot, ensure you are rotating the polarizer around the lens slowly. Changes in polarization will be most obvious in the sky or in a reflection.

A polarizer achieves maximum intensity when positioning your camera at a 90-degree angle from the sun. To determine the area of the sky that will be most affected, use a technique called "shoot the sun." Extend your thumb and pointer finger as if you were shooting a gun (so that your thumb and pointer finger form a 90-degree angle). Then, point your "gun" directly at the sun and rotate your arm so that your thumb rotates along an imaginary circle around the axis of your finger. The directions where your thumb points are the directions where your polarizer will have maximum effect on your photograph. When photographing in a different direction than where your thumb points, the polarizer will have little to no effect in your photograph.

As you turn the polarizer, watch for uneven polarization, which occurs when shooting at angles in between 45 and 90 degrees, particularly with wide-angle lenses. One part of the sky will be darker blue than the other parts which looks unnatural in nature photographs. To avoid uneven polarization, reduce the intensity of the polarizer by simply turning the filter slightly until the shades of the sky match better.

Since a polarizer will reduce the amount of light your camera sees by about one to two stops of light, it can also double as a neutral density filter to slow shutter speeds.

**EASTERN ARIZONA**

# Forest Service Road 419

*Sego lilies bloom in a strawberry hedgehog cactus. Canon 5DMII, TS-E 24mm, ISO 100, f/22 @ 1/30 sec., diffuser, reflector. Paul Gill*

**BLOOM TIME**
**April to May**

**IDEAL TIME OF DAY**
**Sunrise**

**VEHICLE**
**2WD high-clearance**

**HIKE**
**Easy**

As the sun rises over the Sierra Ancha mountain range on the eastern horizon, the warm rays of golden light sweep across the expansive desert floor at the foot of the glowing rugged Mazatzal Mountains. Along the quiet, unnamed plateau hosting the road to the Barnhardt Trailhead, gorgeous 360-degree vistas and a surprising unmatched high desert wildflower bloom await shutterbugs each spring.

When conditions are optimal, carpets of yellow goldfields and purple owl clover cover the plateau to start the blooming season in April. Shortly thereafter, brilliant pink blooms open at the ends of spiny strawberry hedgehog cacti as Parry's century plants shoot their once-in-their-lifetime flower stalks to the sky at the end of May.

As if that wasn't worth the visit alone, the warmer temperatures usher in perhaps the most prolific sego lily blooming displays in Arizona as well as an equally impressive Engelmann's prickly pear cactus performance. Desert globemallow and paper flower intermix with leafy and blooming ocotillo.

To allow time to scout along the southern cliffs for the perfect flowers to serve as foreground, arrive about 30 minutes before sunrise with a **wide-angle lens**, **polarizer**, **graduated neutral density filter**, **tripod**, and **cable release**. Bring a flashlight or headlamp to help you find the best blooms.

As you compose your scene, decide how much of the valley below—the "middle ground"—to include in your photograph. To make this area more dominant in your frame, raise your camera and tripod. To minimize it, drop your camera closer to the ground. Whichever you decide, remember to keep the horizon line out of the center of your image to abide by the Rule of Thirds.

As the sun rises, replace your wide-angle lens with a **macro lens** to focus on smaller compositions of intermixing or individual flowers. Use a **diffuser** or a **reflector** to help balance extreme contrasts between highlights and shadows in your scene.

**42**

- ✣ Sego Lily
- ✶ Strawberry Hedgehog Cactus
- ✺ Goldfield

Barnhardt Trailhead

FSR 419

Rye

Payson

Phoenix

## DIRECTIONS:

From Phoenix, take the AZ 202 Loop eastward towards Mesa. Take Exit 13 for AZ 87 (Country Club Drive). After exiting the highway, turn left onto AZ 87 and follow it north for about 61 miles (98.2 km) until you see the brown sign indicating the turnoff on the left for Forest Service Road 419 and the Barnhardt Trail. Turn left onto Forest Service Road 419.

Wildflowers will appear on both sides of this sometimes rocky dirt road for 5 miles (8.1 km) until it ends at the gravel parking area for the Barnhardt Trailhead. No other formal parking areas exist, so turn off onto a spur road or into a previously used camp site to safely park while exploring this area.

*Beautiful cloud formation over goldfield flowers along FR 419. Canon 5DMII, 16-35mm at 16mm, ISO 100, f/8 @ 1/1600 sec. Paul Gill*

## Sego Lily

*Calochortus nuttallii*
**Blooms:** May to July on dry mesas and open pine forests in between 5,000 and 8,000 feet (1,524 and 2,438 m) elevation. (Perennial)
**Fun Fact:** The state of Utah adopted the sego lily as their state flower in 1911.

# Making the Photo 6

# Telling a Story

By Colleen Miniuk-Sperry

What do you aim to record with your camera: a snapshot or a story?

Dictionary.com defines a snapshot as, "An informal photograph; a quick shot taken without deliberate aim." In other words, a snapshot is an image you do not think much about capturing. And as a result, most viewers will not think much about it either when they see it!

On the other hand, dictionary.com defines a story as "A narrative designed to interest, amuse, or instruct the hearer or reader." An engaging story-telling image possesses the potential to excite, educate, and/or cause wonder with your viewing audience.

I certainly aim to tell stories with my camera (and I will assume you do as well!), as I believe photographs can help me express important moments and experiences with my viewers. However, I wish to say more than, "I saw these pretty flowers while on a hike." I seek to create a meaningful visual account of things like why the flowers exist, what they might be doing in this location, and their relationship with their surrounding environment.

For example, when I spotted a cluster of sego lilies near the Barnhardt Trail, I noticed several blooms in varying stages of their lifecycle. Some appeared fully opened; others promised their bounty in the days to come. I appreciated this chance to observe a field of flowers at different moments in their lives. I decided to transform this story into a photographic idea.

With a visual message in mind, I began setting up my camera gear. I used my 100mm macro lens on a tripod positioned so low to the ground that I needed to lie on the gravel. Now in a somewhat contorted prone position, I perfected my composition and focus, not by looking through the viewfinder, but rather through using my Live View feature (which displays literally the live view of your scene on a camera's LCD screen).

Originally, the stems rose vertically in a straight line from the ground which felt too static as I arranged the elements in my frame. I turned the camera to the left in a slight Dutch tilt so that the stems created a more dynamic, diagonal line originating from the bottom left corner.

I made some minor tripod movements to minimize the overlaps between the different stems at the bottom of the frame. Then I chose an f/6.3 aperture to blur the background. This short depth of field conveyed a sense of separation between the bud and the flowers which created the illusion of depth in the final image.

Fortunately, there was already back-side lighting from camera left, so I did not need to reposition to render a shapeful scene. However, after clicking a few frames, I felt the direct light from the mid-day sun created too harsh a contrast for my scene. With this in mind, I grabbed my diffuser and experimented with its placement until it covered my scene adequately to soften the light but did not appear in my final photograph.

After 15 attempts, I had recorded the exact story I wished to share: the story of fully open blooms surrounding a single bud as if to encourage the young one to show the world what it had to offer.

*LEFT: Sego lilies near the Barnhardt Trail. Canon 5DMII, 100mm macro, ISO 200, f/6.3 @ 1/80 sec., diffuser. Colleen Miniuk-Sperry*

**EASTERN ARIZONA**

# Black Mesa

*Saguaro cactus, ocotillo, and brittlebush hug the canyon's edge. Canon 5DMII, 24-105mm at 105mm, ISO 100, f/11 @ 0.8 sec. Paul Gill*

**BLOOM TIME**
**March to May**

**IDEAL TIME OF DAY**
**Sunrise**

**VEHICLE**
**Any (with hike);**
**4WD HC (no hike)**

**HIKE**
**Strenuous**

Black Mesa is everything you would expect: a black mesa. But what the name doesn't suggest, though, is that this location produces one of the most diverse exhibitions of wildflowers blooming in Arizona's high desert come springtime.

Located in the rugged Mazatzal Mountains, this volcanic plateau transforms from a dark desert landscape to a polychromatic hillside, flaunting prolific displays of dainty pinkish-white flat-top buckwheat, vivacious orange mariposa lilies, and flashy red—not white—white ratany. Not to be outdone, the banana yucca, strawberry hedgehog cactus, and the New Mexico thistle bloom simultaneously, followed shortly thereafter by ocotillo and Engelmann's prickly pear cactus in April. Saguaro cacti finish the booming bloom through May.

Even with such broad diversity and extensive photographic opportunities, lugging a lot of heavy gear uphill may not appeal to you, so pack only a **wide-angle lens**, **polarizer**, **graduated neutral density filter**, **tripod**, and **cable release** for an outing at sunrise.

Plan to arrive and set up on top of the mesa at least 30 minutes before the sun breaks the mountainous horizon to the east in order to capture optimal lighting conditions. Look to the north to include Black Mountain as your backdrop to a field of flowers in your foreground.

Though ambitious photographers may make the arduous two miles (3.2 km) trek, you don't necessarily need to make the full hike to the saddle to make a great image. Whether you go part or all of the way up, use a flashlight or headlamp to help illuminate your path in the dark.

However, if you plan to visit any time after sunrise, leave the wide-angle lens, polarizer, and graduated neutral density filter behind and instead bring a **macro** or **telephoto lens** with a **reflector** and **diffuser** to concentrate on macro photography during the harsher mid-day light.

If overcast or partly cloudy conditions exist, grab all your camera equipment, extra water, and hiking poles to photograph the wildflowers in ideal conditions - and then take a few days off afterwards to recover! Or, follow the flat lower wash up stream for one mile (1.6 km) to explore a forest of banana yucca worthy of a short visit.

Regardless of the path you choose, if rain is in the forecast, stay clear of the wash, as flash floods can occur here.

*Oversized brittlebush cover the hillsides of Black Mesa. Canon 5DMII, 16-35mm at 17mm, ISO 100, f/8 @ 0.2 sec. Paul Gill*

## DIRECTIONS:

From Phoenix, drive east on the AZ 202 Loop towards Mesa. Take Exit 13 for AZ 87 (Country Club Drive). After exiting the highway, turn left onto AZ 87 and follow it north for 35.6 miles (57.3 km). Turn left onto an unmarked road. When you see a large grouping of saguaros just off the north side of this dirt road, park your passenger car here. Only experienced off-road drivers with four-wheel drive, high-clearance, and a short wheel base should proceed.

Hikers and courageous four-wheel drivers should head westward to the Sycamore Creek wash. Travel along the wash about 0.25 miles (0.4 km) until a jeep trail comes into view on the right. Zig-zag your way up to the top of the plateau for about 1 mile (1.6 km). When you reach the top, veer off the trail to the right to hike cross-country another 1 mile (1.6 km) to the saddle.

## Flat-Top Buckwheat

*Eriogonum fasciculatum var. polifolium*
**Blooms:** February to June on rocky terrain between 1,000 and 4,500 feet (305 and 1,372 m) elevation. (Perennial)
**Fun Fact:** Since this flower grows in both the Sonoran and Mohave deserts, its nickname is the "Eastern Mohave buckwheat."

## Making the Photo 7

# What Else is It?

By Colleen Miniuk-Sperry

Language is the powerful way we bring together our personal observations and perceptions into a common understanding with other human beings. Shortly after birth, babies often point to things enthusiastically (and sometimes not so enthusiastically) and proudly exclaim, "Ball!" or "Tree."

As the years pass, we recite these labels over and over. The labels become so engrained we stop thinking even for a split second what it means to be a "ball" or "tree." For those who share the same language, it becomes difficult to convince another person (or even ourselves) that a "ball" is a "tree" and vice versa.

In documentary photography, photographers might aim to record a particular ball in the context of a beach or baseball game. Nature photographers might seek to bring home a beautiful image of a tree that caught their attention within the confines of a forest. We aim to convey visually what we have experienced along our journey in the world, responding to what the world shows us.

To take this approach into a more creative realm, however, we must consider the wise words of Minor White, "One should not only photograph things for what they are, but for what else they are." Or, in our language of labels, photographers should tap into analogy to help go beyond the common labels we hear every day.

An analogy is a comparison between two things. A metaphor (which is a type of analogy) concludes that one thing "is" another. Similarly, a simile implies that one thing "is like" (or "is as") another. By any name, incorporating analogy as we approach an object or scene can help us go beyond common naming conventions and lead to more creative interpretations—especially since we are all likely to come up with a different answer based on our own perceptions!

To put this idea into context with wildflowers, I happened upon an extensive bloom of fairy duster near the Matzatal Mountains one April. Because of their dainty, cotton-ball-like shape, I have previously found them difficult to photograph. I would characterize most of my previous photographs of this beautiful bloom as a documentary portrait that seemed to merely say, "This is what a fairy duster flower looks like. The end."

This time, however, I felt differently about my scene. As I surveyed the hillside of red and pink, I noticed myself feeling as if I were standing in a magical ground-level display of exploding fireworks. I immediately tapped into this notion. I wanted to fill my image with blooms that conveyed, "A cluster of fairy duster blooms look like exploding fireworks!" (a simile).

I knelt beside a single plant, observing the ways the different blooms intermixed with each other. I spotted one cluster of healthy blooms surrounding a pinwheel-like bloom which had seen its peak glory likely a few days before my arrival. This shape served to break up the repeating pattern and add an element of juxtaposition.

I experimented with different angles until I felt comfortable with an

*Fairy duster blooms resembling exploding fireworks. Canon 5DMII, 100mm macro, ISO 200, f/8 @ 1/20 sec. Colleen Miniuk-Sperry*

energetic arrangement. Then, I added a diffuser overhead, not only to soften the harsh mid-day light, but also to help emphasize the rich and more fiery red and pink hues. To keep an emphasis on the exploding blooms, I used an f/8 aperture to blur the background, but retain enough depth of field so the blooms appear sharp.

While fairy duster blooms appeared to me like exploding fireworks in this particular scenario, the next time I cross this same flower, I may have a different analogy to convey based on what I observe at the time. This is one of the ways we can stand in front of a similar scene and bring home a variety of different visual messages. What do fairy duster blooms look like to you?

**EASTERN ARIZONA**

# Cline Cabin Road

*A carpet of purple nightshade grows near a charred ponderosa pine tree. Canon 5D, 24-105mm at 75mm, ISO 100, f/22 @ 1/30 sec.*
*Paul Gill*

**BLOOM TIME**
March to June

**IDEAL TIME OF DAY**
Early afternoon to sunset

**VEHICLE**
2WD high-clearance

**HIKE**
Easy

When admiring the majestic Four Peaks from the metropolitan Phoenix area, it's difficult to imagine that anything other than desert graces its flanks. However, the surrounding area supports a wide range of life zones where visitors can see the transition in plant life from the Sonoran Desert to a ponderosa pine tree forest in the space of 20 miles (32.2 km). Because of this extreme environmental diversity, the areas along the Cline Cabin Road enjoy a prolonged blooming season with extensive flower variations.

In March, Mexican gold poppies, blue dicks, Coulter's lupine, and owl clover cover the lowlands after bountiful winter rains. In April, brittlebush, staghorn cholla, and Engelmann's prickly pear cactus flourish followed by the brilliant blooms of the saguaro cactus and littleleaf paloverde in May. Among rolling hills and jumbo rocks through classic Sonoran Desert scenery, brittlebush intermix with ocotillo, paper flower, and desert globemallow.

From March and May, this is the spot to be about 30 minutes before sunset with a **wide-angle lens**, **polarizer**, **graduated neutral density filter**, **tripod**, and **cable release** in hand to capture spectacular landscape photographs at sunset looking towards the Four Peaks or south towards the Superstition Mountains. By June, the summer heat has cooked the wildflowers at the lower elevations, but other great blooms continue to thrive as the road climbs higher.

After about eight miles (12.9 km), cacti disappear while purple nightshade, Goodding's verbena, fairy duster, and sacred datura burst onto the scene as the desert transitions to shrubby pinyon-juniper woodland. A **normal focal length** (e.g. 50mm), **telephoto**, or **macro lens** works best in this brushy and busy setting. Simplify your compositions by clearly identifying a primary subject, composing tightly, and scanning your frame's edges for unwanted branches or leaves.

A mile (1.6 km) later, skeletons of scorched trees from a wildfire serve as graphic backdrops if you can find hidden wildflowers among the catclaw acacia and mesquite trees hugging the ground.

Before reaching the saddle, flowers more characteristic to Arizona's higher elevations like Colorado four o'clocks, Hill's lupine, and New Mexico locust compete for your attention as you are treated to sprawling views of the desert hills below. Though a macro or telephoto lens will help isolate clusters of wildflowers near the road, a wide-angle lens will render the expansive roadside views best.

★ **Purple Nightshade**
✿ **Saguaro Cactus**
❋ **Globemallow**

Desert globemallow and purple nightshade. Canon 5DMII, 24-105mm at 105mm, ISO 400, f/4 @ 1/200 sec. Paul Gill

## DIRECTIONS:

From Phoenix, drive east on the AZ 202 Loop towards Mesa. Take Exit 13 for AZ 87 (Country Club Drive). Turn left onto AZ 87 and follow it north for 26.7 miles (43 km). Turn right onto Forest Service Road 143 (also known as Four Peaks Road and Cline Cabin Road). Travel this well-maintained dirt road for 2 miles (3.2 km), and then veer left at the split to stay on Cline Cabin Road. Continue an additional 8.8 miles (14.2 km) and then veer right when the road splits again. As the road twists another 6.9 miles (11.1 km) up to the saddle, blooms typically occur all along this bumpy, rocky section. No formal parking areas exit along this popular route, so find a wide spot off the road to safely park before photographing.

## Purple Nightshade

*Solanum xanti*
**Blooms:** April to November in chaparral and on rocky slopes in between 3,500 and 5,500 feet (1,067 and 1,676 m) elevation. (Perennial)
**Fun Fact:** Many people originally assumed tomatoes were deadly to eat since edible tomatoes and this lethal flower are in the same Solanum genus.

## EASTERN ARIZONA

# The Rolls

*Mexican gold poppies, bladderpod mustard, broad-leaved gilia and Coulter's lupine bloom at sunset in the low areas of the Rolls. Canon 5DMIII, TS-E 17mm, ISO 100, f/22 at 0.6 sec., three-stop graduated neutral density filter. Paul Gill*

**BLOOM TIME**
March to April

**IDEAL TIME OF DAY**
Early morning to sunset

**VEHICLE**
2WD high-clearance

**HIKE**
Easy

At a distance, the Sonoran Desert landscape along AZ 87 at the foot of the majestic Four Peaks and rugged Superstition Mountains looks flat. However, ambitious photographers willing to look more closely will see there is much more than meets the eye. As the name suggests, the Rolls area conceals undulating mounds which harbor profuse amounts of Mexican gold poppies, lupine, owl clover, broad-leaved gilia, bladderpod mustard, and more, intermingling along its many valleys after abundant winter rains.

Because of the long trek up and down rocky hills, keep your pack light. That said, Murphy's Law suggests the lens you leave behind will inevitably be the exact one you need! At a minimum, pack a **wide-angle lens**, **polarizer**, **tripod**, and **cable release**. If possible, time your visit to coincide with a cloudy day to help decrease the amount of harsh contrast in your landscape compositions. Or consider using the High Dynamic Range (HDR) technique to make multiple frames at varying exposure levels and blending them later during post-processing. If you plan to photograph through sunset, also bring **graduated neutral density filters** and a headlamp or flashlight. Do not forget **extra charged batteries** and **memory cards**!

Despite the variety of flowers that bloom here, only haul in a **telephoto** and/or **macro lens** if you are willing to carry the weight. If a blue sky prevails overhead, bring a **diffuser** and **reflector** to manage contrast in your smaller scenes.

## 45

## DIRECTIONS:

From Mesa, travel northbound on AZ 87 for about 27 miles (43.5 km). Take Exit 199 for the Bush Highway. Turn right and proceed another 2.5 miles (4 km). Turn left into the Pobrecito Staging Area, but stay straight towards the Rolls OHV Parking Area (if you reach the turnoff for the Butcher Jones Recreation Area, you have traveled too far south). Follow the pavement until it turns to dirt. Park in the dirt parking area.

Wildflowers are most abundant on the east side of the dirt lot and to the north towards AZ 87 (outside of the fenced OHV area). ATV traffic can be heavy, especially on weekends, so take great care walking along their paths.

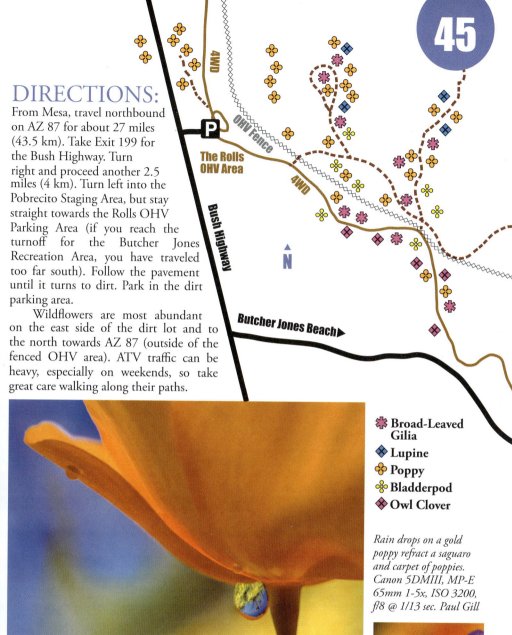

- Broad-Leaved Gilia
- Lupine
- Poppy
- Bladderpod
- Owl Clover

*Rain drops on a gold poppy refract a saguaro and carpet of poppies. Canon 5DMIII, MP-E 65mm 1-5x, ISO 3200, f/8 @ 1/13 sec. Paul Gill*

## Broad-Leaved Gilia

*Gilia latifolia*
**Blooms:** From February to April in desert washes and rocky hills below 2,000 feet (610 m). (Annual)
**Fun Fact:** The leaves surrounding the dainty pinkish-purple flower give off a skunk-like odor.

## EASTERN ARIZONA

# Apache Trail

*Mexican gold poppies on the foothills of Bronco Butte. Pentax 67II, 55-100mm, Kodak VS 100, f/32 @ 1/30 sec., polarizer. Paul Gill*

**BLOOM TIME**
**March to June**

**IDEAL TIME OF DAY**
**Late morning to sunset**

**VEHICLE**
**Any**

**HIKE**
**Easy**

Until 1922, the Apache Trail served as the only direct route for intrepid motorists traveling from Globe to Phoenix. It followed a historic wagon road built in 1903 to support the construction of Roosevelt Dam. Today, the only federally-designated Scenic Historic Byway in Arizona is one of the state's most breathtaking drives as it weaves its way through the rugged Superstition Mountains and past remarkable manmade desert lakes en route to Roosevelt Lake.

Starting in mid-March, the pristine Sonoran Desert landscape along this picturesque route comes alive with the uplifting colors of spring. The best wildflowers can be found along the paved section of road from Lost Dutchman State Park to Canyon Lake, which lies about eight miles (12.9 km) to the north. On the west side of the road, about three miles (4.8 km) away from the Lost Dutchman State Park, the Willow Springs Canyon area offers hillsides of spectacular Mexican gold poppies, desert-chicory, and Coulter's lupine in March, followed by a brilliant yellow bloom of brittlebush throughout April.

Before you reach Canyon Lake, turn left onto the dirt Mormon Flat Dam Road and travel about 500 yards (457.2 m) to see a vibrant display of

Mexican gold poppies and scorpionweed. Because these blooming annuals open in response to sunlight, plan to visit here a couple hours after sunrise or before sunset.

Continue past Canyon Lake and deeper into the Superstition Mountains, as beautiful blooming Parry's century plants show off elongated stalks in May and June among the soaring cliffs. After driving 4.3 miles (6.9 km) beyond Tortilla Flat, turn left onto the dirt Horse Mesa Dam Road and travel about two miles (3.2 km) north until you reach the gate, scanning both sides of the road for owl clover, Mexican gold poppies, scorpionweed, and chia blooming in March.

After this short detour, return to the Apache Trail and continue driving east on what becomes an even tighter dirt road. Though difficult to do with the gorgeous desert scenery, keep your eyes on the road as you drive down the infamous Fish Creek Hill which drops 1,500 feet (457 m) in elevation in about three short miles (4.8 km) through numerous unsettling hairpin turns.

Prior to Apache Lake, turn right onto Forest Service Road 212 towards the Reavis Ranch Trailhead and drive until views of Apache Lake come into sight on the left-hand side of the road. Poppies bloom at the feet of gigantic saguaro cacti which produce the official state wildflower of Arizona near Bronco Butte in May.

Since the photographic opportunities vary tremendously

*Yellow paloverde trees and Parry's century plants bloom on Horse Mesa Dam Road. Canon 5DMII, 24-105mm at 45mm, ISO 400, f/8 @ 1/160 sec. Paul Gill*

# Engelmann's Prickly Pear Cactus

*Opuntia englemannii*
**Blooms:** April to June on sandy deserts and grasslands between 1,500 and 7,500 feet (457 and 2,286 m) elevation. (Perennial)
**Fun Fact:** After flowering, this cactus produces magenta fruit often made into delectable jellies, candy, and margarita mix!

**EASTERN ARIZONA**

# Apache Trail

and your vehicle will be nearby, you can afford to pack a broader set of equipment for your photographic outing along the Apache Trail. Pack **wide-angle**, **telephoto**, and **macro lenses** along with a **polarizer**, **tripod**, and **cable release**. If you plan to stay in the area for sunset, also bring **graduated neutral density filters**, especially if clouds grace the typically clear blue sky. You may also find use for a **reflector** and **diffuser** in setting up close-up compositions during the high contrast, mid-day light.

If you have extra time, you might consider a stop at the Lost Dutchman State Park (see page 120)—the perfect place to wrap up your photography outing at sunset.

*Banana yucca bloom at sunset above Fish Creek. Canon 5DMIII, 24-105mm at 40mm, ISO 100, f/22 @ 0.8 sec. Paul Gill*

*Mexican gold poppies on the hillsides above Apache Lake. Canon 5D, 24-105mm, at 105mm. ISO 100, f/22 @ 1/8 sec., polarizer. Paul Gill*

## DIRECTIONS:

From Phoenix, take US 60 east towards Apache Junction. Take Exit 196 for AZ 88 (Idaho Road). Turn left onto Idaho Road and drive about 2.5 miles (4 km) before veering right onto the Apache Trail (AZ 88). The Apache Trail winds along the northern edge of the Superstition Mountains Wilderness Area for about 40 miles (64.4 km) to the Roosevelt Dam.

Though flowers bloom beside the road all along the Apache Trail, getting to them safely can be a challenge due to the steep cliffs on both sides of the narrow, winding road and heavy vehicle traffic, particularly on the weekends. Look for an obvious wide spot in the road to cautiously pull off and park, then watch your step as you exit your vehicle.

Because services are limited along the trail, it is best to fill up on gas in Globe or Apache Junction before embarking on your trip. Food, including scrumptious prickly pear ice cream, is available at Tortilla Flat.

## Making the Photo 8

# Working Freehand
By Paul Gill

*Ladybug on the edge. Canon 5DMIII, 100mm macro, ISO 800, f/5 @ 1/500 sec. Paul Gill*

My favorite way to work in macro mode is to leave the tripod, focusing rail, reflectors, and diffuser behind. I like to set the camera on 1/500th of a second in shutter speed priority mode with continuous shoot mode enabled. Then, I strap on knee pads and "freehand" it.

This approach opens the creative flow by moving through small scenes and groupings of wildflowers. I am able to see and compose quickly, capturing images I would have never seen from six feet (1.8 m) away while loaded up with all my camera gear.

If you are a compulsive photographer like me, this style could work perfectly for you. Sometimes I will start off working this way if I am feeling creatively blocked or if the good landscape light has left and I do not want to laboriously construct images anymore. This freeing method can be somewhat exhausting, as you crawl around on the desert floor (where everything either stings, pokes, or bites you!), but you will discover how the small world beneath your feet can hide wonderful surprises.

During spring and early summer, many convergent ladybugs begin migrating towards mountainous areas. In these summit swarms, you will frequently notice the ladybugs congregating in the hundreds, if not the thousands. Mid-March through April is my favorite time to catch these wildflowers and ladybugs. Another chance arrives in May when the paloverde trees, century plants, and saguaro cacti bloom. Morning is the best time to capture bugs on wildflowers because they are not very active yet.

I photographed the ladybug crawling along the edge of an orange mariposa lily (on the left) on the Apache Trail (see page 170) near the Apache Lake Dam Road turn-off. I had finished the early morning light landscapes and had some intermittent cloud cover so I switched out my wide-angle lens to a 100mm f/2.8 macro lens. I strapped on my camera (with a hand strap) and then went hunting—freehand style. Blooming banana yucca, strawberry hedgehog cactus, and orange mariposa lilies (all of which had hundreds of ladybugs just starting to warm up in the sunlight) covered the area.

*Five ladybugs gather on the sunny side of a banana yucca bloom. Canon 5DMIII, 100mm macro, ISO 1250, f/5 @ 1/200 sec. Paul Gill*

I also snapped the second image above without a tripod. For this image, I intentionally positioned my camera to record an odd number of subjects in the composition to avoid conveying symmetry. Odd numbers create a visual tension which keeps the eye moving within the frame. In addition, a collection of one, three, five, etc., objects create unifying asymmetrical balance. Even numbers create a sense of symmetrical balance, which divides the viewer's focus.

Also, as I hand-held my camera, I took extra care in keeping my lens parallel with the bugs and petal to keep everything sharp. Moving away from parallel can give a better sense of depth in macro photography (as with the image on the left). In doing so, however, it is almost impossible to keep a sharp focus throughout the entire frame, given the extremely narrow depth of field macro lenses yield.

For most outdoor photographic work, a tripod is an essential item and not an accessory. However, if you want to handhold your camera, you will have to work with either a wide aperture and/or a high ISO. The rule of thumb for shutter speed is that if you want a sharp image, the shutter speed should be no slower than the same fraction as your focal length – that is, if you're using a 100mm lens, set your shutter speed to 1/100th second or faster. If available, use image stabilization or vibration reduction to allow an decrease in your the shutter speed by two or three stops.

Some of the most beautiful wildflower macro photographs are made in the moment, so learning these techniques will help you take advantage of all opportunities and get that great image even when you do not have a tripod.

## EASTERN ARIZONA

# Workman Creek

*Yellow columbine bloom along Workman Creek. Canon 5D, 24-105mm at 40mm, ISO 100, f/11 @ 1/20 sec., polarizer. Paul Gill*

**BLOOM TIME**
June to July

**IDEAL TIME OF DAY**
Early morning

**VEHICLE**
2WD high-clearance

**HIKE**
Easy to moderate

In the spring of 2000, the Coon Creek Fire charred almost 10,000 acres (4,047 hectares) across the Tonto National Forest, changing the landscape surrounding Workman Creek. After this significant disturbance, however, the forest began immediately regenerating. Under a canopy of healthy ponderosa pine, sycamore, and maples trees, the resulting nutritious, fertile soil now supports an abundance of wildflowers along the peaceful Workman Creek each summer.

Start at the Creekside Recreation Area and carefully drop down to the creek to look for showy flowers like yellow columbine, monkeyflower, and cutleaf coneflower along the water. Prevalent individual blooms in June and July lend themselves well to close-up style photographs using a **macro lens**.

If enough rain has fallen in the spring, intermingling species present excellent opportunities to capture broader compositions with a photogenic mix of color along the forested watercourse using a **wide-angle lens**. A **polarizer** will help bring out the natural color of the flowers

*Purple myrtle and yellow columbine line the shores of Workman Creek. Canon 5DMIII, TS-E 17mm, ISO 100, f/18 @ 4.0 sec., reflector. Paul Gill*

## EASTERN ARIZONA
# Workman Creek

*Yellow columbine surrounds a spring. Canon 5D, 24-105mm at 24mm, ISO 100, f/11 @ 1/8 sec., polarizer. Paul Gill*

and help give a silky appearance to the flowing water when used in conjunction with slower shutter speeds (around one quarter of a second or slower). With exposure times this slow, you will need to stabilize your camera with a **tripod** and **cable release**.

Once you have worked this location, return to your vehicle and continue east to Forest Service Road 487 to the Falls Recreation Area. As you make your way to the next stop, steep drop-offs on the right-hand side of the narrow road make it difficult to stop or park. Take advantage of the wider spots in the road to pull off and scan for flowers like wild bergamot and scarlet bugler in the immediate vicinity.

At the Falls Recreation Area, explore both up- and down-stream as flowers tend to congregate along the shoreline in hordes. Occasionally, you will find natural debris has collected in the creek and makes arranging clean scenic compositions a difficult, but not impossible, challenge. Before photographing, scan the edges of your photograph in your viewfinder or your camera's Live View screen (if available) to ensure there are no out of focus branches or other visually disturbing objects cluttering your composition.

Wearing water shoes will not only help cool you off in the refreshing stream during the more humid month of July, but will also enable you to more easily work your way up or down the creek from either parking area in search of the best blooms. And, because of your proximity to water, wear long pants to guard against poison ivy lining the creek and bring bug spray to ward off any mosquitoes.

After photographing at the Falls Recreation Area, you might consider driving another mile (1.6 km) or so up Forest Service Road 487 to catch a glimpse of the 100-foot (30.5-m) waterfall called Workman Falls plunging out of the rocks. The pools above the falls often offer bundles of wildflowers like yellow columbine, but bring a **telephoto lens** to capture these flowers, as they can be difficult to reach without deep wading.

## DIRECTIONS:

From Globe, drive north on AZ 188 for approximately 14.5 miles (23.3 km). Turn right onto AZ 288 (the Globe-Young Highway) and continue northbound on this mostly paved road for about 25.7 miles (41.4 km) until you see milepost 284. Immediately after milepost 284, you should see a brown sign for the Workman Creek Recreation Area (Forest Service Road 487). Turn here and drive three-quarters of a mile (1.2 km) on this dirt road to the Creekside Recreation Area. The Falls Recreation Area is another three-quarter miles (1.2 km) further along Forest Service Road 487. Workman Falls is an additional mile (1.6 km) or so up this bumpy dirt road.

- ❋ Yellow Columbine
- ● Wild Bergamot
- ◆ Cutleaf Coneflower
- ⬢ Wild Geranium
- ★ Myrtle

Western wallflower along the road near Workman Falls. Canon 5DMII, 100mm macro, ISO 400, f/4.5 @ 1/200 sec. Colleen Miniuk-Sperry

## Yellow Columbine

*Aguilegia chrysantha*
**Blooms:** April to September in moist soil and near water in forests between 3,000 and 11,000 feet (914 and 3,353 m) elevation. (Perennial)
**Fun Fact:** The word "columbine" derives from a Latin word meaning "dove."

**EASTERN ARIZONA**

# Peridot Mesa

*Fields of Gold Poppies cover the hillsides of Peridot Mesa, Canon 5DMIII, 24-105mm at 65mm, ISO 100, f/13 @ 1/30 sec. Paul Gill*

**BLOOM TIME**
**Late February to May**

**IDEAL TIME OF DAY**
**Early morning to late afternoon**

**VEHICLE**
**2WD high-clearance**

**HIKE**
**Easy to moderate**

The name "Peridot" derives from the presence of the olive green gemstones found in the basalt rock found atop aptly-named Peridot Mesa. Some estimates suggest that the San Carlos Indian Reservation holds the world's largest deposit of the August birthstone and consistently produces a substantial amount of the world's commercial-grade supply of this stone.

While only members of the tribe may mine for the prized mineral, those visiting Peridot Mesa in search of wildflowers in late February through early April will find their own gems—that is, expansive blankets of Mexican gold poppies dotted by lupine, desert-chicory, and blue dick across rolling desert hillsides for as far as the eye can see.

Arrive late in the morning to allow the poppies enough time to transition from their tight overnight buds into full, vibrant blooms admiring the sky overhead. Since you will be close to your vehicle (unless you decide to hike cross-country), bring a broad range of lenses from **wide-angle** to **telephoto** to **macro**. A **polarizer** will help reduce the reflected light from the flowers and increase the saturation across your entire frame. Also, carry a **diffuser**, **reflector**, and/or **artificial flash** to manage any harsh contrasts in your smaller compositions resulting from the mid-day sun.

Once something catches your eye in such a visually stimulating scene, pause and ask, "What stopped me? What am I seeing here that I like?" With the answer in mind, fill your frame with your answer (your primary subject).

## DIRECTIONS:

From Globe, follow US 70 eastbound for approximately 19 miles (30.6 km). Just past mile marker 268, turn left onto an unnamed dirt road (marked by a cattle guard framed by two white H-shaped poles). Continue an additional 0.5 miles (0.8 km), where you should start seeing flowers along the road and hillsides. Pull off the side of the road to park.

A recreation permit (issued by the San Carlos Apache Indian Reservation) is required to visit this area. Purchase a permit at the Basha's grocery store in Peridot (2 miles (3.2 km) east of the turnoff to Peridot Mesa). Permits are also available in Globe at Express Stop at 1501 E. Ash Street and the Circle K at 2011 E. Ash Street.

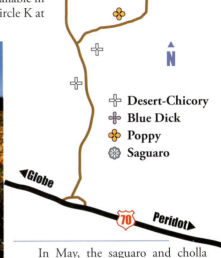

In May, the saguaro and cholla cactus put on a second, but equally impressive, colorful showing as they sprout their own blooms. Sunrise and sunset offer the best time to experience and photograph this late spring bloom, but pack **graduated neutral density filters** to balance the exposures in the sky and land.

*Gold poppies cover the hillsides of Peridot Mesa. Canon 5DMIII, TS-E 17mm, ISO 100, f/11 @ 1/125 sec. Paul Gill*

## Desert-Chicory

*Rafinesquia neomexicana*
**Blooms:** From February to May in desert landscapes below 3,000 feet (914 m). (Annual)
**Fun Fact:** Often mistaken for white tackstem, this white flower also goes by "New Mexico plumeseed."

# When Natural Light Isn't Enough

Artificial flash is useful in situations when the sun does not provide the right quantity or quality of light you desire. Specifically, the flash can help balance a large contrast between the highlights and shadow areas much like a reflector does, only more so. Flash also creates more dramatic light in diffused lighting set-ups.

On-camera flash (through either a pop-up flash or a flash added to the hot shoe on top of the camera) is most effective in backlit situations where the subject is dark and the surrounding ambient light is lighter than the subject. This type of artificial light adds an even amount of light to the shadow and helps to balance the contrast with the rest of the scene.

Off-camera flash acts the same as on-camera flash, except the flash is physically separated from the camera by a cord or wireless transmitter (infrared or radio). Not only does this provide the most flattering light in most applications, but it also provides seemingly endless creative options in creating and capturing side or backlight in your scene.

A ring flash (a circular light that fits around the camera's lens) produces light that surrounds the subject. Like on-camera flash, this helps evenly illuminate the entire subject when odd shadows or highlights fall on the subject with natural light. To create a similar shadow-less effect as a ring light, some manufacturers offer twin lights, where two separate lights sit on either side of the camera's lens.

The biggest challenge in using artificial flash is balancing the natural ambient light with the flash output to expose the entire scene properly. To do this, consider lighting your photograph in two different layers – first, an ambient or background layer, and second, a flash or foreground layer, controlling the light and exposure level for both of these layers separately.

Starting with the ambient layer, adjust your shutter speed and aperture to get a desired exposure for the background. Then snap a "test" shot for ambient exposure, keeping the flash unit turned off. Check your histogram to ensure a balanced ambient exposure. Your flower in the foreground might be dark, and that's OK!

Next, turn on your flash unit and select either Through-The-Lens (TTL) or Manual mode. The various TTL modes available will automatically calculate and provide the necessary flash output for you. Selecting Manual mode is much like shooting in Manual camera mode: you decide the appropriate flash output setting given your distance from the subject, ISO speed, the focal length of your lens, and set aperture.

An off-camera flash held on camera right adds a touch of illumination to a claret cup hedgehog cactus bloom at the Desert Botanical Garden. Canon 5DMII, 100mm macro, ISO 250, f/3.5 @ 1/200 sec., diffuser, off-camera flash triggered by Pocket Wizards on Manual 1/2 power set manually to 24mm zoom, covered with an Omni-Bounce and bounced off a gold reflector to soften the artificial light. Colleen Miniuk-Sperry

**Without Flash**     **With Flash**

*A yellow columbine sitting in shade at the Boyce Thompson Arboretum (left) blends with the background, and a slow shutter speed could not freeze the swaying bloom. To highlight the flower, I used a faster shutter speed to darken the background and then held an off-camera flash above the flower. Canon 5DMII, 100mm macro, ISO 200, f/4.5 @ 1/80 sec., off-camera flash triggered by Pocket Wizards on Manual 1/8 power set manually to 24mm zoom, covered with an Omni-Bounce. Both by Colleen Miniuk-Sperry.*

Now make an exposure with the flash. What do you see on your histogram? Evaluate your foreground to determine how to adjust the flash output only, not the ambient light in the background.

If the bloom in the foreground looks too dark, increase flash output by adding light through the Flash Exposure Compensation (FEC) button (often labeled with a "+" symbol) on the flash or camera if you're using TTL mode. If you're in Manual flash mode, you have other options:

- Increase the flash output in Manual flash mode
- Move the flash closer to subject
- Select a faster ISO speed setting
- Open up the aperture (speed up the shutter speed to keep the ambient light unchanged)

If the foreground is too bright, subtract light through the Flash Exposure Compensation (FEC) button (often labeled with a "-" symbol) on the flash or camera if you're using TTL mode. If you're in Manual flash mode, you have other options:

- Decrease the flash output in Manual flash mode
- Move the flash away from subject
- Select a slower ISO speed setting
- Stop down the aperture (slow the shutter speed to keep the ambient light unchanged)

When photographing wildflowers, the effect of artificial light on the subject should be subtle, not nuclear. If you feel the flash is adding light sufficiently, but it's creating too much contrast, soften the light even further with a flash diffuser or the bounce card built into the flash unit. Or if you wish to soften and warm the artificial light simultaneously, point the flash at a reflector positioned to redirect light back onto your bloom.

*Atop a saguaro cactus bloom almost 30 feet (9.1 m) above the ground, an ant collects nectar. Canon 5DMII, 100mm macro, ISO 100, f/11 @ 1/30 sec. Paul Gill*

# *Wildflowers of* SOUTHERN ARIZONA

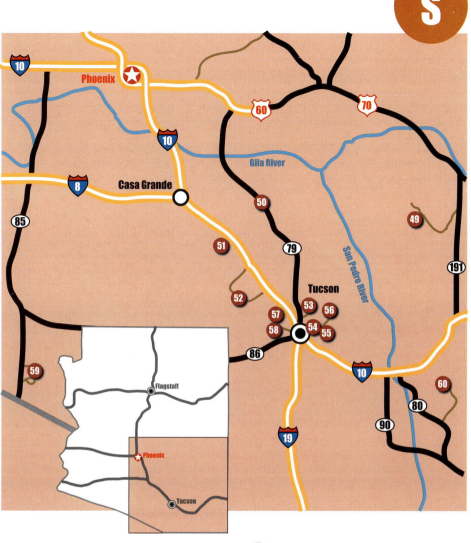

- **49** Treasure Park.............. 186
- **50** Pinal Pioneer Parkway..188
- **51** Picacho Peak State Park ................... 192
- **52** Ironwood Forest National Monument.....194
- **53** Catalina State Park.....198
- **54** Tohono Chul Park.........200
- **55** Tucson Botanical Gardens.......................204
- **56** Mount Lemmon...........206
- **57** Saguaro National Park - West.................210
- **58** Arizona - Sonora Desert Museum ......... 214
- **59** Organ Pipe Cactus National Monument.....220
- **60** Dragoon Mountains....224

## SOUTHERN ARIZONA

# Treasure Park

*Meadow of Dakota verbena high in the Pinaleno Mountains. Canon 5DMIII, 16-35mm at 21mm, ISO 100, f/22 @ 2 sec. Paul Gill*

**BLOOM TIME**
**July to September**

**IDEAL TIME OF DAY**
**Sunrise and sunset**

**VEHICLE**
**2WD high-clearance**

**HIKE**
**Easy**

Legend holds that a buried treasure of stolen gold and silver from the 1800s remains in the heart of the Pinaleno Mountains. The bandits supposedly marked their stash with three colored granite stones formed in a triangle. In the early 1900s, a Forest Service employee, named T. T. "Ted" Swift (for which the Swift Trail Highway is named) located a trail that led to three colored rocks at Treasure Park. Despite significant digging efforts, Swift never found the riches—nor has anyone else to date.

Today, a visit to Treasure Park is still worth the trip up the winding road, not for the pursuit of three colored rocks or the cache of gold and silver, but rather for a natural treasure of vibrant wildflowers! From July through September, blooms from Rocky Mountain iris, fleabane, western wallflower, New Mexico locust, and Dakota verbena grace the conifer-lined, serene meadow.

Bring a **wide-angle lens** to help convey the expansive nature of this scene. Move close to the flowers and focus at the hyperfocal distance (check the tables at **dofmaster.com**) while using a smaller aperture like f/16 or f/22 to maximize your depth of field. To increase the emphasis on the flowers in the mid-ground, raise your tripod. To minimize the mid-ground, lower your equipment instead.

**Macro** and **telephoto lenses** can help you isolate a single wildflower among intermixing species. No matter your lens, use a **polarizer** to help reduce the sheen on the flowers and increase the saturation of colors across your frame. The higher elevations of Mount Graham often experience fog

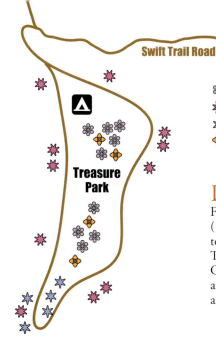

# 49

- Dakota Verbena
- New Mexico Locust
- Rocky Mountain Iris
- Western Wallflower

## DIRECTIONS:

From Safford, travel south on US 191 for 7.3 miles (11.8 km). Turn right onto AZ 366 (also referred to as the Swift Trail). Drive 22.6 miles (36.4 km). Turn left at the signed turnoff for Treasure Park. Continue driving on the dirt road until it reaches at the Treasure Park Campground-North. Park anywhere along the loop road.

in the summer, so pack **graduated neutral density filters** to darken the light sky and **extra lens cloths** if the mountain looks socked in by clouds.

Those not acclimatized to the thinner air at this 9,000-foot (2,743-m) elevation may feel dizzy or short of breath. If you experience either, return to lower elevations. As you enjoy your visit here, stay hydrated and move slowly.

Because much cooler temperatures provide a welcome respite from the scorching desert summer temperatures, this area is popular for camping and hiking, especially on the summer weekends. Plan to arrive at sunrise or early in the day to get a parking spot.

*Dakota verbena surround orange western wallflowers. Canon 5DMIII, 100mm macro, ISO 100, f/22 @ 1/30 sec. Paul Gill*

## Dakota Verbena

*Verbena bipinnatifida*
**Blooms:** At elevations in between 5,000 and 10,000 feet (1,524 and 3,048 m) in clearings in coniferous forests from May to September. (Perennial)
**Fun Fact:** Like many flowers within the verbena (or vervain) Family, the stems of this bloom are quite hairy.

**SOUTHERN ARIZONA**

# Pinal Pioneer Parkway

*A balanced rock reflects last light over Coulter's lupine and ocotillo along 96 Ranch Road. Canon 5DMII, 24-105mm at 45mm, ISO 100, three exposure HDR. Paul Gill*

**BLOOM TIME**
**March to May**

**IDEAL TIME OF DAY**
**Sunrise to sunset**

**VEHICLE**
**Any**

**HIKE**
**Moderate**

Known as one of the first Hollywood cowboys, famed actor Tom Mix wowed audiences with his death-defying stunts in silent movies during the early 1900s. In 1940, though, his successful acting career came to a screeching halt when he died in an unfortunate car accident while driving along this scenic stretch of the Pinal Pioneer Parkway.

Today, a tall stone memorial capped with a lone metal horse marks the approximate location of the accident. Each spring, a mix of wildflower blooms prolifically along this desolate stretch of highway and at the Tom Mix Rest Area as if to celebrate this legendary actor's life.

Make a stop at the historical marker or at one of the many unofficial dirt turnouts along the road since it is tough to fully appreciate the desert wildflowers if you're zipping by at high speeds. Pleasing even the toughest critics, Mexican gold poppies, Coulter's lupine, chuparosa, Parry's penstemon, and desert globemallow put on a performance in March and April worthy of photographing through a **macro** and/or **telephoto lens** with a wide aperture ranging from f/2.8 to f/5.6.

Bring a **reflector**, **diffuser**, or **off-camera flash** to help spotlight an individual or small grouping of flowers. As you search for a healthy specimen on which to focus, also look for an uncluttered, simple backdrop. A natural-colored shirt, mat board, or old photo can serve as an out-of focus artificial background (see page 136).

In May, the buckhorn cholla stages a multi-colored bloom of yellow, red, and orange flowers along the Freeman Road. Later, the flowers of the

# 50

## DIRECTIONS:

From Florence, AZ 79 (known as the Pinal Pioneer Parkway) stretches 42 miles (67.6 km) south toward Tucson. Wildflowers bloom all along the entire route, but the best places to stop are around the Tom Mix Rest Area, about 18 miles (29 km) south of Florence on the west side of the road. Visit the dirt 96 Ranch and Freeman roads about 15.3 miles (24.6 km) and 21.9 miles (35.3 km) respectively south of Florence on the east side of the road.

✸ Buckhorn Cholla
◆ Lupine
❄ Paloverde
✳ Ocotillo

saguaro cactus, littleleaf paloverde, and ironwood hold an encore performance among the jumbo boulders along the more northerly 96 Ranch Road. A **wide-angle lens**, **tripod**, and **cable release** will best capture these prized shows. Also, use a **polarizer** and a **graduated neutral density filter** to keep your exposure balanced and to add more drama in the sky, especially if clouds are overhead.

*A purple scorpionweed blooms next to a young prickly pear pad. Canon 5DMIII, 100mm macro, ISO 100, f/22 @ 0.5 sec. Paul Gill*

## Buckhorn Cholla

*Opuntia acanthocarpa*
**Blooms:** Mid-April to May in between elevations of 500 and 3,500 feet (152 and 1,067 m) in sandy slopes and washes. (Perennial)
**Fun Fact:** Named for its shape, "deer horn cactus" is another term for the buckhorn cholla.

# PHOTO TIP 14

# Get Perfect Exposures
## With Graduated Neutral Density Filters
*Sponsored by Singh-Ray, www.singh-ray.com*

*On the hillsides above the Silver King Mine Road, I wanted to record a well-exposed sky and landscape. After capturing this frame, my camera's histogram suggested the sky was overexposed by showing a spike on the right-hand side of the graph and blinking highlights on the LCD screen when I reviewed the photo. Canon 5DMII, 24-105mm at 24mm, ISO 100, f/22 @ 1/4 sec. Paul Gill*

Cameras "see" a fairly broad dynamic range of light and shadow. However, sometimes the scene we compose contains areas that are too bright for the camera to record while still properly exposing the rest of the scene. This frequently results in images where the foreground looks perfect, but the over-exposed sky looks white and washed-out. Your camera may also have a highlight alert feature that warns of this scenario.

A graduated neutral density filter to the rescue! Also called a split neutral density filter, this tool reduces the bright areas of the frame while exposing the rest of the photograph properly.

To use a graduated neutral density filter, start by switching the camera's shooting mode to Manual so you can more easily adjust the exposure settings as you decide which strength of filter to apply. In addition, change your metering mode to spot metering to precisely understand the correct exposure for the foreground and background.

Next, to determine if you need a one-, two-, three-, four- or five-stop graduated neutral density filter, first decide the correct exposure for the dark area by aiming your camera at the darker spots in your foreground. Note the shutter speed and aperture that appear in your meter. Then, meter for a bright area (most commonly in the sky). Again, note the exposure readings.

Lastly, calculate the number of stops between the two exposures. The difference in exposure equals the strength of the graduated neutral density filter to use. For example, a three-stop

*To preserve detail in the foreground but also capture a well-exposed sky, I positioned a two-stop graduated neutral density filter over the sky so the graduated line just touched the horizon and a one-stop graduated neutral density filter diagonally above the foreground hill. Canon 5DMII, 24-105mm at 24mm, ISO 100, f/22 @ 1/4 sec., one- and two-stop graduated neutral density filters stacked. Paul Gill*

difference in exposure indicates a three-stop filter would work best.

Remember to reset the exposure settings to the aperture and shutter speed you metered in the dark area once you have decided which filter to put in front of your lens.

Look for a natural horizontal or diagonal line between the light and dark areas to place the graduated line. Soft-edged filters are more forgiving with an odd-shaped horizon than hard-edged ones. If the horizon line falls at an angle, tilt the filter to match the horizon line.

To get a better idea of where to place the filter, hold down the depth of field preview button (if available on your camera) while positioning the filter. Stopping down to a small aperture such as f/16 or f/22 will make the placement of the graduated line more apparent.

Instead of using graduated neutral density filters, some photographers prefer capturing multiple images at different exposure levels to later blend in post-processing software to create High Dynamic Range (HDR) images. Specialized filters within post-processing software can also re-create the effect of a graduated neutral density filter for a single image.

**SOUTHERN ARIZONA**

# Picacho Peak State Park

*A fallen saguaro cactus lies in a bed of closed Mexican gold poppies and Coulter's lupine at sunset. Wista 4x5, 90mm, Fuji Velvia 50, f/32 @ 1/2 sec. Paul Gill*

**BLOOM TIME**
March

**IDEAL TIME OF DAY**
Sunrise to sunset

**VEHICLE**
Any

**HIKE**
Moderate

On April 15, 1862, the westernmost Civil War battle began near the towering 3,374-foot (1,028-m) eroded volcanic plug called Picacho Peak. Today, Picacho Peak is one of the most dominating features in the Sonoran Desert landscape for travelers driving along I-10 in between Tucson and Phoenix.

In a celebration of life each March, seemingly everywhere you look within this park you will see a mix of wildflowers in a good bloom year, with vibrant Mexican gold poppies prevailing.

Start your day with a pre-dawn hike along the Nature Trail, Calloway Trail, or the first half mile (0.8 km) of the more difficult Hunter Trail to position yourself north of the peak. From these spots, focus on placing wildflowers in your foreground with the scenic spire as your backdrop. Use a **wide-angle lens** as the sun illuminates your scene.

To keep sharp focus across the entire image, use a small aperture such as f/16 of f/22 to ensure the broadest depth of field possible. This setting will likely translate into slower shutter speeds, so pack your **tripod** and **cable release** before you head out for your morning shoot. **Graduated neutral density filters** may also be helpful to reduce light in the bright sky and perfectly expose your foreground.

During the middle of the day, when the light is harsher, seek out carpets of flowers any place within the park where you can isolate individual blooms, as well as patterns and shapes, with your **macro** and **telephoto lenses**. Intentionally placing flowers close to your lens while focusing on distant blooms with a wide aperture (e.g. f/4.0 or f/5.6) will create a sense of depth in your photographs. If the sky is clear, consider using a diffuser or **reflector** to tame high contrast.

If you still have some energy left after a full day of photographing, pack up your camera gear, including your wide-angle lens, tripod, cable release, **polarizer**, and **graduated neutral density filters**, and head out about a mile or two (1.6 to 3.2 km) along the moderately difficult Sunset Vista Trail. Though the view of Picacho Peak is not as stunning as on the east side of the park, this aptly named trail offers excellent opportunities to photograph a rich and vibrant sunset above the wildflowers gracing the bajada.

## DIRECTIONS:

From Phoenix: take I-10 east towards Tucson to Exit 219 for Picacho Peak Road. Turn right onto Picacho Peak Road and drive straight into the park.

From Tucson: take I-10 west towards Phoenix to Exit 219 for Picacho Peak Road. Turn left onto Picacho Peak Road. Cross under the highway and into the park.

Entrance to the park requires a fee which the park waives if visitors show an Arizona State Parks Annual Pass. For more information, visit the Picacho Peak State Park website at **www.pr.state.az.us/parks/PIPE/index.html**.

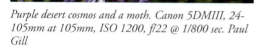

*Purple desert cosmos and a moth. Canon 5DMIII, 24-105mm at 105mm, ISO 1200, f/22 @ 1/800 sec. Paul Gill*

## California Poppy

*Eschscholzia californica*
**Blooms:** March to May on dry desert flats and slopes below 4500 feet (1,372 m) elevation. (Annual and perennial)
**Fun Fact:** The California poppy, which resembles the smaller Mexican gold poppy, became California's state flower in 1903.

**SOUTHERN ARIZONA**

# Ironwood Forest National Monument

*Stormy morning skies over Ragged Top Mountain during the saguaro cactus and ironwood bloom. Wista 4x5, 120mm, Fuji Velvia 100, f/32 @ 1 sec., two-stop graduated neutral density filter. Paul Gill*

**BLOOM TIME**
**May**

**IDEAL TIME OF DAY**
**Sunrise**

**VEHICLE**
**2WD high-clearance**

**HIKE**
**Easy**

Established in 2000, the Ironwood Forest National Monument honors the Sonoran Desert's slow-growing and longest-living tree, the ironwood. Because many ironwood trees serve as a protective nurse plant to young saguaro cacti, the two often occur side by side in the park. Coincidentally, they also bloom simultaneously.

Each May, the pale lavender blossoms of the elderly tree provide a subtle, but photogenic, splash of color to the expansive desert valley dotted with blooming prickly pear cactus, ocotillo, and paloverde trees. In contrast, the saguaro cactus produces bold white flowers.

Although the ironwood bloom duration is short-lived at 10 to 18 days, the saguaro bloom duration is even shorter. The saguaro cactus produces a bundle of blooms throughout the entire month, but each flower opens independently in the morning, only to close that evening.

Plan to arrive about 30 minutes before sunrise with a flashlight or headlamp so you can locate an ironwood and saguaro cactus blooming together on either side of the dirt road. At day break, point your camera south towards the rugged Ragged Top Mountain. To emphasize the flowering ironwood tree and/or saguaro cactus as the primary subject, get close to the tree and cactus, and then photograph using a **wide-angle lens**, framing Ragged Top Mountain with the tree branches. Alternatively, if you wish to show the scale of the scene, back away from the ironwood tree and use a **telephoto lens**.

However you compose the image, bring along a **polarizer**, **graduated**

*Backlit ironwood tree. Canon 5DMII, 100-400mm at 400mm, ISO 800, f/4 @ 1/400 sec. Paul Gill*

**neutral density filter**, **tripod**, and **cable release** to help capture your scene at first light.

If you are lucky enough to find an unusual bouquet of saguaro cactus blooms clustered together occurring at eye level, pull out your **macro lens** to photograph this magnificent display of Mother Nature. If available on your camera, use your depth of field preview button to ensure all the flowers in the bloom are in focus.

## DIRECTIONS:

From Tucson, take I-10 west towards Marana. Take Exit 236 for Sandario Road and turn left onto Sandario Road. Drive under the highway and past the Frontage Road, and then take an immediate right onto Marana Road. Head west for just short of 6 miles (9.7 km) to Silver Bell Road. Turn right onto Silverbell Road, and then drive about 13 miles (20.9 km) to the Ironwood Forest National Monument for the best blooms (the road turns from paved to dirt after the first 7.6 miles (12.2 km)). No formal parking areas exist, so look for previously used pullouts or wide spots in the road to park.

Encounters with the U. S. Border Patrol and/or illegal immigrants are possible within the national monument. Do not intervene with border patrol activities and report any suspicious activity to the local authorities.

For more information, visit the Ironwood Forest National Monument website at **www.blm.gov/az/st/en/prog/blm_special_areas/natmon/ironwood.html**.

## Desert Ironwood

*Olneya tesota*
**Bloom:** May to June below 2,500 feet (762 m) elevation along sandy desert flats, washes, and canyons. (Perennial)
**Fun Fact:** Producing one of the densest woods in the world, ironwood is so heavy, even a small piece will not float in water.

# Rain, Rain, Don't Go Away!

*Dew on a Mexican gold poppy bud next to a Coulter's lupine. Canon 5DMII, MP-E 65mm 1-5x, ISO 400, f/4 @ 1/4 sec., diffuser. Paul Gill*

Some photographers like to tote a spray bottle of water around while photographing wildflowers, as a few drops of water sprayed on a bloom can make the flower look as if it's been freshly kissed by a passing storm. If it is raining outside, let Mother Nature do the work for you!

Before photographing in the rain, pack rain gear for you and your camera. A large golf umbrella can serve as a dry cover for you and your camera as you shoot. For more protection, purchase a Think Tank Hydrophobia rain cover or Op/Tech USA Rainsleeve made specifically to fit around your camera. A dry lens cloth tucked in your rain jacket's pocket can help wipe off any water drops that fall on your lens during your outing.

Because the natural light tends to be lower when it's cloudy, set your camera to a faster ISO

*Rain droplets cover a Mexican gold poppy and a strawberry hedgehog cactus bloom. Canon 5DMII, MP-E 65mm 1-5x, ISO 400, f/4 @ 1/30 sec. Paul Gill*

speed and shutter speed to freeze the rain drops and your subject, especially if wind accompanies the rain. A slower shutter speed will blur any motion, including the rain or movement of your subject in the wind.

Compositions ranging from abstracts to moody broad scenic views offer endless possibilities during a rainy day. To capture abstracts of flower shapes and patterns, use a macro lens with a short depth of field. Use extension tubes, bellows, or a close-up filter to capture water droplets and the tiny refractions they often produce. On the other hand, a strong graduated neutral density filter in combination with a wide-angle lens can add a more ominous feeling to a broad scene.

After the storm passes, look for puddles that create reflections of the surrounding scenery and sky. If you are fortunate to see the sun poke her head out of the clouds, put a polarizer on your lens quickly and look in the sky directly opposite the sun. A rainbow might reward you for your extra efforts!

*A single drop of rain hangs from the stamen of a Mexican gold poppy, refracting an image of a desert cosmos. Canon 5DMII, MP-E 65mm 1-5x, ISO 800, f/2.8 @ 1/8 sec. Paul Gill*

**SOUTHERN ARIZONA**

# Catalina State Park

Stately saguaro cactus grow among Mexican gold poppies. Canon 5DMII, TS-E 24mm, ISO 100, f/11 @ 1/80 sec. Paul Gill

Though many people flock to the Saguaro National Park across town to see the iconic cactus of Arizona's Sonoran Desert, color-chasers should not overlook the smaller, but equally impressive, Catalina State Park when it comes to stunning desert-in-bloom landscapes. Located a stone's throw away from the city lights of Tucson, the rocky hills within the park come alive with a symphony of colorful wildflowers each spring.

At the foot of the rugged Santa Catalina Mountains jutting out of the desert on Tucson's northwest side, a chorus of Mexican gold poppies, Coulter's lupine, fiddleneck, wild heliotrope, fairy duster, desert-chicory, and owl clover bloom together starting in March. Golden brittlebush chimes in towards the beginning of April, while littleleaf paloverde and stands of gigantic saguaro cacti express their vibrant blooms in May.

No matter what time of year you arrive, start with a **macro** or **telephoto lens** to study a solo bloom along the Sutherland Trail, one of the best places in the park to see what the winter rains have produced. Because shade is tough to come by in this cactus forest, bring a **diffuser** to create consistent light over your selected scene.

Along the dirt path, find a saguaro to get up close and personal with, then drop your **tripod** low to the ground and angle your **wide-angle lens** towards the sky, keeping the horizon in the bottom third of your frame. A vertical composition will emphasize the height of the spiny green giants, while a horizontal composition can show a repetitive pattern.

As the sun drops, the last rays of the day permeate the west-facing slopes and turn the Santa Catalina Mountains into a radiant backdrop for a melody

**BLOOM TIME**
March to May

**IDEAL TIME OF DAY**
Late afternoon to sunset

**VEHICLE**
Any

**HIKE**
Moderate

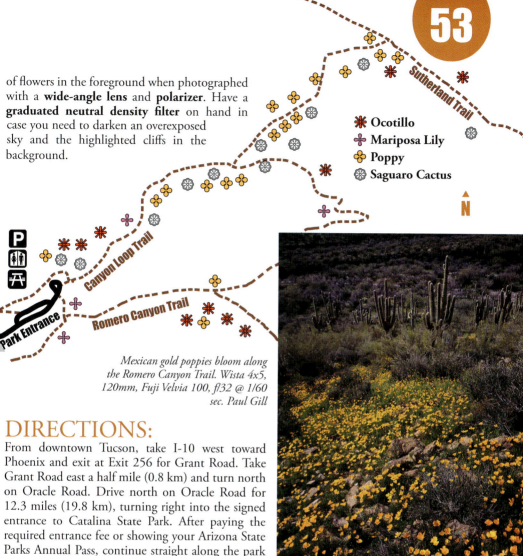

of flowers in the foreground when photographed with a **wide-angle lens** and **polarizer**. Have a **graduated neutral density filter** on hand in case you need to darken an overexposed sky and the highlighted cliffs in the background.

*Mexican gold poppies bloom along the Romero Canyon Trail. Wista 4x5, 120mm, Fuji Velvia 100, f/32 @ 1/60 sec. Paul Gill*

## DIRECTIONS:

From downtown Tucson, take I-10 west toward Phoenix and exit at Exit 256 for Grant Road. Take Grant Road east a half mile (0.8 km) and turn north on Oracle Road. Drive north on Oracle Road for 12.3 miles (19.8 km), turning right into the signed entrance to Catalina State Park. After paying the required entrance fee or showing your Arizona State Parks Annual Pass, continue straight along the park road until it ends at the easternmost trailhead. The entrance to the Canyon Loop Trail, which intersects with the Sutherland Trail, is on the northeastern side of the parking area.

To learn more about this park, visit **www.pr.state.az.us/parks/cata/index.html**.

## Ocotillo

*Fouquieria splendens*
**Blooms:** March to June on dry rocky slopes and deserts below 5,000 feet (1,524 m). (Perennial)
**Fun Fact:** Homeowners in Arizona often use ocotillo limbs to build fences. However, harvesting stems from the wild is illegal.

**SOUTHERN ARIZONA**

# Tohono Chul Park

*A night-blooming trichocereus hybrid sprouts its vibrant flower. Canon 5DMII, 100mm macro, ISO 100, f/4.5 @ 1/400 sec. Colleen Miniuk-Sperry*

**BLOOM TIME**
March to August

**IDEAL TIME OF DAY**
Early morning to late afternoon

**VEHICLE**
Any

**HIKE**
Easy

The name 'Tohono Chul' is from the Native American Tohono O'odham language and means "desert corner." It should come as no surprise, then, that one finds the park nestled on a corner within a residential area—a seemingly unlikely place for such an impressive garden.

In 1966, benefactors Richard and Jean Wilson began patching together what would eventually total 37 acres (15 hectares) for preservation purposes. Declining numerous offers from commercial developers for this valuable spread, the couple dedicated their first parcel of land as a park in 1985. Then, in 1988, they deeded the property to a new non-profit foundation, the Tohono Chul Park. In 2005, then-Governor Janet Napolitano deemed the park an "Arizona Treasure."

Today, the now 49-acre (19.8-hectare) desert oasis and living museum features a broad variety of wildflowers, offering petal peepers a premiere location to celebrate the desert's bounty. With stunning views of the distant Santa Catalina Mountains, a maze of well-defined dirt paths crisscross the urban natural preserve. Although you will not go wrong on any trail here, venture to the Sonoran Seasons Garden, the Cactus/Succulent Ramada, or the South Loop Trail to see splashes of Mexican gold poppies, owl clover, desert globemallow, and desert marigolds sprout during March and April. As temperatures warm, yellow columbine, chuparosa, yucca, and paloverde trees offer their colorful flowers to the seasonal celebration. Water-loving plants, like yerba mansa, bloom more subtly in the Riparian Habitat.

Bring a **diffuser** and **reflector** to help you manage the harsh, direct mid-

## DIRECTIONS:

From downtown Tucson, follow I-10 north and take Exit 248 for Ina Road. Turn right and drive 4.8 miles (7.7 km). Turn left onto Paseo del Norte. Turn right at the first driveway, which is the park's main entrance.

The park charges an entrance fee. The park opens its gates from 8 a.m. to 5 p.m. daily (except for New Years Day, July 4th, Thanksgiving, and Christmas). Learn more about the park at **tohonochulpark.org**.

*Western wallflower stands out among Goodding's verbena. Canon 5DMII, 100-400mm at 400mm, ISO 400, f/9 @ 1/250 sec. Colleen Miniuk-Sperry*

day sun. A **macro lens** and **artificial backgrounds** will come in handy for the blooms along the trail. The park does not permit off-trail travel, so bring a **telephoto lens** to help you record wildflowers beyond the low fences.

While the abundance of wildflowers throughout the year offers a mecca for macro photographic opportunities, by far the biggest draw to Tohono Chul Park is the annual bloom of the world's largest private collection of desert night-blooming cereus. Aptly referred to as the "Arizona Queen-of-the-Night" cactus, over 300 plants in the garden bloom on a single "Bloom Night" in between late May and July. The park's staff monitors the progress closely and sends "Bloom Watch" email announcements about the event until it occurs. Learn more and join the mailing list at **tohonochulpark.org/cereus**.

## Yerba Mansa

*Anemopsis californica*
**Blooms:** May to August in wet riparian areas in between 2,000 and 5,500 feet (610 and 1,676 m). (Perennial)
**Fun Fact:** Also known as "bear root," Native Americans tapped into the roots of this plant for medicinal purposes.

## Making the Photo 9

# Visualizing the Possibilities

By Colleen Miniuk-Sperry

*My final vision. Canon 5DMII, 100-400mm at 400mm, ISO 200, f/11 @ 1/200 sec. Colleen Miniuk-Sperry*

Visualization is the act of creating an image in your mind prior to photographing it. This could happen years or seconds (or some time in between) before you snap the shutter. While this process cannot (and should not) replace observing and reacting serendipitously to your scene once you arrive to a place, visualization can help prepare you for a wide variety of scenarios you may encounter, allow you to practice your craft without the pressure of changing conditions, and get more emotionally connected with your desired subjects—all before you ever pick up a camera. In other words, as Louis Pasteur suggested, "Luck favors the prepared."

When I visited Tohono Chul Park in late April, I knew I would be arriving after the peak of the desert's spring bloom. Flowers like Mexican gold poppies, lupine, chuparosa, and desert globemallow would have had their brilliant moment in the sun earlier in the year. Instead, I was hoping to catch the start of the second act—the desert's vibrant cactus bloom.

Upon seeing my tripod and camera riding on my shoulder, volunteer docents and wandering visitors made similar enthusiastic suggestions,

"There's an echinopsis cactus bloom near the Exhibit House that you absolutely must see and photograph!"

I rushed to the recommended location, and as promised, four stunning large blooms appeared beneath the canopy of trees. Three appeared no further than a few feet from the path, clustered together within a few inches of each other and hiding beneath the cactus branches giving them life. The other one reached to the sky but was growing in the desert landscape about 100 feet (30.5 m) from the path.

Although I arrived at Tohono Chul with no preconceived notion of what I might find, seeing this single bloom grabbed my attention. I immediately began developing an imaginary photograph in my mind. This vision guided my gear, compositional, and lighting decisions in the field. Since visualization does not stop at the moment of image capture, I also imagined how I might tap into the digital darkroom when I returned home to help bring my vision to life.

*The original, untouched photo as recorded in the field. Canon 5DMII, 100-400mm at 400mm, ISO 200, f/11 @ 1/200 sec. Colleen Miniuk-Sperry*

What I envisioned was a dramatic, chiaroscuro-like lighting effect to draw attention to this magnificent display of nature. Because of its distance from my position, I attached my 100-400mm lens onto my camera. I placed my camera on top of my tripod and affixed a cable release to ensure I did not introduce any shaking while depressing the shutter.

I liked the spatial relationship between the cactus branch and the bloom, but I composed the image using a Dutch tilt so that the arms served as a diagonal line from the bottom left corner. I danced around the path (trampling on the desert landscape is prohibited) to try different arrangements between the foreground and background. After a couple steps to the left – and then to the right – I settled on the composition.

However, after arranging the elements to my liking, it became painfully obvious that the lighting conditions were not going to help me render my final vision. I enjoyed the subtle direct light falling on the cactus bloom. However, while the background elements fell into shadow, the mid-day light kept the backdrop brighter than I preferred.

Knowing that I could darken the background during my post-processing activities at home, I continued moving around until I placed the bloom against the darkest – and most consistent in tones – backdrop I could find while preserving the general composition. The image above represents the RAW photograph I brought home.

Then, I converted the RAW image via Adobe Bridge and opened it in Adobe Photoshop. Through a Curves adjustment layer, I selected the dark tones in the background and moved the curve downward so as to darken the image (without affecting the highlighted areas). I repeated this process until the entire background turned black, using masks to paint in the effects with the Brush tool and block the adjustments from affecting the white bloom.

While I was able to record the best image possible in the field, by keeping my visualization in my mind from image capture through post-processing activities, my vision (on the left) finally came to light.

**SOUTHERN ARIZONA**

# Tucson Botanical Gardens

*An echinopsis hybrid called "First Light" blooms in the Cactus and Succulent Garden. Canon 5DMII, 100mm macro, ISO 400, f/11 @ 1/80 sec. Colleen Miniuk-Sperry*

**BLOOM TIME**
March to August

**IDEAL TIME OF DAY**
Early morning to late afternoon

**VEHICLE**
Any

**HIKE**
Easy

The idiom "Good things come in small packages" certainly helps describe the Tucson Botanical Gardens when it comes to wildflowers. Though small in size (just over 5 acres (2 hectares)), this little desert sanctuary in the middle of a bustling urban area showcases a bountiful bloom each spring and summer, offering a perfect mid-day get-away while exploring other Tucson hot spots like Catalina State Park (see page 198) and Saguaro National Park-West (see page 210).

Depending on the winter rains and warmth, beginning in late February through March, popular desert annuals and perennials like Mexican gold poppies, Coulter's lupine, owl clover, desert marigolds, and chuparosa make appearances in the appropriately named Wildflower Garden, Aloe Alley, and the Butterfly Garden. A fast shutter speed (e.g. 1/200th of a second or faster) while using either a **macro** or **telephoto lens** can help freeze butterflies in mid-flight as they search for nectar from the season's bounty.

Each April, while yellow columbine and fairy duster bloom in these same areas, the Iris Garden begins to boast an impressive array of photogenic iris. Showy flowers like Mexican hat and blanketflower continue to sprout through May. As summer temperatures rise during June and July, so do the number of cacti in bloom, especially in—not surprisingly—the Cactus and Succulent Garden. Flowering paloverde trees provide welcomed relief from the hot sun but also can create uneven dappled light across colorful scenes.

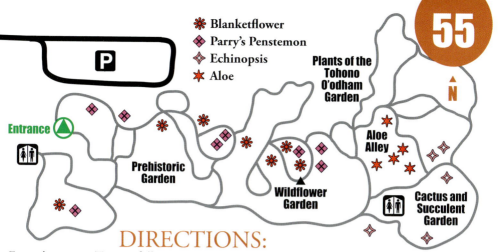

## DIRECTIONS:

From downtown Tucson, follow I-10 north to Grant Road (exit #257). Turn right and drive 4.8 miles (7.7 km). Turn right onto Alvernon Way. Drive 0.1 miles (0.2 km) and then turn left into the small gravel parking lot. If this lot is full, visitors are permitted to park in the shopping center parking area to the north.

Tucson Botanical Gardens opens its gates every day year-round from 8:30 a.m. until 4:30 p.m., except for Independence Day, Thanksgiving Day, Christmas Eve and Day, and New Year's Day. An admission fee is charged. For more information, visit **www.tucsonbotanical.org**.

*White evening primrose blooms among verbena. Canon 5DMII, 100mm macro, ISO 400, f/6.3 @ 1/100 sec. Colleen Miniuk-Sperry*

Pack a **diffuser**, **reflector**, and/or **artificial flash** to manage any unwanted contrasts you might find.

Although the garden restricts travels to the defined paths, ample trailside flowers allow photographers to explore blooms from a multitude of close-range angles—varying from top-down to a bug's perspective. Should you wish to photograph a flower from the side, keep the front of your lens parallel to the plane of the stem (which gives the photographer a better chance of keeping the stem and center part of the flower in focus given the narrow depth of field inherent to macro and telephoto lenses).

The garden encourages photography for personal usage. However, commercial and advertising uses are prohibited unless the photographer has obtained previous written consent from the Tucson Botanical Gardens.

## Blanketflower

*Gaillardia pulchella*
**Blooms:** April to September along roadsides, fields, and forests at elevations between 3,500 and 5,500 feet (1,067 and 1,676 m). (Annual)
**Fun Fact:** Likely due to its resemblance to woven Native American blankets, this fiery-colored flower is also referred to as "Indian blanket."

**SOUTHERN ARIZONA**

# Mount Lemmon

*During monsoons, western sneezeweed thrive in the wet soil near the peak. Canon 5DMII, 24-105mm at 24mm, ISO 100, f/22 @ 1/60 sec. Paul Gill*

**BLOOM TIME**
**July to August**

**IDEAL TIME OF DAY**
**Sunrise to late afternoon**

**VEHICLE**
**Any**

**HIKE**
**Moderate**

No doubt you have heard the idiom, "If you can't take the heat, get out of the kitchen." With the scorching hot temperatures and soaring humidity common during the monsoon season, those living in the Arizona desert might instead say, "If you can't take the heat, head to Mount Lemmon."

Though the Aspen Fire in June 2003 forever changed this idyllic landscape, this high-alpine oasis situated at nearly 9,000 feet (2,743 m) elevation offers not only a convenient escape from summer's wrath but also an excellent chance to see bountiful sun-loving wildflowers during July and August.

Start at sunrise along the easy-going Meadow Trail with a **wide-angle lens**, **polarizer**, **graduated neutral density filter**, **tripod**, and **cable release** in hand. A short 0.4 mile (0.6 km) stroll will quickly reveal serene meadows filled with western sneezeweed and lemon beebalm intermixing with shaded forests dotted with fleabane, Richardson's geranium, and wood sorrel. When you reach the large fallen log across the trail, venture into the recovering burned area on the left-hand (southeast) side of the track to photograph an endless sea of yellow western sneezeweed sprouting next to charred stumps.

Though tempting, do not dwell too long if you wish to visit other locations atop Mount Lemmon. Start heading to the Marshall Gulch Trailhead by mid-morning before the parking area fills with desert dwellers trying to escape the heat. From this popular trailhead, two different trails offer abundant flowering subjects perfect for macro photography: the Sunset and the Marshall Gulch trails.

The moderately difficult Sunset Trail starts along the creek, where yellow columbine and scarlet cinquefoil flourish but quickly rises out of

*Backlit wood sorrel along the Marshall Gulch Trail. Canon 5DMII, 100-400mm at 400mm, ISO 400, f/11 @ 1/160 sec. Colleen Miniuk-Sperry*

**SOUTHERN ARIZONA**

# Mount Lemmon

ABOVE: Yellow columbines bloom next to a small cascade in Marshall Gulch. Canon 5DMII, 24-105mm at 41mm, ISO 100, f/22 @ 1/8 sec.
RIGHT: Cutleaf coneflowers in Marshall Gulch. Canon 5DMII, 24-105mm at 41mm, ISO 100, f/11 @ 1/25 sec., reflector. Both by Paul Gill

the stream bed to skirt the side of the mountain. When the trail makes a hairpin turn about a half mile (0.8 km) from the parking area, hillsides of wild geranium, wood sorrel, and western yarrow appear in areas where the Aspen Fire left its mark.

Alternately, the informal Marshall Gulch Trail follows a shallow perennial creek teeming with photogenic wildflowers like cutleaf coneflower, yellow columbine, and monkeyflower. Large patches of wood sorrel and Indian paintbrush grow on the southern hillsides overlooking the trail within the first half mile (0.8 km). Water shoes aren't necessary, but you might bring a hiking pole or use your tripod to help you cross rockier sections of the creek bed. Since poison ivy grows along the trail, wear long pants.

No matter which path you choose, put your **macro** and **telephoto lenses** in your backpack along with **extension tubes**, **close-up filters**, or **bellows**. Since the flowers grow beneath a canopy of conifers, dappled light often occurs on the blooms, so also bring a **diffuser** and **reflector** to help even the mid-day contrast between highlights and shadows. A tripod and cable release will also come in handy as you compose scenes low to the ground.

As you drive out of the trailhead, watch for Hooker's evening primrose along the roadside. True to its name, the yellow blooms open and reach to the sky towards the end of the day.

Afternoon storms commonly roll through this "sky island," so dress in layers and pack rain gear for you and your camera to shoot through a passing shower. Head indoors if lightning is in the area.

Also, stay "bear-aware." Since this is black bear country, avoid hiking alone or at dark. As you hike, make some noise to help prevent a surprise encounter.

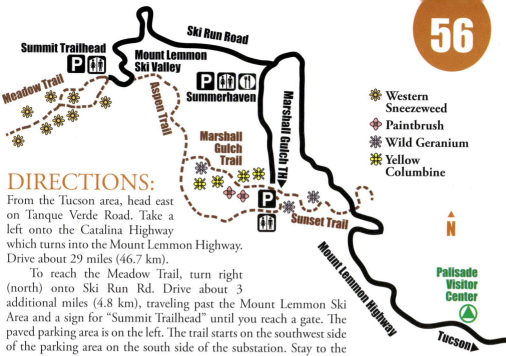

- ❋ Western Sneezeweed
- ✣ Paintbrush
- ❋ Wild Geranium
- ❋ Yellow Columbine

## DIRECTIONS:

From the Tucson area, head east on Tanque Verde Road. Take a left onto the Catalina Highway which turns into the Mount Lemmon Highway. Drive about 29 miles (46.7 km).

To reach the Meadow Trail, turn right (north) onto Ski Run Rd. Drive about 3 additional miles (4.8 km), traveling past the Mount Lemmon Ski Area and a sign for "Summit Trailhead" until you reach a gate. The paved parking area is on the left. The trail starts on the southwest side of the parking area on the south side of the substation. Stay to the right on the signed Meadow Trail when the trail splits.

To reach the Marshall Gulch Trailhead, veer left instead when the Mount Lemmon Highway splits towards Summerhaven. Continue another 1.4 miles (2.3 km), passing several parking areas on the left, before reaching the last dirt parking area. The unmarked Sunset Trail starts on the southernmost end of this parking area.

The formal Marshall Gulch Trail starts on the northwest side of this same lot. While there are flowers on this signed higher trail, follow the creek on an unmarked trail (informally referred to as the Marshall Gulch Trail as well) that begins behind the pit toilets.

A federally-issued "America the Beautiful" annual pass or a Coronado Recreational Pass is required. For more information, visit the Coronado National Forest website at **www.fs.fed.us/r3/coronado**.

## Lemon Beebalm

*Monarda citriodora*
**Blooms:** July to October in oak woodlands and ponderosa pine forests between 3,000 and 9,600 feet (914 and 2,926 m) elevation. (Annual)
**Fun Fact:** When rubbed together, the leaves of lemon beebalm have a distinct citrus or lemony aroma.

**SOUTHERN ARIZONA**

# Saguaro National Park - West

*Backlit blooming yellow paloverde trees and saguaro cacti. Canon 5DMII, 100-400mm at 115mm, ISO 400, f/11 @ 1/80 sec. Colleen Miniuk-Sperry*

**BLOOM TIME**
Late February to May; August

**IDEAL TIME OF DAY**
Early morning ; sunset

**VEHICLE**
Any

**HIKE**
Easy to moderate

Established in 1994, Saguaro National Park protects vast stands of saguaro cactus in two distinct sections located 30 miles (48.3 km) apart on either side of Tucson. When late February rolls around, photographers should heed the mantra of the early pioneers and "Go West!"

A short one mile (1.6 km) round-trip hike up stone steps on the Signal Hill Petroglyph Trail in the Saguaro West district leads not only to views of ancient writings pecked into the volcanic rocks—worth seeing with or without wildflowers—but also astounding views of the bajada, where desert annuals, perennials, and stately saguaro cacti bloom beneath the Tucson Mountains.

Starting in late February, gatherings of Coulter's lupine, Mexican gold poppies, and desert globemallow scatter across the desert floor, creating a picture-perfect medley of purples, yellows, and oranges through March. In April, the brittlebush bursts into gold, adding a splash of color to the surrounding Signal Hill petroglyphs and saguaros near the Cactus Wren Trail.

A **wide-angle lens**, **tripod**, **polarizer**, and **graduated neutral density filters** will help to capture an expansive scene when facing south at sunset. As the sun drops below the horizon, turn to the west and find a shapely saguaro to silhouette against the colorful sky.

In May, as the weather warms up, the saguaro cacti begin showing off delicate creamy-white flowers. Each morning, the saguaro cactus flower opens, then closes as the sun goes down, which ironically is the best time to photograph here. A neighboring flower opens the next morning until the entire bouquet has bloomed. Because the time frame to photograph these flowers is short, if you see a composition you like, shoot it immediately, because you won't get a second chance!

Since each flower blooms independently, it is unusual to find a collection of saguaro cactus flowers blooming simultaneously in a large bunch. If you do run into this gorgeous work of art by Mother Nature, find a way to photograph it using side or back light regardless of the time of day.

*A gilded flicker perches on saguaro cactus blooms. Canon 5DMII, 100-400mm at 400mm, 1.4 teleconverter, ISO 1000, f/5.6 @ 1/600 sec. Paul Gill*

You may be surprised to find that many cactus blooms are higher than you are tall and require you to stand on your car roof, a step-stool, or a large rock to get at eye-level with most of the blooms. Your best bet is to bring a **telephoto lens** and tripod to photograph individual blooms or bouquets from a distance with your feet on the ground. If you find flowers lower to the ground, use a **macro lens** to isolate the single bloom or take a few steps backwards to get a slightly broader view of the whole bunch together.

Look for clumps of odd numbers—three or five blooms together—to produce a more balanced composition. If the horizon is not in your frame, consider tilting your camera to one side or the other in a "Dutch tilt" (see page 150) to create a diagonal line with the flowers and consequently a more dynamic, pleasing composition.

Return to this same area again in August as dramatic storms usher in a spectacular monsoon bloom of barrel cacti and Arizona caltrops. Because temperatures here can easily exceed 100 degrees Fahrenheit (38 degrees Celsius), bring along a wide-brimmed hat, sunscreen, and plenty of drinking water.

## Saguaro Cactus

*Carnegiea gigantea*
**Blooms:** May to June on rocky slopes and dry flats in between 600 to 3,600 feet (183 to 1,097 m) in the Sonoran Desert. (Perennial)
**Fun Fact:** In 1903, scientists from the Carnegie Institution of Washington assigned the scientific name to this cactus.

# Saguaro National Park - West

SOUTHERN ARIZONA

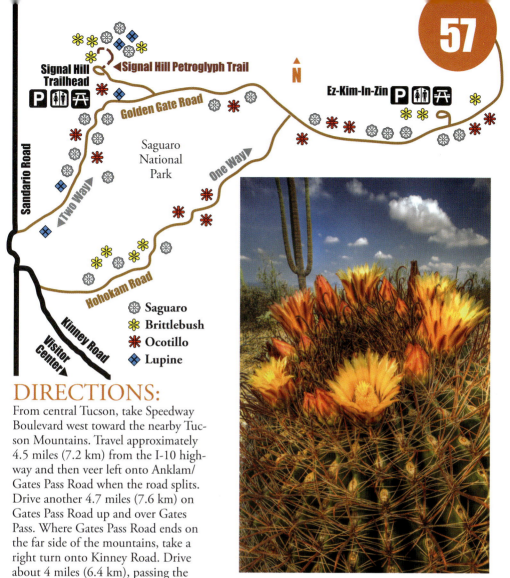

ABOVE: Barrel cactus blooming in August. Canon 5DMII, TS-E 24mm, ISO 100.
LEFT: Cluster of saguaro cactus blooms. Canon 5DMII, TS-E 24mm, ISO 100. Both by Paul Gill

## DIRECTIONS:

From central Tucson, take Speedway Boulevard west toward the nearby Tucson Mountains. Travel approximately 4.5 miles (7.2 km) from the I-10 highway and then veer left onto Anklam/Gates Pass Road when the road splits. Drive another 4.7 miles (7.6 km) on Gates Pass Road up and over Gates Pass. Where Gates Pass Road ends on the far side of the mountains, take a right turn onto Kinney Road. Drive about 4 miles (6.4 km), passing the Arizona-Sonora Desert Museum on the left, until the road splits. Veer right to continue following Kinney Road.

The Saguaro National Park Visitors Center will be on the right hand side of the road. Stop here first to pay your entrance fee or show your "America the Beautiful" annual pass issued by the National Park Service.

From the Visitors Center, continue on Kinney Road until it ends at Sandario Road. Take a right onto Sandario Road and drive around the bend for less than a half mile (0.8 km), taking a right onto the first unpaved road on the right hand side of the road, which is Golden Gate Road. Drive 1.5 miles (2.4 km) until you see the turnoff to the Signal Hill Picnic Area. Turn left at the turnoff, and drive about a half mile (0.8 km) to the parking area for Signal Hill. The Signal Hill Petroglyph Trailhead is on the northeastern side of the parking area.

For more information, visit the Saguaro National Park website at **www.nps.gov/sagu/index.htm**.

## SOUTHERN ARIZONA
# Arizona-Sonora Desert Museum

*Blanketflower in the Desert Garden. Canon 5DMII,100mm macro, ISO 200, f/29 @ 0.3 sec., diffuser. Colleen Miniuk-Sperry*

**BLOOM TIME**
March to May; August to September

**IDEAL TIME OF DAY**
Early morning to late afternoon

**VEHICLE**
Any

**HIKE**
Easy

Established in 1952, the Arizona-Sonora Desert Museum celebrates Arizona's largest desert and aims to encourage visitors to have a better appreciation for this magnificent ecosystem. Located about 25 miles (40.2 km) west of Tucson, this world-renowned zoo, museum, and botanical garden offers a convenient place to shoot an excellent collection of wildflowers and cactus blooms beginning in early March and often lasting through September.

Plan on a full day here, as there are three distinct locations that offer a multitude of intimate compositions best captured through a **macro** and **telephoto lens**. Though the gardens are beautiful, broad landscape scenes are not the main feature, so you can leave the wide-angle lens at home. Pack instead a **tripod**, **cable release**, **reflector**, and **diffuser**.

Start your visit at opening time (7:30 a.m. from March to May and 7:00 a.m. from June to September) to capture the flowers at their freshest and to beat the afternoon heat. Upon entering the museum, turn left onto the Desert Loop Trail and head to the Pollination Gardens. As you mosey down the easy-to-follow, well-maintained gravel path, keep an eye out for the red-tipped ocotillo and delicate cactus blooms along either side of the trail.

The abundant wildflowers found in the Pollination Garden provide excellent opportunities for close-up work. Using a macro lens, get close to an individual flower and use a wide aperture such as f/4.0 or f/5.6 to blur the busy backgrounds. Check your photograph on your camera's screen to ensure the center of the flower, particularly the stamen and pistol, is in focus before moving onto another composition.

For added appeal, follow a butterfly, bee, or hummingbird through a telephoto lens, patiently waiting for these pollinators to land on a blooming desert sand verbena, evening primrose, or bird-of-paradise. Before tracking the flying creatures, though, set your camera to a higher ISO speed (such as ISO 400 or faster) and ensure a fast enough shutter speed to freeze action, especially since some of the flower boxes reside under shady mesquite trees

*Mexican bird-of-paradise in the Pollination Garden during August's monsoon bloom. Canon 5DMII, 24-105mm at 85mm, ISO 200, f/11 @ 1/100 sec. Paul Gill*

and thus have less available natural light.

After exhausting the possibilities in the Pollination Garden, locate the dirt shortcut deviating southwest from the main Desert Loop Trail to the Cactus Garden. This area features hundreds of different cactus species ranging from the familiar to the bizarre and often offers the best bloom display in the park. Starting in early March, wildflowers like Mexican gold poppies, desert globemallow, and Coulter's lupine intermingle with their taller cactus neighbors, making possible photographs of single blooms, multiple blooms intermixed with each other, and flowers mixing with nearby cactus. Then in late April and into early May, the cactus blooms start peaking. Finally, in August and September, barrel cactus and Arizona caltrop blooms flourish. To help isolate these various types of scenes, use a short depth of field (such as f/4 or f/5.6) in conjunction with a macro or telephoto lens.

When you've finished photographing the Cactus Garden, visit the small Desert Garden area to see chocolate flower, blanketflower, and scorpionweed bursting with color in flower boxes under littleleaf paloverde trees. These native trees provide some shade, but a diffuser or reflector may help balance any uneven light falling on your scene.

Since the museum closes before sunset, those interested in additional photography opportunities on this side of the mountain should visit nearby Saguaro National Park (see page 210).

## Chocolate Flower

*Berlandiera lyrata*
**Blooms:** April to October in disturbed soil along roads in between 4,000 and 5,000 feet (1,219 and 1,524 m) elevation. (Perennial)
**Fun Fact:** Known also as "greeneyes," the chocolate flower gives off a faint chocolate smell.

**SOUTHERN ARIZONA**

# Arizona-Sonora Desert Museum

## DIRECTIONS:

From Tucson, take Speedway Boulevard west toward the nearby Tucson Mountains. Travel approximately 4.5 miles (7.2 km) from the I-10 highway, veering left onto Anklam/Gates Pass Road when the road splits. Drive another 4.7 miles (7.6 km) up and over Gates Pass on Gates Pass Road. When the Gates Pass Road ends on the west side of the mountains, take a right onto Kinney Road. Drive about 4 miles (6.4 km), turning left into the museum's parking area.

The museum charges an entrance fee. For more information visit their website at **www.desertmuseum.org**.

*Century plants bloom in the Cactus Garden. Nikon N90s, 24-70mm at 24mm, Fuji Velvia 50, f/11 @ 1/100 sec. Paul Gill*

**PHOTO TIP 16**

## Extend Your Opportunities

While a macro lens is perhaps the best known way to maximize close-focusing capabilities, photographers can also utilize close-up filters, extension tubes, and bellows to shorten their working distance while keeping perfect focus on a beautiful bloom.

The cheapest way to achieve closer focus is through a close-up filter. This filter fits on the front of your lens and does not affect the lens-to-sensor distance. Like a magnifying glass, close-up filters come in a variety of strengths or diopters.

If you are more serious about macro photography, consider investing in extension tubes. This hollow accessory's only purpose is to move the lens away from the camera. Available in a variety of sizes, the longer the extension tube, the closer you can get to your subject and stay in focus. Extension tubes are compatible with a variety of lenses of different focal lengths, not just with a macro lens.

Using multiple extension tubes simultaneously increases magnification, but at a small cost. Exposure times may increase and auto-focusing capabilities may not work with more than one

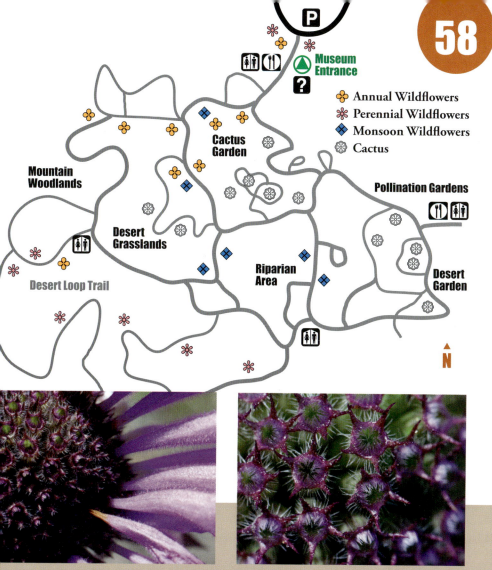

*Using a macro lens with extension tubes can change the composition, as seen with this wild bergamot bloom. LEFT: Pentax 67II, 135mm macro. MIDDLE: Pentax 67II, 135mm macro with #1 extension tube. RIGHT: Pentax 135mm with #1 and #2 extension tubes stacked. All by Paul Gill*

extension tube stacked in between your camera and lens. To resolve these minor challenges, shoot from a tripod, increase your ISO speed, and manually focus. When stacking, make sure the thickest (strongest) one is closest to the base of the camera while the thinnest (weakest) is furthest away.

Unlike fixed-length extension tubes, bellows create space between the lens and the digital sensor in varying degrees of extension as controlled by the photographer. Bellows enable greater capabilities for getting closer to your subject, but at a higher price. They tend to be bigger and heavier than extension tubes.

Any time you extend the lens, focusing gets a little more challenging so you may find using a tripod with focusing rails helps in achieving sharp focus whether you are using close-up filters, extension tubes, or bellows.

# Making the Photo 10

# Focus Stacking

By Paul Gill

*A fishhook barrel cactus thorn with a raindrop. The refraction seen in the water drop is of another fishhook barrel cactus bloom. I made three images at three different depths of field, and then combined them together for the final image seen above. Canon 5DMIII, MP-E 65mm 1-5x, ISO 2000, f/8 @ 1/20 sec. Paul Gill*

Focus stacking is a process in which the photographer records multiple images at varying focus distances and then blends those frames during post-processing to achieve the appearance of extended depth of field. This technique is especially helpful for macro photography, since macro lenses tend to have extremely shallow depth of field—especially as you move closer to your subject matter.

When I first saw the water droplet form at the tip of a fish-hook barrel cactus, I knew I would not be able to record both the cactus spine and drop in focus, even with my smallest aperture. Focus stacking to the rescue!

I started with the sharpest aperture for my 65mm macro lens. Lenses generally produced the sharpest image when set to one or two f-stops smaller than the widest aperture for that lens (a larger aperture may blur due to diffraction, while a smaller aperture requires more light to cover the same depth of field). For example, if your lens' widest aperture is f/2.8, then your sharpest aperture is likely f/4- f/8. Conducting tests at each of the different apertures, though, can help determine the exact setting for your equipment.

Fortunately, calm winds prevailed as I set up my scene. Choosing a non-moving subject also helped! I used a Wimberley Plamp to hold my thorn in place while photographing. I also employed a sturdy tripod and cable release - two essential pieces of equipment to keep the camera steady and all of your frames sharp.

While composing, I positioned my primary subject such that a little extra room was left on all sides (as I would later crop off the outer edge in post-processing). I adjusted the ISO speed and shutter speed settings after taking a few test shots and monitoring my histogram to confirm an appropriate exposure.

I started with the focusing rail positioned as far back as possible to achieve focus on the closest part of the subject. Then, I moved the camera by turning the focus rail dials through the varying depth of fields for my composition—making an image with each small turn. Most focusing rails possess small marks on the axis line to help guide your adjustments between exposures.

Instead of using the focus rail, I could have simply turned the lens' barrel and manually focused on the closest element to the frame. Then, I would use the Live View mode (if available) or a tethered laptop to help confirm my adjustment. I would start to turn the lens barrel ever-so-slightly until the furthest element in my frame is in focus—once again, recording a photograph at each small turn of the lens at different focus points. I don't prefer this method, as changing the focus through the lens barrel can also lead to unsharp images if I accidentally touched the lens while photographing.

After I had a series of multiple images (I aim to record at least eight to ten frames), I selected the set of images in Adobe Bridge. Afterwards, I picked Tools/Photoshop/Load Files Into Photoshop Layers. Once in Adobe Photoshop, I selected File/Auto Blend Layers and used the Stack Images option to result in a blended image.

Adobe Lightroom does not currently have the ability to perform automatic blending of images (without the use of Photoshop), but third-party software like Helicon Soft's Helicon Focus (to which you can export images from Adobe Lightroom) and Zerene Stacker offers similar functionality.

Photo #1 represents a single exposure of this composition. Photo #2 shows the final image after blending three images at three different depths of field. Canon 5DMIII, MP-E 65mm 1-5x, ISO 2000, f/8 @ 1/20 sec. Paul Gill

**SOUTHERN ARIZONA**

# Organ Pipe Cactus National Monument

*Thick carpets of Mexican gold poppies and Coulter's lupine along Ajo Mountain Drive in early March. Super Graphlex 4x5, 135mm, Fuji Velvia 50, f/22 @ 1/8 sec. Paul Gill*

**BLOOM TIME**
Late February to June

**IDEAL TIME OF DAY**
Early afternoon to sunset

**VEHICLE**
2WD high-clearance

**HIKE**
Easy to moderate

Abundant in Mexico, the organ pipe cactus rarely grows in the United States. Not surprisingly, the highest concentration of organ pipe cactus in the country is located in southern Arizona along the Mexico border. The Organ Pipe Cactus National Monument protects and honors this unique pea-green cactus with thin spiny arms rising into the air like a majestic pipe organ. Though winter rains are as rare as the organ pipe cactus in this part of the country, each spring, vivid wildflowers splash color onto an otherwise brown and dry desert.

Start your adventure into this remote backcountry area by driving on the beautiful 21-mile (33.8-km) one-way Ajo Mountain Drive. This maintained dirt road puts you in the heart of the arid Sonoran Desert and spectacular organ pipe cactus territory. Plan on three to four hours to drive this loop *twice*.

*Mexican gold poppies surround the skeleton of a chain fruit cholla. Wista 4x5, 120mm, Fuji Velvia 50, f/32 @ 1/2 sec., warming polarizer. Paul Gill*

Two trips around this road will help you take advantage of the best light for macro and broad scenic shots. It will also allow you enough time to explore other off-the-beaten path spots, depending on where the best blooms are happening during your visit. If you see a good set of flowers during your drive, stop and photograph it as it may not be there next year.

On the first loop, start by capturing smaller scenes with a **macro lens** during the harsher afternoon light not well suited for landscape photography. Wildflowers are best typically in the mostly unnamed washes as you start the drive along Ajo Mountain Drive, as well as on the hillside of the Diablo Mountains near Birdseye Point and the area around Bull Pasture Trailhead.

Keep a keen eye open for flowers near organ pipe or saguaro cactus, using the base of these prickly giants as a background and context for your Mexican gold poppies, Coulter's lupine, or owl clover, which are the dominant blooms in the park starting in late February and lasting through March. Also consider looking for the skeletons of dead saguaro cactus or chain-fruit cholla to add a more dramatic "life versus death" message to your photograph.

Other stops worth checking out include Arch Canyon Trailhead, the bajadas in between miles 10 and 11 (kilometers 16.1 and 17.7) on the Ajo Mountain Drive, and the desert areas about 13 miles (20.9 km) along the loop looking out at Diaz Spire.

If you don't have the time or interest in driving the loop a second time, stopping along the southern part of the Ajo Mountain Drive can yield excellent opportunities to photograph saguaros, organ pipes, or teddybear cholla silhouetted against the colorful sky of the setting sun. As you continue down Ajo Mountain Drive, watch for possible backlit scenes in between miles 15 and 17 (kilometers 24.1 and 27.4) near Teddybear Pass. While a second pass around the one-way loop may sound like a lot of driving, the view from

## Organ Pipe Cactus

*Stenocereus thurberi*
**Blooms:** May to June on rocky hillsides and deserts in between 1,000 and 3,500 feet (305 and 1,067 m). (Perennial)
**Fun Fact:** The Tohono O'odham Indians harvest organ pipe cactus fruit which they eat raw and make into syrups.

**SOUTHERN ARIZONA**

# Organ Pipe Cactus National Monument

*Poppies and owl clover with cholla, saguaro and organ pipe cacti. Super Graphlex 4x5, 135mm, Fuji Velvia 50, f/22 @ 1/100 sec. Paul Gill*

Birdseye Point at sunset is worth every mile. When the one-way section meets the two-way section, turn right and head back around the loop.

Plan on being at Birdseye Point about 30 minutes before sunset to capture an unforgettable broad scenic view of the Diablo Mountains and the expansive bajada below dotted with organ pipe cactus and wildflower blooms. Using a **polarizer** and **graduated neutral density filter** on a **wide-angle lens** will be your best bet in this location. Use a small aperture such as f/16 or f/22 if you place flowers in the foreground to ensure the mountains in the background also appear to be in focus.

Another option if a second time around the loop drive doesn't appeal to you, is to head to Alamo Canyon to the north for sunset instead. Here a plethora of Mexican gold poppies, Coulter's lupine, and owl clover bloom among the organ pipe cacti beneath the rugged Ajo Mountains. Bring a wide-angle lens, polarizer, graduated neutral density filters, and **tripod** to record a magical scene of the desert in bloom.

During your spring visit to the national monument, take notes about photogenic saguaro and organ pipe cacti as well as scenic locations featuring these two desert plants. You will want to return to these locations within the park in May with the same camera gear for the saguaro cactus blooms (which open in the morning) and then again in June for the organ pipe cactus flowers (which open at night). Plan to visit the park early morning or late evening with a macro lens to capture these spectacular moments in nature and to beat the summer heat.

## DIRECTIONS:

From Ajo, travel south on AZ 85 for approximately 33 miles (53.1 km) to Ajo Mountain Drive. The park prohibits vehicles over 24 feet (7.3 m) on this drive.

Before driving the Ajo Mountain Drive, visit the Kris Eggle Visitor Center. Here, you can pick up the inexpensive informative guidebook to Ajo Mountain Drive and pay your required entrance fee to the Organ Pipe Cactus National Monument. This fee is waived when you present an "America the Beautiful" interagency pass.

The turn-off for Alamo Canyon is located 9.9 miles (15.9 km) north of the Ajo Mountain Drive along AZ 85. Travel east onto this bumpy dirt road for about 4 miles (6.4 km).

Because of the remoteness and limited services available near Organ Pipe Cactus National Monument, fill up on gas in Ajo, Why, or Lukeville before visiting the park. Due to the park's close proximity to the Arizona-Mexico border, you may encounter U. S. Border Patrol agents and/or illegal immigrants. Do not intervene with border patrol activities and report any suspicious activity to park rangers immediately.

For more information, visit the Organ Pipe Cactus National Monument website at **www.nps.gov/orpi**.

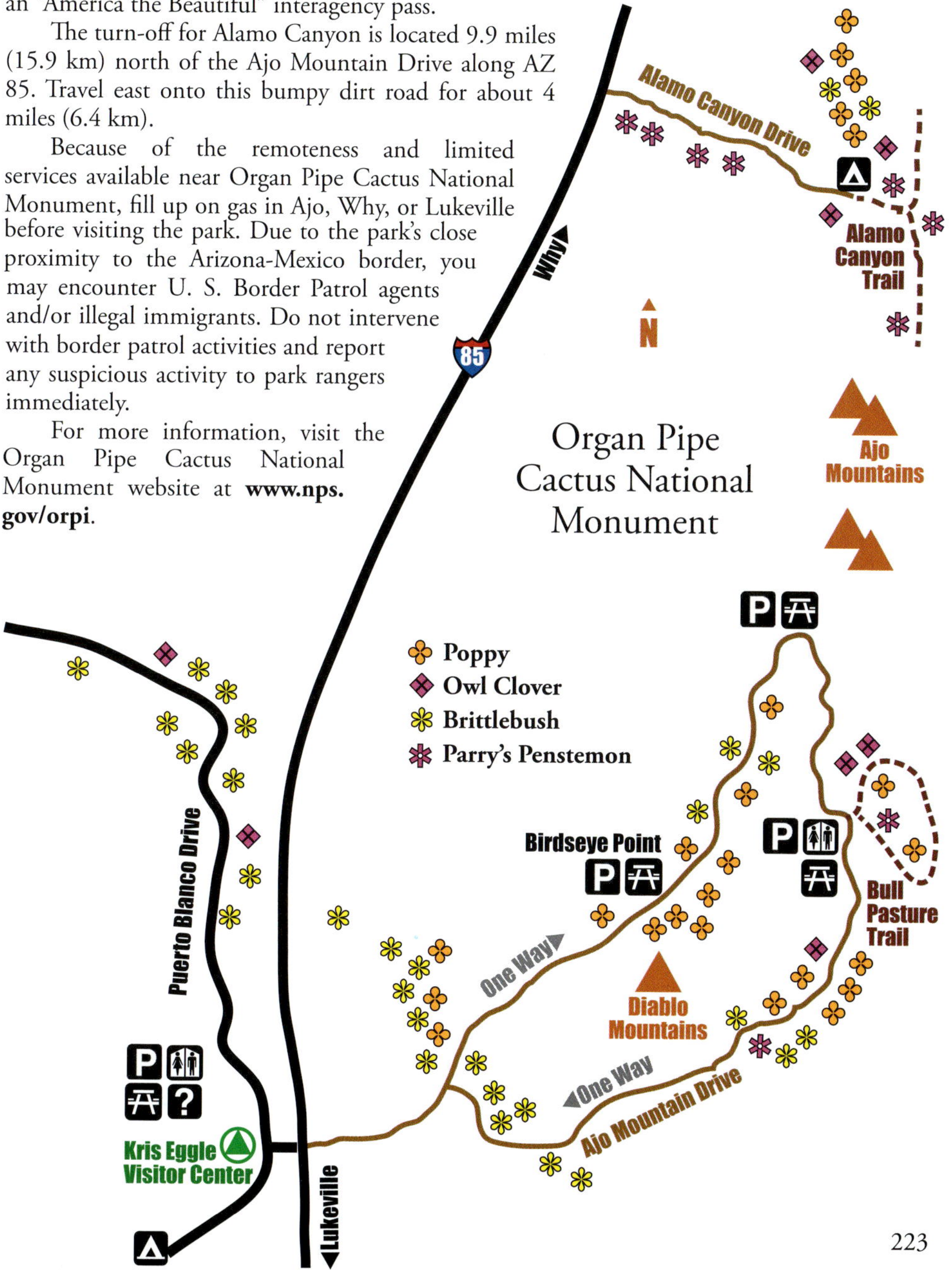

**SOUTHERN ARIZONA**

# Dragoon Mountains

*Arizona caltrop basks in sunset light in August. Wista 4x5, 120mm, Fuji Velvia 100, f/32 @ 1 sec., two-stop graduated neutral density filter. Paul Gill*

**BLOOM TIME**
**May; August to September**

**IDEAL TIME OF DAY**
**Sunset**

**VEHICLE**
**2WD high-clearance**

**HIKE**
**Easy**

Part of the Madrean sky islands, the dramatic Dragoon Mountains once gave refuge to Cochise, a Chiricahua Apache chief, as he battled the United States Army in the late 1800s. Today, while the Cochise Stronghold on the eastern side celebrates his efforts, the western side harbors beautifully blooming wildflowers each spring and summer. And fortunately, you won't have to look as hard as the U. S. Army did for Cochise to discover the best blooms here.

Among the collection of car-sized jumbo rocks, spiny banana yucca scattered across the grasslands beneath the rocky peaks reveal flower stalks overflowing with soft, bulbous blooms in May. Then in August, the same area uncovers a showy low-desert monsoon bloom of Arizona caltrop, a Mexican gold poppy look-alike. After driving ten miles (16.1 km) on Forest

*New Mexico thistle blooms near a banana yucca. Canon 5DMII, 100mm macro, ISO 400, f/11@ 1/2 sec. Paul Gill*

Road 687 from the intersection with Middlemarch Road, the petite white western pepperweed also makes a conspicuous appearance as sacred datura and bluestem pricklepoppy pop up along the roadside.

Though each of these flowers begs a closer look through a macro lens, the best photographic opportunities come at sunset when the radiant last light of day transforms the beige boulders into a lustrous backdrop worthy of filling a memory card. Compose looking north or south with a **wide-angle** or **tilt-shift lens** aimed towards the field of blooms in the foreground. Have a **polarizer** and **graduated neutral density filter** on hand to balance the exposure between the sky and land. Because of the slow shutter speeds common in low light, use a **tripod** and **cable release** to keep your camera steady.

Both of these bloom times occur during hot weather, so pack a hat, sunscreen, and extra water. Since the monsoon storms can develop overhead, you should also bring rain gear for you and your camera. Stay in your vehicle if lightning is present.

## Arizona Caltrop

*Kallstroemia grandiflora*
**Blooms:** July to October in open plains, mesas, desert slopes, and roadsides below 5,000 feet (1,524 m). (Annual)
**Fun Fact:** Called the "summer poppy," this flower blooms during monsoon season after abundant rain.

**SOUTHERN ARIZONA**

# Dragoon Mountains

*Western pepperweed covers the desert along Middlemarch Road. Wista 6X9 back on a Wista 4x5. Nikkor 90mm, Kodak VS 100, f/32 @ 1/2 sec., two-stop graduated neutral density filter. Paul Gill*

**PHOTO TIP 17**

## Breaking the Rules

Composition rules provide instruction on how to put together unrelated visual elements, while exposure guidelines explain how to capture just the right amount of light with our exposure settings. Following these standard rules of composition and exposure often yield pleasant, well-executed, and technically-sound photographs. But sometimes these so-called "perfect images" look a little boring. They might lack emotion or that indefinable "wow" factor.

Rules were made to be broken, right? Once you have a solid understanding and consistently deliver to the composition and exposure principles, throw out the entire rule book! The less you conform to any rules, the more creatively you're likely to see. Plan on a little experimentation and a lot fun in the field with these rule-breaking techniques.

First, look for a bloom with a subtle pattern, color, or form to emphasize, and then intentionally add two to three stops of light from what the camera meter suggests to make the entire background white. Don't worry about your resulting histogram if it shows you have severely overexposed the frame. You meant to do it this way!

Then, try photographing out of focus on purpose. Turn off autofocus (AF) and manually

## DIRECTIONS:

From Benson, head southeast on AZ 80 towards Tombstone. Follow AZ 80 for about 14.5 miles (23.3 km) until you reach the unpaved Middlemarch Road on the left hand side of the road. Turn left onto Middlemarch Road and drive about 10 miles (16.1 km). Turn left onto Forest Service Road 687 and drive about 5 miles (8.1 km) for the best flowers.

There are no formal parking areas, but previously used pullouts and multiple side tracks along the route provide a safe place to park.

- Banana Yucca
- Arizona Caltrop
- Western Pepperweed
- New Mexico Thistle

*Moving the camera in a fluid motion from top to bottom during the exposure creates an abstract view of the wildflowers. The wind moved the lupine from side to side during the exposure, creating unexpected wavy lines. Canon 5D, 100mm macro, ISO 50, f/32 @ 1 sec. Colleen Miniuk-Sperry*

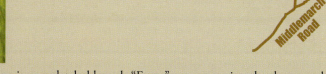

adjust your focus until the scene is completely blurred. "Focus" on composing the shapes and colors in a harmonious way.

Or take your camera off your tripod and move the camera during your exposure for a more impressionistic perspective. Slow your shutter speed down to one quarter of a second or slower. As you press the shutter, move your camera in any direction. Experiment with a variety of movements at different speeds as each attempt will render slightly different results.

Similarly, if you have a zoom lens, you can twist the zoom in or out while the shutter is open. Center your subject and slow your shutter speed down to one quarter of a second or slower to allow enough time to record the motion. Post-processing software can recreate this effect (called a radial blur).

Keep in mind that breaking the rules should be an intentional activity aimed to achieve a specific effect or emotion. Before you photograph, think deeply about your subject matter and how your subject could benefit from going outside the traditional boundaries of photography.

*Wild common sunflowers on the hillsides of Robinson Crater near Sunset Crater National Monument. Canon 5DMIII, 16-35mm at 16mm, ISO 800, f/22 @ 1/100 sec., polarizer. Paul Gill*

# APPENDIX

# Additional Resources

Ayer, Eleanor. H., *Arizona Wildflowers* (Phoenix, AZ: Renaissance House Publishers, 1989)

Bowers, N., Bowers, R., & Tekiela, S., *Wildflowers of Arizona Field Guide* (Cambridge, MN: Adventure Publications, 2008)

Desert Botanical Garden Staff and Arizona Highways Staff, *Arizona Wildflowers: A Year-Round Guide to Nature's Blooms* (Phoenix, AZ: Arizona Highways Books, 2006)

Epple, A., *A Field Guide to the Plants of Arizona.* 2nd edition (Helena, MT: Falcon Publishing Inc., 2012)

Spellenberg, R., *Sonoran Desert Wildflowers: A Guide to Common Plants.* 2nd edition (Helena, MT: Falcon, 2012)

*A hanging saguaro arm blooms against the sky in Saguaro National Park. Canon 5DMII, TS-E 24mm, ISO 100, f/8 @ 1/25 sec., reflector. Paul Gill*

# Bloom Calendar

| # | Location | Pg. | Feb | Mar | Apr | May |
|---|---|---|---|---|---|---|
| 23 | Cabeza Prieta National Wildlife Refuge | 94 | W | W | | |
| 14 | Oatman | 68 | W | W | W/S | |
| 48 | Peridot Mesa | 180 | W | W | W | W/C |
| 59 | Organ Pipe Cactus National Monument | 220 | W | W | C/S | C |
| 57 | Saguaro National Park - West | 210 | W | W | W/C/S | C/T |
| 16 | Buckskin Mountain State Park | 72 | | W/C | | |
| 51 | Picacho Peak State Park | 192 | | W/S | | |
| 22 | Kofa National Wildlife Refuge | 90 | | W/C/S | | |
| 18 | Eagletail Mountains Wilderness | 76 | | W | W | |
| 19 | Saddle Mountain | 78 | | W | W | |
| 36 | Silver King Mine Road | 134 | | W | W | |
| 17 | Gibraltar Mountain Wilderness | 74 | | W | W/S | |
| 31 | Lost Dutchman State Park | 120 | | W | W/S | |
| 32 | Silly Mountain | 124 | | W | W/S | |
| 45 | The Rolls | 168 | | W | W/S | |
| 20 | Lake Pleasant Regional Park | 82 | | W/S | W/S | |
| 25 | Bartlett Lake | 102 | | W/S | W/S | |
| 26 | Lost Dog Wash Trail | 108 | | W/S | W/C/S | |
| 15 | Tres Alamos Wilderness | 70 | | W/S | W/T/S | |
| 34 | Hewitt Canyon | 128 | | W | W/S | C/T |
| 21 | White Tank Mountain Regional Park | 88 | | W | W/C/S | W/C/T |
| 30 | San Tan Mountain Regional Park | 118 | | W | W/C/T/S | W/C/T/S |
| 29 | Pass Mountain Trail | 116 | | W/S | W/S | C |
| 53 | Catalina State Park | 198 | | W/S | W/S | C/T |
| 24 | Go John Trail | 100 | | W/S | W/C/S | C/T |
| 33 | Peralta Road | 126 | | W/S | W/C/S | C/T |
| 50 | Pinal Pioneer Parkway | 188 | | W/S | W/C/S | C/T |
| 43 | Black Mesa | 162 | | W/S | W/C/S | W/C |
| 27 | Desert Botanical Garden | 110 | | W | W/C | W/C/T |
| 28 | South Mountain Park | 114 | | W | W/C/S | C |

**Bloom Time:** **W**=Wildflower; **C**=Cactus; **T**=Tree; **S**=Shrub

| Jun | Jul | Aug | Sep | Ideal Time of Day | Vehicle | Hike |
|---|---|---|---|---|---|---|
| | | | | Sunrise and sunset | 4WD HC | M |
| | | | | Late afternoon to sunset | Any | E |
| | | | | Early morning to late afternoon | 2WD HC | E / M |
| **C** | | | | Early afternoon to sunset | 2WD HC | E / M |
| | | **W/C** | | Early morning; sunset | Any | E / M |
| | | | | Sunrise and sunset | Any | S |
| | | | | Sunrise to sunset | Any | M |
| | | | | Early morning; sunset | 2WD HC | M |
| | | | | Sunrise | 2WD HC | E |
| | | | | Sunrise and sunset | 2WD HC | E |
| | | | | Sunset | 2WD HC | S |
| | | | | Sunrise and sunset | Any | E |
| | | | | Early afternoon to sunset | Any | M |
| | | | | Early afternoon to sunset | Any | M |
| | | | | Early morning to late afternoon | 2WD HC | S |
| | | | | Late afternoon to sunset | Any | M |
| | | | | Sunrise to late morning; sunset | Any | E |
| | | | | Early to late morning | Any | M |
| | | | | Sunrise and sunset | 2WD HC | E |
| | | | | Sunrise and sunset | 2WD HC | M |
| | | | | Sunrise; late afternoon | Any | E |
| | | | | Sunrise and sunset | Any | M |
| | | | | Sunrise to late morning | Any | M |
| | | | | Late afternoon to sunset | Any | M |
| | | | | Early morning; late afternoon to sunset | Any | M |
| | | | | Sunrise to late morning | Any | E |
| | | | | Sunrise to sunset | Any | M |
| | | | | Sunrise | Any/4WD HC | S |
| **C** | | | | Early morning to late afternoon | Any | E |
| **C** | | | | Early morning; late afternoon to sunset | Any | E |

231

# Bloom Calendar

| #  | Location | Pg. | Feb | Mar | Apr | May |
|----|----------|-----|-----|-----|-----|-----|
| 35 | Boyce Thompson Arboretum | 132 |  | W/S | W/C/S | W/C |
| 46 | Apache Trail | 170 |  | W/S | W/C/S | W/C/T |
| 44 | Cline Cabin Road | 166 |  | W | W/C/S | W/C/T/S |
| 54 | Tohono Chul | 200 |  | W/S | W/C/S | W/C/T/S |
| 55 | Tucson Botanical Gardens | 204 |  | W/S | W/C/S | W/C/T/S |
| 58 | Arizona-Sonora Desert Museum | 214 |  | W/S | W/C/S | W/C |
| 42 | Forest Service Road 419 | 158 |  |  | W | W/C |
| 37 | General Crook Trail | 142 |  |  | W/C | W/C |
| 52 | Ironwood Forest National Monument | 194 |  |  |  | C/T |
| 10 | Red Canyon | 56 |  |  |  | W/C/S |
| 8  | West Fork of Oak Creek | 50 |  |  |  | W |
| 41 | Hannagan Meadow | 152 |  |  |  | W |
| 12 | Mormon Lake | 60 |  |  |  | W |
| 60 | Dragoon Mountains | 224 |  |  |  | W/C |
| 9  | Schnebly Hill Road | 54 |  |  |  | W/S |
| 47 | Workman Creek | 176 |  |  |  |  |
| 5  | The Arboretum at Flagstaff | 42 |  |  |  |  |
| 38 | Fool Hollow Lake Recreation Area | 144 |  |  |  |  |
| 1  | Grand Canyon National Park - North Rim | 30 |  |  |  |  |
| 40 | Thompson Trail | 148 |  |  |  |  |
| 56 | Mount Lemmon | 206 |  |  |  |  |
| 3  | Hart Prairie | 38 |  |  |  |  |
| 4  | Arizona Snowbowl | 40 |  |  |  |  |
| 13 | Ashurst Lake | 64 |  |  |  |  |
| 7  | Sunset Crater National Monument | 48 |  |  |  |  |
| 2  | Grand Canyon National Park - South Rim | 36 |  |  |  |  |
| 49 | Treasure Park | 186 |  |  |  |  |
| 6  | Robinson Crater | 46 |  |  |  |  |
| 11 | Lake Mary | 58 |  |  |  |  |
| 39 | Scott Reservoir Area | 146 |  |  |  |  |

**Bloom Time:** **W**=Wildflower; **C**=Cactus; **T**=Tree; **S**=Shrub

| Jun | Jul | Aug | Sep | Ideal Time of Day | Vehicle | Hike |
|---|---|---|---|---|---|---|
| W/C | | | | Early morning to late afternoon | Any | E |
| W/C | | | | Late morning to sunset | Any | E |
| W/C/T/S | | | | Early afternoon to sunset | 2WD HC | E |
| W/C/T/S | W/C | W/C | | Early morning to late afternoon | Any | E |
| W/C/T/S | W/C | W/C | | Early morning to late afternoon | Any | E |
| | | W/C | W/C | Early morning to late afternoon | Any | E |
| | | | | Sunrise | 2WD HC | E |
| | W | W | | Sunrise to sunset | Any | E |
| | | | | Sunrise | 2WD HC | E |
| | | | | Late afternoon to sunset | Any | E / M |
| W | W | W | | Early morning | Any | E |
| W/S | W | W | | Late afternoon to sunset | Any | E |
| W | W/S | W/S | W/S | Late afternoon to sunset | Any | E |
| | | W | W | Sunset | 2WD HC | E |
| W/S | W | W | | Early afternoon to sunset | 2WD/4WD HC | E |
| W | W | | | Early morning | 2WD HC | E / M |
| W | W | W | | Mid-day | Any | E |
| W | W | W | W | Sunrise and sunset | Any | E |
| | W | W | | Early afternoon to sunset | Any | E |
| | W | W | | Early morning | Any | M |
| | W | W | | Sunrise to late afternoon | Any | M |
| | W/S | W/S | | Sunset | 2WD/4WD HC | E |
| | W | W | W | Late afternoon to sunset | Any | M |
| | W/C | W | W | Late afternoon to sunset | Any | E |
| | W/S | W/S | | Sunrise and sunset | 4WD HC | E |
| | W/S | W/S | W/S | Sunrise and sunset | Any | E |
| | W/T | W/T | W/T | Sunrise and sunset | 2WD HC | E |
| | | W | | Late afternoon to sunset | 4WD HC | M / S |
| | | W | | Sunrise and sunset | Any | E |
| | | W/S | W/S | Sunset | Any | E |

*If you enjoyed this book, you will love this one too!*

# Discover the most photogenic locations in
# ACADIA NATIONAL PARK

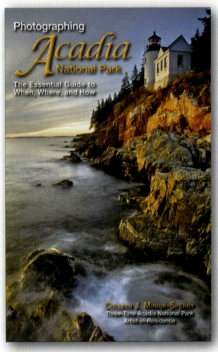

Make your own spectacular photographs of Acadia with the award-winning guidebook, ***Photographing Acadia National Park: The Essential Guide to When, Where, and How*** by three-time Acadia Artist-in-Residence, author, and photographer, Colleen Miniuk-Sperry!

- 224 pages with over 180 inspiring color photographs
- 50 locations with photo tips & directions
- 18-page "Photography Basics" section
- 12 "Making the Photo" stories
- A Shoot Calendar to help plan your visit

TRAVEL/TRAVEL GUIDE BOOK | BEST TRAVEL GUIDE/ESSAY | BEST INTERIOR DESIGN

TRAVEL: GUIDES & ESSAYS | BEST INTERIOR DESIGN

*10% of this book's profits are donated to the* **SCHOODIC EDUCATION ADVENTURE,** *a residential program in Acadia National Park for children!*

ANALEMMA PRESS

Order the book/eBook today at
# WWW.PHOTOACADIA.COM

# ARIZONA
## HIGHWAYS
### Photo Workshops

### EDUCATE    MOTIVATE    INSPIRE

Arizona Highways Photo Workshops are exciting photo adventures for small groups of photographers of all skill levels. We provide unique photographic experiences in Arizona, the Southwest and all over the United States Our photographers will teach you techniques in the field that will enrich your photography, getting you "to the right place at the right time" for the best possible photographs.

*For more information call or visit our website for a complete schedule or to request our current brochure.*

### ahpw.org

Register for any four-plus day photo workshop and receive 10% off.
Enter promo code AHPWAZ2. Valued up to $250. Applies to new customers only.

## 602-712-2004 or toll free 888-790-7042

*Images courtesy of Colleen Miniuk-Sperry*

# ENLARGE YOUR VISION...

When you've finally got the perfect image, our Photo Imaging Center can help you turn it into something extrodinary. From framed photographic prints to archival inkjet prints on canvas, to giant prints that will cover your wall, we have the expertise to make your vision stand out - in your home, office, website or gallery show.

PHOTO IMAGING CENTER • SALES • RENTALS • REPAIRS
606 and 530 W University Drive, Tempe Arizona
480.966.6954    800.836.7374    TempeCamera.com

*Exclusive Offer- Get 10% off Clik Elite™ gear!*

The Venture 35 from Clik Elite™

Use the promo code: **CEB10** at www.clikelite.com for 10% off your order!

**for adventure photographers**
clikelite.com | 888.532.2545

With over 25 years of experience in the outdoor industry, Clik Elite™ has built photography packs for some of the most challenging and demanding activities. Made with only the best materials, our products are designed to provide an effective workflow, with both comfort and stability in mind.

## Flower Viewing Duo

**Inspired Imaging Tools**tm

www.HoodmanUSA.com     800.818.3946

# Boyce Thompson Arboretum

Against the stunning backdrop of Picketpost Mountain, visit this paradise for plant lovers, photographers, birders, and nature enthusiasts.

### Only an hour's drive from downtown Phoenix

520.689.2811     37615 E US Highway 60, Superior, AZ 85173     arboretum.ag.arizona.e

# Singh-Ray Filters
*capture what you imagine*

## www.singh-ray.com

Jack Graham shot this photo with the Singh-Ray Mor-Slo™ 10-stop solid neutral density filter.

Just minutes later, Jack shot this photo with a leading competitive solid neutral density filter. Note the pronounced blue cast.

**Save 10% on Singh-Ray filters with discount code EVmag10**

800-486-5501 or 863-993-4100
2721 SE Highway 31, Arcadia, FL 34266-7974

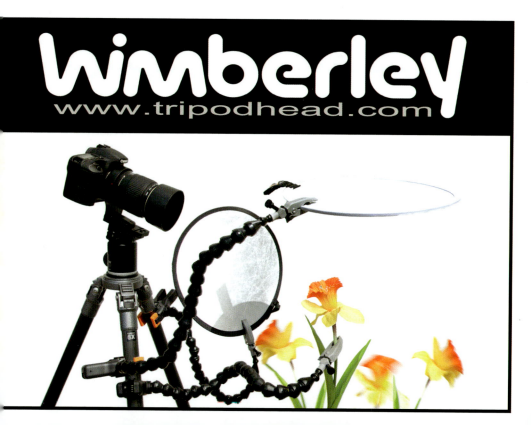

# Tohono Chul

www.tohonochul.org
7366 N. Paseo del Norte
Tucson, AZ 85704
Phone: (520)742-6455
Email: Marketing@tohonochul.org

Tohono Chul is a 49 acre nature preserve whose mission is to enrich people's lives by connecting them with the wonders of nature, art and culture in the Sonoran Desert region and inspiring wise stewardship of the natural world. The park features nature trails, demonstration gardens, art galleries, museum shops and The Garden Bistro restaurant.

# Valued Individual Contributors

Ambika Balasubramaniyan
Jacqueline D. Doyle
Ena Flynn
Harry and Caraleen Ford
Gene and Peggy
Grand Photo Friends
Brian Hayward
Martin and Shirley Hill
Catherine S. King
Tina Litteral
Jeff Maltzman
Josef Mikulas
Robert and Jacqueline Miniuk
Rob "Sluggo" Miniuk, Jr.
Amy Minton
Matt Nickell
Denise Schultz
Kerry Smith
Lynette Tritel
Joe Webster
Wickenburg Art Club - Photography Group
Gwen Williams
Rebecca Wilks

*A monsoon storm billows on the horrizon as sunflowers bloom near Robinson Crater. Canon 5DMIII, 16-35mm @ 27mm, ISO 100, f/22 @ 1/100 sec. Paul Gill*

# Index

Ajo Mountain Drive 221, 223
Alamo Canyon 222-3
Annual goldeneye 30, 58-61, 142-3, 146-7
Annual Penstemon Festival 42
Antelope horns 60, 105
Apache Lake 171, 173
Apache-plume 5, 36-7, 48-9
Apache Trail 22, 123, 170-3, 175
Aperture 21, 23-5, 30-1, 35-6, 38, 45, 51, 56, 60, 63-5, 72, 78, 84, 86-7, 97, 116, 136, 142, 144, 148, 161, 165, 175, 182-3, 186, 190-2, 214, 218, 222
Arboretum at Flagstaff, The 42, 44
Arizona caltrop 15, 211, 215, 224-5, 227
Arizona gilia 15, 38-9, 47-9
Arizona Highways Photography Workshops 10, 235, 256
Arizona Snowbowl 40-1
Arizona-Sonora Desert Museum 213-14, 216
Artificial background 26, 43, 53, 65, 103, 110, 133, 136, 188, 201
Ashurst Lake 52, 64-5
Aspen fleabane 30, 43, 144, 146, 148

Balance
  asymmetrical 52, 175
  symmetrical 53, 175
Bartlett Lake 34, 102-6
Bellows 26, 38, 45, 130, 197, 208, 216-17
Bird-of-paradise, Mexican 214-15
Blackfoot daisy 56-7
Black Mesa 162-3
Bladderpod mustard 76-8, 90-1, 93, 168-9
Blanketflower 131-2, 204-5, 214-15
Blue dicks 14, 56, 78, 108, 114, 116, 118, 126, 129, 131-2, 166, 180-1
Blue flax 42
Bluestem pricklepoppy 74, 144-5, 225
Blur, radial 227
Boundary Cone 68-9
Boyce Thompson Arboretum 10, 131-3, 183, 238
Brittlebush 9, 14-15, 21, 68-71, 74-5, 82, 88-91, 100, 102-3, 105, 109, 114-17, 119-20, 122-7, 129, 131, 162-3, 166, 170, 193, 198, 210, 213, 223

Broad-leaved gilia 168-9
Broom snakeweed 30-1, 33, 48-9
Buckskin Loop Trail 72-3
Buckskin Mountain State Park 72-3
Bulb mode 22
Bull thistle 146
Butter and eggs 28, 58-60, 85

Cabeza Prieta National Wildlife Refuge 94, 97
Cactus
  Arizona Queen-of-the-Night 201
  barrel 16, 211, 213, 215
  beavertail 72-3
  Boyce Thompson hedgehog 133
  claret cup 10, 113, 182
  echinopsis 203-5
  Engelmann's prickly pear 16, 56, 64, 100-1, 116, 129, 132, 142, 158, 162, 166, 171, 173, 189, 194-5
  fishhook barrel 218
  golden barrel 132
  grizzly bear 36
  night blooming 112-13
  night-blooming cereus 201
  night-blooming trichocereus 200
  organ pipe 220-2
  pincushion 16, 108, 126-7
  saguaro 12, 82, 88, 97, 100, 103, 116, 118-19, 121, 124-7, 129, 131, 133, 139, 162, 166-7, 169, 173, 175, 181, 184, 189, 194-5, 198, 201, 210-11, 213, 221-2, 229
  torch 113
Cactus, strawberry hedgehog 5, 16, 25, 56-7, 88-9, 100, 108-11, 113-16, 118, 127, 133, 158-9, 162, 175, 193, 197
Calliopsis 52, 58-61, 64-5, 144-5
Camera mode
  aperture priority (Av) 19, 21, 25
  Manual (M) 21, 25, 182, 190
  program (P) 21
  shutter speed priority (S or Tv) 21, 25
Catalina State Park 198-9, 204
Cave Creek Regional Park 100-1
Century plant 142, 171, 175, 216
  Parry's 142-3, 158, 171

*Cluster of sego lilies along Forest Service Road 419. Canon 5DMII, 100mm macro, ISO 200, f/10 @ 1/100 sec., diffuser. Colleen Miniuk-Sperry*

Chia   14, 100-1, 116, 129, 171
Chocolate flower   110, 215
Cholla   181
   buckhorn   188-9
   staghorn   166
   teddy bear   82, 91
Chuparosa   34, 82, 90-1, 93, 102-3, 105, 116-17, 120, 123, 188, 200, 202, 204
Cinquefoil   38, 206
Cline Cabin Road   166-7
Clik Elite   26, 237
Colorado four o'clocks   54-5, 123, 167
Columbine
   Rocky Mountain   30, 42-3, 45
   yellow   132, 176-9, 183, 200, 204, 206, 208-9
Composition   20, 23, 30, 34, 40, 52-3, 63, 81, 83, 87, 91, 93-4, 97, 103, 106, 116
   border patrol   63
   breaking the rules   226
   horizon line   34-5, 46, 53, 158, 191, 198, 211
   horizontal vs. vertical   70, 74, 121, 198
   lines   150-1
   middle ground   40, 63, 106, 158, 186
   near-far technique   138
   primary subject   34, 43, 106, 136, 166, 180, 194, 219
   Rule of Thirds   35, 45, 52-3, 150, 158
Coneflower
   cutleaf   51, 176, 179, 208
   purple   44
Continuous shoot mode   84
Cooper's goldflower   43
Cowboys' fried egg   45, 74, *See also* bluestem pricklepoppy
Cream cups   56-7, 106-7
Creosote bush   108-9, 125

DeMotte Park   30
Depth of field   23-4, 31, 35-6, 48, 63, 124, 131, 142, 152, 165, 186, 218-19
   Depth of Field Master (dofmaster.com)   23, 35-6, 186
   hyperfocal   23, 35-6, 78, 144, 186
   lens parallel   88, 175, 205
   preview   35, 191, 195
Desert bluebells   110
Desert Botanical Garden   19, 110, 112-13, 182

# Index (continued)

Desert-chicory   117, 170-1, 180-1, 198
Desert cosmos   14, 197
Desert marigold   14, 83, 91, 123, 125, 132-3, 200, 204
Desert primrose   94-5, *See also* evening primrose, dune
DesertUSA Wildflower Report   19
Diffraction   86, 218
Diffuser   26, 30, 38, 40, 42, 48, 51, 54, 56, 59-60, 68, 73, 76, 78, 82, 94, 100, 103, 106, 108, 110, 114, 118, 122-3, 127, 133, 135, 142, 146, 149, 154, 158, 161-2, 168, 172, 174, 180, 188, 192, 198, 200, 205, 208, 214-15
Disturbance wildflowers   17, 30, 148, 154
Dragoon Mountains   15-16, 224, 226
Dutch tilt   60, 150, 161, 203, 211

Eagletail Mountains Wilderness   4, 6, 16, 67, 76-7
El Niño   18
Evening primrose, dune   95, 97, 205, 214, *See also* desert primrose
Exposure   20-5, 31, 35, 54, 85, 87, 97, 108, 116, 146, 181-3, 189-91, 219, 225-7
  balance   25, 31, 35-6, 54, 61, 82, 146, 158, 181-2, 215, 225
  Exposure Value (EV) compensation   24-5
  multiple   65, 87, 131
Extension tubes   26, 33, 38, 45, 121, 130, 197, 208, 216-17

Fairy duster   100, 105, 116, 120, 164-6, 198, 204
Fiddleneck   27, 66, 68, 76-9, 81, 88, 114, 120, 132, 198
Filaree   116
Filter
  close-up   38, 130, 197, 208, 216-17
  graduated neutral density   26, 31, 35-6, 39-40, 46, 48, 54, 58, 61, 63, 65, 68, 71, 74, 76, 78, 90-1, 97, 100, 102-3, 114, 116, 118, 127-8, 142, 144, 146, 158, 162, 166, 168, 172, 181, 187, 189-92, 199, 206, 210, 222, 225
  polarizer   26, 31, 36, 40, 46, 48, 51, 56, 61, 68, 71, 74, 76, 78, 82-3, 88, 91, 100, 103, 108, 114, 116, 118, 121, 127, 129, 135, 142, 144, 149, 152, 156-8, 162, 166, 168, 172, 176, 180, 186, 189, 192, 194, 197, 199, 206, 210, 222, 225
Fireweed   17, 42, 51, 150
Flash   85, 112, 180, 182-3, 205, 242
  balance with ambient light   182-3
  diffuser   183, 242
  Flash Exposure Compensation (FEC)   183
  manual mode   182-3
  off-camera   26, 48, 113, 121, 182-3, 188
  on-camera   93, 182
  pop-up   182-3
  ring   182
  second curtain sync   85
  Through-The-Lens (TTL)   182-3
Flat-top buckwheat   108, 126-7, 162-3
Fleabane   14, 30, 43, 46-7, 144-8, 186, 206
  aspen   30, 43, 144, 146, 148
Focus   23, 30, 35, 38, 43, 45, 48, 56, 60, 62, 64, 73, 78, 87, 127, 130-1, 139, 142, 158, 161, 175, 186, 188, 192, 195, 205, 214, 216-19, 222, 226-7
  autofocus (AF)   130, 226
  focus stacking   218
  manual focus (MF)   45, 131, 217, 219
Focusing rail   26, 45, 130-1, 174, 217, 219
Fool Hollow Lake Recreation Area   144-5
Foreground   31, 34-6, 38-40, 48, 53, 56, 61, 63, 68, 72, 78, 88, 91, 97, 106, 121, 124, 128-9, 135, 139, 144, 158, 162, 182-3, 190-2, 199, 203, 222, 225
Forest Service Road 419   25, 158-9
F-stop *See* aperture

General Crook Trail   142
Gibraltar Mountain Wilderness   74
Globemallow, desert   15, 36-7, 54-6, 60-1, 82, 85, 100, 116, 118-21, 131-2, 158, 166-7, 188, 200, 202, 210, 215
Go John Trail   100-1
Goldenrod, tall   30-1, 33, 146
Goldfields   143, 158-9
Grand Canyon National Park, North Rim   30-2

244

Grand Canyon National Park, South Rim  36-7

Hannagan Meadow  148, 152, 154-5
Hart Prairie  38, 40
Helicon Focus  131, 219
Hewitt Canyon  128-30
High Dynamic Range (HDR)  4, 35, 65, 168, 191
Highlight Alert function  25, 190
Highlights  24, 68, 73, 80, 146, 158, 182, 208
Histogram  24-5, 35, 48, 182-3, 190, 219, 226
Hoodman Corporation  10, 92, 130, 238
Hoodman HoodLoupe  26, 93, 131, 139
Humphreys Trail  40-1
Hydroseeding  17
Hyperfocal *See* depth of field, hyperfocal

Ironwood, desert  129, 189, 194-5
Ironwood Forest National Monument  194-5
ISO/film speed  21-2, 24-5, 35, 39, 51, 63, 84, 86, 94, 149, 157, 182-3, 196, 214, 217, 219

Jacob's Crosscut Trail  120, 122
Joshua tree  70-1
JPEG file format  20, 24

Kofa National Wildlife Refuge  90, 92-3

Lake Pleasant Regional Park  82, 84-5
La Niña  18
Larkspur  30, 40-1, 54, 133, 151
"Leave No Trace" principles  26-7
Lemon beebalm  206, 209
Lens
  macro  30, 38, 40, 42, 44-5, 48, 51, 54, 56, 59-60, 64, 68, 71, 73-4, 76, 78, 82, 86-8, 94, 100, 103, 108, 110, 112, 114, 116, 118, 120, 124, 127, 129-30, 133, 135, 142, 146, 149, 152, 154, 158, 161-2, 167-8, 172, 175-6, 180, 186, 188, 192, 195, 197-8, 201, 204-5, 208, 211, 214-18, 221-2, 225
  micro  26
  normal  30, 70, 88, 108, 144, 149
  telephoto  26, 30, 35-6, 45, 48, 51, 54, 59-60, 64, 68, 70, 73-4, 76, 78, 82, 88, 91, 94, 108, 112, 114, 116, 124, 129, 133, 135, 142, 146, 152, 162, 166-8, 172, 178, 180, 186, 188, 192, 194, 198, 201, 204-5, 208, 211, 214-15
  tilt-shift  35, 91, 126, 139, 225
  wide-angle  30-1, 35-6, 38, 40, 46, 48, 54, 58, 60, 63, 65, 68, 70, 72, 74, 76, 78, 82-3, 87-8, 91, 94, 97, 100, 103, 108, 112, 114, 116, 118, 121, 124, 126, 128-9, 135, 139, 142, 144, 146, 148-9, 152, 157-8, 162, 166-8, 172, 175-6, 180, 186, 189, 192, 194, 197-9, 206, 210, 214, 222, 225
Lens flare, prevent  65, 81-2, 87-8
Lesser yellow throat gilia  78
Light
  back  64, 80-1, 110, 133, 182, 210
  dappled  30, 204, 208
  diffused  73, 105, 182
  front  81
  mid-day  54, 87, 122-3, 162, 165, 172, 203
  reflected  104
  side  56, 68, 80-1, 97, 125, 133, 161
  top  81
Lightning Bolt Trail  73
Light tent  26, 85, 122
Live View mode  87, 93, 131, 139, 178
Locoweed  28, 43, 46-7
Lost Dog Wash Trail  108-9
Lost Dutchman State Park  120, 122-3, 156, 170, 172
Lower Lake Mary  58-9, 63
Lupine
  Arizona  90
  Coulter's  4, 8, 14, 22, 35, 68-9, 72-3, 76, 78, 82, 85, 88, 93, 98, 100, 102, 104-7, 109, 114, 116, 118-20, 126, 129, 131-2, 134-7, 166, 168-71, 173, 188-9, 192-3, 196, 198, 202, 204, 210, 213, 215, 220-2
  Hill's  30, 38, 40, 51, 167
  King's  28, 152

# Index (continued)

Macro, magnification ratios  44
Manfrotto  26, 240
Mariposa lily  162-3, 175, 199
Mexican hat  132, 137, 204
Milkweed  144
Monkeyflower  51, 176, 208
Mormon Lake  60-4, 85
Motion  22, 24, 85, 197, 227
Mount Lemmon  23, 206, 208-9
Mullein  146
Myrtle  51-3, 177, 179

Narrow-leaved popcorn flower  114
Navajo Point  36-7
Newberry's twinpod  48
New Mexican checkermallow  148-9, 151
New Mexican vervain  30, 144
New Mexico butterweed  60
New Mexico locust  54, 167, 186-7
New Mexico thistle  225, 227
Nightshade, purple  27, 166-7

Oatman  68-70
Ocotillo  8, 74-5, 88, 90-3, 95, 108, 115, 126, 158, 162, 166, 188-9, 194, 199, 213-14
Odora  108
Organ Pipe Cactus National Monument  16-17, 95, 220, 222-3
Owl clover  4, 8, 14, 16, 56-7, 66, 70-1, 76-82, 88, 114, 126, 158, 166, 168-9, 171, 198, 200, 204, 221-2

Paintbrush
  desert  38, 42, 51, 54, 60, 142
  Indian  14, 28, 33, 36-7, 40, 43, 45, 53, 56-7, 61, 65, 145, 148, 152, 155, 208
  Kaibab  30, 33
  Mogollon Indian  148, 155
  woolly  40-1, 144-7
Palm Canyon Trail  90
Paloverde, littleleaf  73, 88-9, 109, 118, 126, 129, 166, 175, 189, 194, 198, 200, 204, 210, 215
Paper flower  158, 166
Pass Mountain Trail  116-17
Penstemon  113, 144

Parry's  15, 45, 110, 132, 188, 205, 223
red firecracker  148
Rocky Mountain  48
Pepperweed, western  94-5, 97, 226-7
Peralta Road  126-7
Peridot Mesa  180-1
Photographer's Ephemeris  81, 97
Picacho Peak State Park  12, 192-3
Pinal Pioneer Parkway  188-9
Pinta Dunes  94-5, 97
Polarization  156-7
  over  156
  uneven  157
Poppy
  albino  102-3, 105
  California  193
  Mexican gold  4, 12, 14, 16, 22, 35, 45, 66, 68-70, 76-8, 81-3, 85-8, 92-4, 100-5, 108-10, 114-18, 120-3, 126, 129-32, 134, 136-7, 166, 168-71, 173, 180-1, 188, 192-3, 196-200, 202, 204, 210, 215, 220-4
  summer See Arizona caltrop
Primrose
  desert  94
  dune  14, 56, 74, 95
  Hooker's evening  208

Rabbit brush  36-7, 48-9
Rainbow  142, 197
RAW file format  20, 24, 203, 221
Red Canyon  12, 56
Reflector  26, 38, 40, 42, 48, 54, 68, 78, 82, 93-4, 100, 104-5, 108, 110, 114, 118, 123, 127, 135, 142, 146, 154, 158, 162, 168, 172, 174, 180, 182-3, 188, 192, 200, 205, 208, 214-15
Refraction  197, 218
Richardson's geranium  23, 206
Robinson Crater  46, 228
Rocky Mountain iris  61, 155, 186-7
Rolls, The  168
Rule of Thirds See composition, Rule of Thirds

Sacred datura  41, 51, 166, 225
Saddle Mountain  16, 66, 78-81

246

Saguaro National Park   12, 198, 210, 212-13, 215, 229
San Tan Mountain Regional Park   118-19
Scarlet bugler   54, 178
Schnebly Hill Road   54-5
Scorpionweed   27, 72, 74-5, 78, 91, 102, 104, 108-9, 116-17, 120, 123, 126, 132, 171, 189, 215
Scott Reservoir   146-7
Sego lily   8, 25, 54-6, 158-9, 161, 243
Shadows   24, 30, 56, 68, 73, 80-1, 83, 88, 91, 93, 106, 121-2, 128, 146, 158, 182, 190, 203, 208
Shutter speed   21-2, 24-5, 31, 35, 38-9, 51, 63-5, 84-5, 91, 93-4, 146, 149, 157, 175, 178, 182-3, 190-2, 197, 204, 214, 219, 225, 227
Silly Mountain   124-5
Silver King Mine Road   4, 35, 98, 134, 136-7, 190
Singh-Ray   10, 156, 190, 239
Siphon Draw Trail   122
Skyrockets   15, 30, 39
Sneezeweed, western   38-40, 148, 151-2, 154-5, 206, 209
South Mountain Park   114-15
Sunburst   65, 86
Sunflower
  common   34, 46-7, 58-9, 61, 228
  prairie   13, 62-3
Sunset Crater National Monument   5, 47-9, 228
Sun shade   81-2, 88
Superstition Mountains   9, 14, 116, 120-1, 126, 166, 168, 170-1
Sutherland Trail   198-9

Tempe Camera   10, 236
Thompson Trail   17, 148, 150-1
Tobacco-root   42
Tohono Chul Park   200-2, 240
  bloom night   201
Tohono Chul Park, Bloom Watch   201
Tom Mix Rest Area   188-9
Treasure Park   186-7
Tres Alamos Wilderness   70-1, 76
Tucson Botanical Gardens   204-5

Upper Lake Mary   58-9, 63

Verbena
  Dakota   186-7
  desert sand   14, 95, 97, 214
  Goodding's   12, 56, 110, 166, 201
Visualization   97, 202-3

Wallflower, western   51, 54, 179, 186-7, 201
Water knotweed   64-5, 140, 144-5
West Fork of Oak Creek   17, 50-2
West Fork of the Black River   148, 151
White balance   25, 39
  Auto White Balance (AWB)   25
White ratany   118-19, 162
White tackstem   116-17, 181
White Tank Mountain Regional Park   88-9
Wild bergamot   50-1, 53, 178-9, 217
Wildfire   17, 148, 166
  Aspen Fire   206, 208
  Coon Creek Fire   176
  Rodeo–Chediski Fire   17
  Slide Fire   17, 50-1
  Wallow Fire   17, 148, 154
Wild geranium   9, 46-7, 51, 60, 179, 208-9
Wild heliotrope   114-15, 198
Wild in Arizona blog   19
Wild onion   14
Wild rose   15, 152
Wimberley   10, 84, 239
Wimberley Plamp   26, 64, 85, 94, 219
Wind, photographing in   26-7, 39, 63, 84, 87, 97, 197, 227
Woodbane phlox   54
Wood sorrel   206-8
Workman Creek   17, 176-9

Yarrow, western   42, 208
Yellow cups   68-9, 72-3
Yellow salsify   53
Yellow sweet clover   60-1
Yerba Mansa   200-1
Yucca   70, 163, 200
  banana yucca   36, 162-3, 172, 175, 224-5, 227

Zerene Stacker   219

247

# About the Authors

*Photo by Paul Gill*

## Paul Gill
**www.paulgillphoto.com**

Since 1975, Paul has turned all of his attention to photographing the grandeur of nature. Paul is the founding director of the Arizona Nature Photographers, Arizona Photo Scouts, and Arizona Photo Guides. Paul's photographs have graced the covers and pages of the world-renowned *Arizona Highways* magazine, calendars, and books; *National Geographic* calendars; *Nature's Best;* Smith-Southwestern calendars and postcards; and many other scenic publications, calendars, and books. His work has also been displayed in numerous fine art galleries. Paul's photographs are featured within the Smithsonian Museum's permanent collection of nature photography.

A native of the Arizona desert, nature photographer Paul Gill received his Bachelors of Fine Arts from Arizona State University and worked as an art director for 17 years, designing and producing publications and fine art books for companies like the Scottsdale Center for the Arts.

In addition to traveling extensively in western North America with his camera, Paul also captures high definition videography for the Discovery Channel and other clients.

*Photo by Ivan Martinez Photography*

## Colleen Miniuk-Sperry
**www.cms-photo.com**

As an award-winning, internationally published outdoor photographer and writer, Colleen supports a wide range of assignments for editorial clients, fine art, and stock. Her work has been published in *National Geographic* calendars; *Arizona Highways* magazine, books, and calendars; *AAA Highroads*; *AAA Via*; *National Parks Traveler*; Smith-Southwestern calendars; and a broad variety of other publications.

In addition to this book, in early 2014, she authored the award-winning guidebook, *Photographing Acadia National Park: The Essential Guide to When, Where, and How.*

Colleen also leads photography workshops for the Arizona Highways Photography Workshops, The Nature Conservancy, Through Each Others Eyes (TEOE), and numerous private clients. She is an Associate of TEOE and a board member of the Outdoor Writers Association of America (OWAA).

Armed with a Bachelor of Business Administration degree from the University of Michigan, Miniuk-Sperry moved to Phoenix to begin a 10-year project management career at Intel Corporation. As an outlet to corporate life, she began making photographs of the western United States' landscapes in late 2001. In early 2007, she left Intel to pursue a full-time career in photography and writing.

Originally hailing from Ohio, Arkansas, and Illinois, Colleen currently resides in Chandler, Arizona with her husband, Craig, and cat, Nolan.